Michelle Muratori
Robert Haynes

Coping Skills for a Stressful World

A Workbook for Counselors and Clients

AMERICAN COUNSELING
ASSOCIATION

6101 Stevenson Avenue • Suite 600
Alexandria, VA 22304
counseling.org

Coping Skills for a Stressful World

A Workbook for Counselors and Clients

American Counseling Association
6101 Stevenson Avenue, Suite 600
Alexandria, VA 22304

Associate Publisher • Carolyn C. Baker

Digital and Print Development Editor • Nancy Driver

Senior Production Manager • Bonny E. Gaston

Copy Editor • Kay Mikel

Cover and text design by Bonny E. Gaston

Library of Congress Cataloging-in-Publication Data

Names: Muratori, Michelle C., 1965–author. | Haynes, Robert (Robert L.), 1945–author.
Title: Coping skills for a stressful world : A workbook for counselors and clients / Michelle Muratori, Robert Haynes.
Description: Alexandria, VA : American Counseling Association, [2020] | Includes bibliographical references.
Identifiers: LCCN 2019053885 | ISBN 9781556203893 (paperback)
Subjects: LCSH: Life skills. | Stress management. | Therapist and patient.
Classification: LCC HQ2037 .M87 2020 | DDC 646.7—dc23
LC record available at https://lccn.loc.gov/2019053885

Dedication

To clients who are struggling to navigate and make sense of these troubled times,
and to their counselors who are braving the journey with them.

• • •

Contents

Part I
Introduction and Central Role of Resilience

Part II
Addressing Common Mental Health Issues

Part III
Coping With Trauma, Disaster, and Adversity

Part IV
Emerging Crises and Intensifying Stressors

Part V
Going Forward: Counselor Self-Care and Client Life After Counseling

Foreword

Emerging crises have ruptured our nation along lines of ethnicity, race, sexual orientation, gender identity, social class, culture, religion, values, partisanship, and more. Those seeking counseling report an increase in the stress and anxiety associated with these crises. Coauthors Michelle Muratori and Bob Haynes have written a workbook unlike any other in the field, providing a comprehensive toolkit to assist counselors as they work with clients coping with both traditional and emerging crises and stressors. This uniquely focused workbook provides narrative material for counselors and clients along with a comprehensive assortment of exercises and activities for out-of-session work to further enhance and facilitate a client's counseling experience.

This workbook addresses these topics and many others in a user-friendly and practical way for both counselors and clients. Here are some key features:

- Practical exercises and activities for clients to reflect on, to explore, and to practice outside the counseling session are a basic part of most chapters.
- Each topical chapter contains a *narrative overview for the counselor*. The authors share what they have learned about working therapeutically with themes in the lives of clients.
- Chapters contain practical *narrative information for clients* to explain the concepts they are working on in counseling (such as depression or coping with crisis) and to provide the basis for the exercises.
- The client sections in the workbook may be freely photocopied and given to clients for their work outside of the counseling session.
- A separate chapter addresses counselor compassion fatigue, burnout, and vicarious trauma, which can result from working with trauma victims, and focuses on self-care exercises and activities to enhance counselors' wellness.

This is a practical toolbox for counselors. Counselors are free to adapt the exercises and activities to meet the needs of their clients, which affords increased flexibility and creativity. Clients have the opportunity to carefully consider their pressing concerns, and the exercises and activities will actively engage clients in self-reflection and guide them in practicing new skills beyond the counseling session. Many of the common reasons clients seek counseling are addressed in this workbook, and the importance of developing resilience and focusing on wellness are emphasized.

Counselors providing brief therapy can use the out-of-session activities to enable clients to extend their work into daily life. In addition, client feedback from these activities will provide significant material for counselors to explore with their clients at the next session. This can only make the counseling endeavor more effective and efficient for both client and counselor.

We have not seen a workbook that offers narrative for counselors, narrative for clients, and exercises and activities for clients for such a large range of counseling topics. In addition, the authors address the newly emerging topics facing our country, our culture, and our clients. The exercises and activities tie nicely into the narrative discussions, and they reflect a variety of theoretical perspectives.

A unique feature is the contributions by experts in the counseling and psychology fields, who share their experience with exercises and activities they have found effective in their work with clients. These experts describe a variety of exercises and activities pertinent to reality therapy, pain management, trauma recovery, and activities for hospice clients, just to name a few.

Michelle and Bob bring their varied clinical backgrounds to the development of this workbook. They are deeply concerned about the human cost of recent divisive trends across American society and around the world today, which are making clients' lives increasingly more stressful. They have written a timely book that provides counselors with tools to help their clients navigate these stressful times. This team has combined their abilities and years of professional experience to produce a top-quality practical guide for counselors and their clients.

—Marianne Schneider Corey, MA
—Gerald Corey, EdD

Preface

We are writing this workbook to aid counseling clients living in a world in distress. People are experiencing "global anxiety" at levels rarely, if ever, seen before. Our world is increasingly plagued by political upheaval, divisiveness and tribalism, interpersonal violence, hate crimes, terrorism, social injustice, the omnipresence of social media, cybercrimes, and speed-of-light news cycles bombarding our televisions, computers, and smartphones. In addition, the tangible effects of climate change are increasing the size and severity of natural disasters. The 2018 Camp Fire, the most destructive wildfire in California history, caused 86 deaths, led to the evacuation of 52,000 people, destroyed more than 18,000 structures, and left an estimated 100,000 people traumatized by the event, the losses, and the aftermath. In 2019, California experienced the two largest earthquakes in 20 years (of magnitudes 6.4 and 7.1, respectively) within the span of 2 days that set off nearly constant aftershocks for weeks and caused widespread damage. Although lives were spared, these massive quakes left people terrified, anxious, and afraid to sleep in their homes. In recent years, catastrophic storms and hurricanes have caused widespread devastation from Maine to Florida and throughout the states along the Gulf of Mexico. Hurricanes Harvey, Maria, and Dorian damaged the environment in addition to destroying homes and businesses. The loss of life from these and other natural disasters are painful reminders of our vulnerability and our limits as human beings.

Tragedies of a different sort—those that are self-inflicted—have also spiked in recent times. According to the Centers for Disease Control and Prevention (2019), death from alcohol, drugs, and suicide in the United States in 2017 hit the highest level since 1999, the year these statistics were first collected. Counselors are seeing an increase in the number of clients who report living in a state of hypervigilance, suspicion, and distrust (Meyers, 2017). As the frequency and intensity of these forces and events increase, a growing number of clients will need the support and direction of counseling and therapy to deal with these crises and resultant long-term stress.

Our hope is that this workbook will support counselors in working with clients who must navigate these stressful times. The primary focus of this workbook is twofold: (a) to assist counselors and therapists by providing materials to use with clients experiencing this increase in global anxiety and stress; and (b) to assist clients in exploring, understanding, and managing crises and stressors in their lives. We wanted to create a counselor- and client-friendly workbook for use as a clinical tool in counseling sessions and for subsequent client homework. We include material to assist counselors in the counseling process and homework material for the client, such as therapeutic activities and exercises that can be completed in or between sessions. This counseling toolbox can greatly enhance the therapy experience and facilitate the work of counselor and client.

We offer our personal and professional perspectives throughout and include a fair amount of scholarly literature to support our claims. In the narrative sections, we share some of our own stories and discuss what we have learned about working with clients therapeutically. We also have invited a number of clinicians to share their experiences with the use of therapeutic exercises and activities in counseling to give you multiple perspectives on using this clinical tool.

We recommend that counselors read through the entire workbook to become familiar with the content and the sections you might most want to make use of in counseling. Exercises and activities represent a variety of theoretical and therapeutic approaches and reflect the wide-ranging needs of clients. Some exercises are preceded by narrative to further explain the concepts addressed by the exercises; others are straightforward and can be easily grasped. Counselors have our permission and that of the publisher to copy the client material to give to your client, and you also have permission to adapt any exercises as you see fit to better meet the unique needs of your clients. We discuss the ethical issues applicable to the utilization of such tools with clients in Chapter 1 and offer guidelines for assigning these activities. We hope this workbook will prove to be a practical and valuable clinical resource in your library of professional books and literature.

About the Authors

Michelle Muratori, PhD, is a senior counselor at the Center for Talented Youth at Johns Hopkins University, in Baltimore, Maryland, where she works with highly gifted middle school and high school students who participate in the Study of Exceptional Talent and their families. She earned her MA in counseling psychology from Northwestern University in Evanston, Illinois, and her PhD in counselor education from the University of Iowa, where she developed her research and clinical interests in gifted education. Her graduate research on the academic, social, and emotional adjustment of young college entrants earned her recognition from the Iowa Talented and Gifted Association, the National Association for Gifted Children, and the Mensa Education and Research Foundation and Mensa International, Ltd. At the University of Iowa, Michelle also earned the Howard R. Jones Achievement Award, the Albert Hood Promising Scholar Award, and the First in the Nation in Education Scholar Award.

Since 2005, Michelle has been a faculty associate in the Johns Hopkins School of Education and teaches courses in the master of science in counseling program. In 2014, she was honored with the Johns Hopkins University Alumni Association Excellence in Teaching Award. Michelle regularly presents at national conferences in counseling and gifted education and is a member of the American Counseling Association, the Association for Counselor Education and Supervision, the Association for Specialists in Group Work, the Maryland Counseling Association, and the National Association for Gifted Children. When not engaged in these professional activities, Michelle enjoys writing, attending concerts, watching late-night comedy shows and movies, and spending time with her family and friends.

Michelle's publications include:

- *Counselor Self-Care* (2018), with Gerald Corey, Jude T. Austin II, and Julius A. Austin, published by the American Counseling Association.
- *I Never Knew I Had a Choice* (11th ed., 2018), with Gerald Corey and Marianne Schneider Corey, published by Cengage Learning.
- *Clinical Supervision in the Helping Professions* (3rd ed., 2021), with Gerald Corey, Robert Haynes, and Patrice Moulton, published by the American Counseling Association.
- *Early Entrance to College: A Guide to Success* (2007), published by Prufrock Press.

• • •

Robert Haynes, PhD, is a clinical psychologist, author, and producer of psychology video programs for Borderline Productions. Bob received his doctorate in clinical psychology from Fuller Graduate School of Psychology in Pasadena, California, and is a member of the American Counseling Association and the Association for Counselor Education and Supervision. He has been actively involved in professional psychology through private practice as well as consulting, leading workshops, and writing on a variety of topics. In addition, Bob taught psychology, criminology, and management courses at the University of California at Santa Barbara, California Polytechnic State University San Luis Obispo, and California State University Sacramento. He also served as Chair of Site Visiting Teams for the Committee on Accreditation of the American Psychological Association. Bob retired after 25 years as training director of the accredited clinical psychology internship program at Atascadero State Hospital in California.

The topic of stress and crisis management has been a focal point in Bob's professional career, and he led stress debriefings and taught stress management classes for more than 20 years. Bob has also provided consultation and training in clinical supervision, criminology, disaster mental health, psychotherapy methods, stress management and burnout, suicide assessment and intervention, and theoretical approaches in counseling.

Bob's publications include:

- Managing Crisis: Personally and Professionally. (2021). Chapter 14 in M. S. Corey & G. Corey, *Becoming a Helper* (8th ed.), published by Cengage Learning.
- *Take Control of Life's Crises Today! A Practical Guide.* (2014), published by Aventine Press.
- *Clinical Supervision in the Helping Professions: A Practical Guide* (2nd ed., 2010), with G. Corey, P. Moulton, & M. Muratori, published by American Counseling Association.

Bob has produced a number of psychology training videos in collaboration with Marianne Schneider Corey and Gerald Corey, including *Groups in Action: Evolution and Challenges* (2006); *Ethics in Action, Student Version CD-ROM* (2003); and *The Art of Integrative Counseling* (2001).

• • •

About the
Contributors

Jude T. Austin II, PhD, assistant professor at University of Mary Hardin-Baylor, Belton, Texas.

Julius A. Austin, PhD, clinical therapist, coordinator of the Office of Substance Abuse and Recovery at Tulane University, New Orleans, Louisiana.

Gerald Corey, EdD, author and professor emeritus of human services and counseling at California State University, Fullerton.

Marianne Schneider Corey, MA, author, licensed marriage and family therapist, and consultant.

Gary Haynes, MA, retired high school science teacher and former volunteer at Saddleback Memorial Hospital in Mission Viejo, California.

Kellie Nicole Kirksey, PhD, holistic psychotherapist and certified rehabilitation counselor, Cleveland Clinic Center for Integrative and Lifestyle Medicine.

Crissa S. Markow, MSW, project director, Volunteer Programs, Sandford Center for Aging, University of Nevada, Reno.

Mark A. Stebnicki, PhD, professor and coordinator of the Military and Trauma Counseling Certificate, Department of Addictions and Rehabilitation, East Carolina University, Greenville, North Carolina.

Judy Van Der Wende, PhD, licensed psychologist in private practice, Simi Valley, California.

Robert E. Wubbolding, EdD, director of the Center for Reality Therapy in Cincinnati and professor emeritus of counseling at Xavier University.

Acknowledgments

This workbook is the result of the collaboration among the authors, guest contributors, reviewers, publisher, editorial staff, and many others who provided valuable input along the way. We would like to thank Jerry Corey and Marianne Schneider Corey, who provided so much to the development and writing of this workbook as reviewers, consultants, and contributors. We also thank those who provided feedback and guidance: Cheryl Haynes, Gary Haynes, Crissa Markow, Jennifer Sullivan, Sage Sullivan, and the peer reviewers.

This workbook has been made possible by the American Counseling Association and the support, guidance, consultation, and editorial wisdom of Carolyn Baker, ACA's associate publisher. We also truly appreciate the attention to detail and the editorial excellence provided by Kay Mikel, our copy editor. This project would not have been possible without the expertise and guidance of the superb editorial team of Carolyn and Kay.

Finally, a heartfelt thank you to those who took the time to share their professional and personal experiences as contributors to this workbook.

Part I

Introduction and
Central Role of Resilience

In Part I you will find foundational materials that set the tone for subsequent parts. Chapter 1 provides a road map for navigating the workbook, offering a rationale for and an overview of the workbook as well as practical tips for using the exercises and activities. One of our overarching goals is to help clients develop greater resilience in an increasingly stressful world, and Chapter 2 is devoted to the topic of resilience. It begins with a brief discussion of the concept of resilience and includes an explanation of resilience especially for clients. The chapter concludes with a series of client activities, exercises, and questions designed to be a catalyst for clients as they explore a variety of topics and issues related to resilience.

Chapter 1

Introduction

Reality is the leading cause of stress among those in touch with it.
— Lily Tomlin

• • •

Coping Skills for a Stressful World: A Workbook for Counselors and Clients is a clinical tool designed for counselors and other mental health practitioners who are looking for exercises and activities that can assist clients struggling with stress and other mental health concerns related to or exacerbated by the stressful times in which we are living. The materials in this workbook can be photocopied and assigned to clients as therapeutic homework and subsequently discussed or processed in session. We have included concrete tools to facilitate productive therapeutic work, and it is our hope that this resource will enhance the therapeutic process with your clients and make your job easier and more efficient.

This chapter is primarily addressed to the counselors, therapists, and other mental health practitioners working in any number of professional settings. We provide our rationale for creating the workbook along with suggestions for how to get the most out of it. We describe how we came to collaborate on this project and the disturbing trends we both see unfolding in society that undoubtedly add to the stress levels of clients and the counselors who serve them. We describe the organization of the workbook, offer information about therapeutic homework compliance, and discuss relevant ethical issues in the use of out-of-session activities. We conclude with instructions and guidelines for using the out-of-session exercises with clients, and we encourage you to refer to this section as often as needed.

Need for and Purpose of the Workbook

Our goal is to provide tools for counselors to use in assisting their clients in navigating stressful situations they encounter in daily life. We emphasize building upon the internal resources clients possess. Clients tend to be much more resilient than they think they are, and they often find strength and creative solutions to the challenges they face even in problem-saturated stories. Most people have some degree of resilience upon which they can build.

Stories of resilience inspire and instill hope in us, but the truth is that people are not all equally resilient. As a mental health professional, you may serve individuals who are fragile or vulnerable (to varying degrees) and who may lack the social support to respond to adversity in a resilient manner. After all, clients tend to seek the support of a therapist when they are having difficulty coping with their circumstances—not when they are handling life's stressors effectively and with ease. We believe resilience is a much-needed skill in today's stressful world. American society is fractured along lines of ethnicity, race, sexual orientation, gender identity, social class, culture, religion, values, and partisanship, and the mental health needs of clients will continue to grow in these divisive times. A driving force behind our decision to collaborate on this workbook was the need to create a resource that would assist clients in developing or strengthening their resilience.

The New Normal

We live in a global community, and we can expect to hear about misfortunes occurring virtually anywhere and at any time. Sometimes this news hits close to home, and other times the news is happening halfway around the world. Within the span of a single day, we may hear stories about the effects of climate change and severe weather events that wreak havoc; crises affecting immigrants, asylum seekers, the LGBTQ+ community, people of color, women, or other vulnerable or marginalized groups; mass casualty tragedies caused by gun violence; terrorist plots carried out or foiled; and accusations of sexual misconduct. To make matters worse, all of these news stories arrive against the backdrop of a constant barrage of "breaking news" about political developments. Disturbing trends have gained momentum in the United States and around the world: an increase of neo-fascism/authoritarianism, cybercrimes, terrorism, hate, racism, xenophobia, homophobia, bullying/cyberbullying, misogyny, and other oppressive forces. It is not an exaggeration to say that it is almost impossible to keep up with the news today. Our exposure to stressful news and information is continuous through the proliferation of social media platforms and 24-hour news channels. Everyday living has become exponentially more stressful in today's world. This is the new normal.

Stress and Resilience in Troubled Times

In today's stressful world, an increasing number of clients will need support in dealing with crises and long-term stress. A recent American Psychological Association (APA, 2017b) survey about the state of stress in the United States found that Americans are stressed about the future of the nation. Some 59% of adults surveyed indicated that they find this to be "the lowest point in our nation's history that they can remember—a feeling that spans generations, including individuals who have lived through World War II and Vietnam, the Cuban missile crisis, the September 11 terrorist attacks, and high-profile mass shootings" (p. 1). A Gallup poll found that 55% of Americans experience stress throughout much of their day, compared to 35% globally, and 45% reported worrying a lot about their lives (Chokshi, 2019). Meyers (2017) noted that counselors are seeing a huge increase in the number of clients who report living in a state of hypervigilance, suspicion, and distrust. One counselor reported that the negative emotional climate in the country—filled with revenge, resentment, and hatred—is harming people's mental health (Meyers, 2017). Others have said that "America is suffering a nervous breakdown" (Frances, 2017). The polarization occurring in our nation, in geographical and online communities, and even in families is exacerbating and causing stress, anxiety, isolation, loneliness, anger, and loss for many people. Based on our conversations with friends and colleagues in the mental health field, we suspect that clinicians may also be vulnerable to heightened stress when listening for hours each week to distressed clients, particularly those who might hold sharply different values and views on certain "hot button" political topics.

Some counselors may feel discouraged and even overwhelmed by the magnitude of their clients' stress and mental health issues coupled with their own stress navigating this polarized and chaotic world. If you fall into this category, it is important to remember that we are also witnessing heroic actions and have reason to feel hopeful. It would be remiss to downplay the positive and selfless actions individuals and groups have taken to defend our hard-earned rights. We have seen advocacy and humanity at its finest. In response to oppressive and discriminatory practices and policies affecting marginalized groups, advocacy groups and ordinary citizens have taken swift action in opposition to such restrictions, demonstrating a new level of social activism. The Me Too (or #MeToo) movement has gained visibility and traction worldwide in response to sexual harassment and assault, and it provides a platform for survivors of abuse to voice their pain and to demand justice.

In the past few years, large-scale protests have been organized to defend human rights and to give voice to the voiceless and those who have been marginalized. "Grounded in the nonviolent ideology of the Civil Rights movement, the Women's March [January 21, 2017] was the largest coordinated protest in U.S. history and one of the largest in world history" (Meyer & Tarrow, 2018, p. 1). Marches, protests, and rallies varying in size and scope have raised awareness of issues ranging from the gun violence epidemic and unjust immigration policies and practices to the protection of the environment and of science itself.

In addition to these widely publicized displays of social activism, we witness smaller acts of kindness and courage on a daily basis that remind us that there is hope for humanity. Paradoxically, as vulnerable as people may be in stressful times, we repeatedly see their capacity for resilience, and we must hold on to that. The nearly miraculous rescue of members of a youth soccer team trapped in a cave in Thailand in July 2018 is a prime example of courage and heroism, the will to survive, and resilience (Suhartono & Paddock, 2018). Many examples of resilience have been described throughout history, and many more challenging and stressful situations will test people's hardiness, resourcefulness, resilience, and ability to cope in the future.

Organization of This Workbook

This workbook is divided into five parts, each focusing on a central theme. The first section introduces the workbook format and explains the concept of resilience. The next three sections focus primarily on client issues (e.g., anxiety, depression, self-esteem, crisis and trauma, and emerging issues of divisiveness, hatred, and tribalism) and provide counselors with an overview of each issue followed by a variety of exercises, activities, and therapeutic homework assignments intended for clients. The final section looks forward and focuses on self-care for counselors and life after counseling for clients.

Part I, "Introduction and Central Role of Resilience," sets the tone for the remainder of the book and includes suggestions for maximizing the use of exercises and activities for clients and ethical issues to consider in the use of homework for clients. Chapter 2 provides critical information about fostering resilience in clients as well as exercises and activities for your clients.

Part II, "Addressing Common Mental Health Issues," contains therapeutic exercises and activities for clients battling anxiety and stress, depression and loneliness, anger, self-esteem issues, and grief and loss. These mental health issues tend to be rooted in intrapersonal or interpersonal conflicts, and similar material may be found in other counseling workbooks. We thought it essential to include this content because clients who are able to strengthen or improve their mental health functioning are likely to fare much better when facing external crises.

Part III, "Coping With Trauma, Disaster, and Adversity," addresses a variety of topics disaster mental health practitioners and crisis counselors routinely encounter. We include exercises for clients coping with natural disasters, climate change, and other environmental issues, as well as human-caused disasters such as mass shootings and terrorism. Material for clients coping with chronic illness and health problems is also included here.

Part IV, "Emerging Crises and Intensifying Stressors," taps into themes such as navigating sharp political differences with family and friends, value conflicts with others, and tribalism in modern society. It also addresses the timely topic of combating social injustice against marginalized groups, such as people of color, immigrants, and the LGBTQ+ population, issues that appear to be rampant in today's world. Although racism, xenophobia, and homophobia have persisted for a very long time and may seem to be too deeply entrenched in society to be considered "emerging," we argue that these injustices have intensified and deserve to be included here. In addition to offering activities for clients who are facing these stressors, we provide exercises for clients dealing with stress associated with the use of social media and technology.

Part V, "Going Forward: Counselor Self-Care and Client Life After Counseling," has reflective activities and exercises for counselors who serve clients burdened by stress and trauma. We recognize that the ever-growing demands placed on counseling professionals may put counselors at greater risk of vicarious traumatization, compassion and empathy fatigue, and burnout. Although counselor self-care is not the primary focus of the workbook, its importance underlies the theme and purpose of the workbook and makes it complete. The final chapter prepares clients for life after counseling and offers tips and strategies for incorporating self-care into their everyday lives.

Appendix A provides additional client exercises applicable to a wide range of issues and problems. We encourage counselors to review this resource along with the exercises at the end of chapters.

Appendix B provides an annotated list of online resources for counselors who want to expand their knowledge on topics and themes we have presented. Collectively, these resources provide a wealth of information that may support clients who not only are dealing with mental health issues but also are struggling with legal issues, marginalization and social injustice issues, and the effects of environmental and public health issues.

Contributors to This Workbook

A unique feature of this workbook is the inclusion of contributions by other counselors and mental health practitioners from a wide range of professional backgrounds who share exercises, activities, and therapeutic homework assignments that have been especially useful and effective in their clinical practice with clients under stress or in crisis. The contributors' writings are sprinkled throughout the workbook and provide homework ideas these practitioners have used and how those ideas worked out for them. Contributors, along with their credentials, are listed in the front of the book.

Therapeutic Homework

Like many counselors and other helping professionals, you may be overextended and may welcome tools and therapeutic activities for clients in distress that will make your job a bit easier. The practical exercises in this workbook can be incorporated into the treatment plans of clients experiencing crisis, and they may be especially appealing if you have limited time to devote to treatment planning. These exercises are intended to assist clients in continuing their therapeutic work outside of counseling sessions, thereby expediting the counseling process. Having clients think about and work outside the counseling session will accelerate their work in session. It will facilitate the therapeutic process by assisting them in further exploring and conceptualizing the various issues discussed in therapy, which may help to generate options for remediation. As noted by Trask, Barounis, Carlisle, Garland, and Aarons (2018), "therapeutic homework is a fundamental skill-building component of the majority of evidence-based therapies and is associated with better treatment outcomes" (p. 821). In a meta-analysis comparing the effectiveness of the same therapy with and without the use of homework, Kazantzis, Whittington, and Dattilio (2010) found that approximately 62% of clients in therapy who did homework improved, compared to 38% of clients who received the same therapy without homework.

Research on Therapeutic Homework Compliance

Perhaps you have encountered client resistance to doing homework. Do any of these excuses sound familiar? "I didn't get around to it last week." "Oh, it slipped my mind." "My dog ate it." (Actually, my [Michelle's] dog once chewed off a sizable chunk of a counseling textbook. It can happen!) Research has demonstrated the value of therapeutic homework for clients (e.g., Kazantzis et al., 2010; Miller 2010; Trask et al., 2018); however, clinicians often wonder how best to motivate their clients to follow through and complete (or at least make significant progress toward completing) out-of-session tasks. Miller (2010) notes that questions remain about the factors that influence client commitment and action. Assuming the client finds the therapeutic homework recommendation acceptable (i.e., appropriate for the problem, fair, reasonable, and nonintrusive), a number of factors may affect whether or not the client implements a suggested exercise or activity. The severity of a client's symptoms may play a role in determining compliance. One group of investigators speculated that "symptom severity acts as a motivator to comply with whatever call to action is suggested by the therapist. The client may perceive the homework as a way to gain control of symptoms or to be actively engaged in symptom relief efforts" (Scheel, Hanson, & Razzhavaikina, 2004, p. 47). However, a client's psychopathology has the potential to "deprive the client of the energy and willingness to act on the therapist's recommendation" (p. 47). Client factors such as personality characteristics may be linked to homework compliance, but more empirical research is needed before any conclusions can be reached. It does seem likely that therapeutic homework completion would be enhanced by assessing the client's readiness for change (Prochaska & DiClemente, 1982) using motivational interviewing techniques or other methods.

Therapist factors and client perceptions of therapists are also likely to have an impact on whether or not clients follow through on therapeutic homework. A study conducted by Weck, Richtberg, Esch, Höfling, and Stangier (2013) showed that "therapist competence in reviewing homework was significantly correlated with patient homework compliance" (p. 169). Another team of researchers showed that clients' perceptions of their therapist's empathy also affects whether a client is amenable to completing homework tasks between sessions. Those who rated their therapists as more empathic reported significantly higher levels of subsequent homework compliance than clients who perceived the same therapist as less empathic (Hara, Aviram, Constantino, Westra, & Antony, 2017). Lenehan, Deane, Wolstencroft, and Kelly (2019) also emphasized the importance of establishing a strong working alliance and the therapist's ability to ensure that therapeutic homework tasks are well aligned with clients' treatment goals.

About the Workbook Activities

We offer exercises (in most chapters and in Appendix A) that can help clients strengthen their coping resources in a multitude of ways. Some exercises focus on the power of using metaphors, humor, or the expressive arts to reframe one's circumstances; others draw on the principles of mindfulness, cognitive restructuring, or emotion regulation to reduce stress and improve functioning.

As you will see, the exercises and activities in the workbook are inspired by and reflect a variety of theoretical perspectives. Therapeutic homework is not confined to a single theoretical orientation; it is now widely regarded as a legitimate practice for psychotherapy in general. To provide counselors with a more comprehensive toolkit of exercises that meet the needs of diverse clients who have experienced unique stressors ranging in severity and duration, offering activities that vary theoretically and afford flexibility and an array of options seems imperative. Clients have different needs and concerns, and they respond well to different methods and interventions. The activities we offer may:

- Promote deep reflection and the exploration of unfinished business from one's family of origin (psychodynamic approaches).
- Assist clients in identifying cognitive distortions and promote cognitive restructuring or the disputation of irrational or inaccurate beliefs with the aid of rational emotive behavior therapy and cognitive therapy (REBT and CT).
- Draw from the principles of third-wave cognitive behavioral therapies such as dialectical behavior therapy or acceptance and commitment therapy (DBT and ACT).
- Guide clients through Wubbolding's WDEP model and help them prepare a plan for reducing their stress (reality therapy).
- Assist clients in resolving their ambivalence about change during stressful times with the aid of motivational interviewing (MI) techniques.
- Help clients deconstruct a problem-saturated narrative and reauthor their story in a more constructive way (narrative therapy).
- Aid clients in reframing their circumstances through the lens of gender socialization and empower them (feminist therapy).

- Tap into clients' creativity as a therapeutic resource through the use of poetry, music, and other artistic mediums (expressive arts therapy).
- Empower clients to generate solutions to their problems by looking for exceptions to the maladaptive ways they have reacted to stress and build on them (solution-focused brief therapy).
- Help clients engage in social action as one avenue for addressing adversity and oppression (social justice and multicultural counseling).

These workbook exercises and activities can, and *should*, be modified to meet the individual needs of clients and *not* be used in a "cookie cutter" fashion. You have our permission to photocopy any of the For Clients materials or create exercises of your own that are inspired by the activities we suggest. These activities are designed to be a tool to augment your clinical work, and they must be selected judiciously based on your professional wisdom and training. Ultimately, you must rely on your clinical judgment to determine whether any exercise or activity is appropriate to use with a particular client.

Ethical Considerations in the Use of Out-of-Session Activities

We believe it is essential to address the ethical issues surrounding the use of therapeutic out-of-session activities in counseling. We asked Marianne Schneider Corey and Gerald Corey, who have written extensively on the topic of ethics in the helping professions (Corey & Corey, 2021; Corey, Corey, & Corey, 2019), to address this topic.

Ethical Issues in Using Out-of-Session Exercises and Activities

Marianne Schneider Corey and Gerald Corey

Exercises and activities used outside of the therapy session can yield many benefits, but ethical considerations in utilizing them effectively and ethically should be addressed prior to their use. In this piece, we provide guidelines for counselors who want to ask their clients to engage in activities outside of the therapy sessions. If you use out-of-session activities, you certainly need to be competent in employing and monitoring these activities. Our hope is that you will have personally experienced any activities and exercises you expect clients to carry out. It is not enough simply to read about therapeutic activities; practicing them and reflecting on their value is of paramount importance.

It is an ethical imperative that you have a theoretical rationale for introducing activities to clients. Not only do you need to know why you are suggesting an exercise, but you also need to explain in simple language why you are inviting clients to practice activities out of sessions. Activities should not be used in a mechanical fashion or without considering the needs of each individual. In short, activities that are a part of this workbook must be customized to fit the goals and needs of each client. It is key for counselors to tailor out-of-session activities to a client's specific problems. These activities need to be geared to what clients hope to achieve, not necessarily what the counselor deems meaningful.

Your relationship with your clients provides the foundation for implementing these activities. It is necessary to prepare and orient your clients to the therapeutic value of exercises and activities that you will collaboratively design with your clients. We find that we need to be mindful that we are not the experts when it comes to the goals of our clients. We have expertise in applying knowledge and skills to assist clients in reaching their life goals, but clients are the experts in terms of knowing who they are and what they want. We do our best to enlist our clients as therapeutic partners and to create a collaborative approach to counseling. Homework is not simply assigned; rather, it is discussed during the therapy hour with the aim of helping clients achieve what they want in life. If the therapist merely gives homework assignments to clients, they are less likely to implement the tasks out of session than if they are involved in making decisions about how they can become actively engaged beyond the therapy office. Clients are more likely to implement the assignments in daily life if they are involved in the process of creating their own assignments. It might be useful to ask clients to think about activities they can carry out between sessions as a way of summarizing the highlights of each therapy session.

Clients are more inclined to practice out-of-session activities if they can see how doing so will move them closer to achieving their goals. The emphasis always needs to be on the client's agenda, not the counselor's agenda for the client. Assignments are best designed collaboratively with the client toward the end of a therapy session and reflect topics that were explored in that session. Follow up is crucial, and a good way to begin a session is by inquiring about the experience of doing (or not doing) the homework. If clients do not complete their homework, it is not helpful to criticize or blame them; rather, the lack of completion of activities provides material for discussion: What got in the way of carrying out the assignment? Is the assignment congruent with the client's personal goals? If clients complete their assignment, they can be asked questions such as these: What was helpful about the out-of-session activity? What was learned from doing the assignment? What challenges were involved in completing the homework?

We need to keep in mind that some activities and exercises can be counterproductive if applied to clients under certain circumstances. For example, some interventions in the therapy office, and in daily life as well, may bring up intense emotions. Activities that are likely to arouse intense emotions need to be assessed carefully to ensure that they are not misused. Encouraging clients to "get out their anger" by pounding on a sofa cushion can boomerang and be somewhat harmful to some clients. Care needs to be used in working with clients with a background of trauma. Exercises or activities used primarily to assist clients in reliving traumatic events can result in retraumatizing them. Clients are sometimes encouraged to carry work into their daily life that was initiated during a therapy session. For example, during a counseling session a client might have explored her hurt and anger toward a parent who failed to provide compassion and caring. The client may have lingering resentment toward the parent for withholding love, and this resentment can be interfering with present-day relationships. Therapists often suggest that these clients write a letter to the parent expressing this hurt and saying what they wish had transpired. These letters have symbolic value through the process of simply writing them and venting feelings that have been suppressed. It is not necessary that these letters be given to the parents; indeed, caution is needed in giving letters such as this to parents. Cultural factors need to be considered in deciding what to do with letters that are drafted as part of therapeutic homework. In some cultures, if adult children were to express painful feelings about the way they were reared or about their early childhood experiences, the outcome could be a source of division within the family. The result could certainly be anything but therapeutic. Giving a letter that was written in emotional circumstances needs to be carefully assessed, and the risks need to be discussed in a therapy session with the client.

Individuals in therapy are sometimes asked to interview members of their family of origin about the family processes or family history. Out-of-session exercises in which clients are encouraged to interview selected family members and the extended family can be viewed as intrusive and be the source of intense conflict. Before such activities are assigned, certain cautions and guidelines need to be addressed in the therapy office. In all cases, feedback from clients who carry out activities between sessions is of the utmost importance. Therapists need to provide a rationale for their clients about the value of the practice of giving regular feedback about their experience during the therapy session. Clients need to understand how their feedback on any activities they are doing outside of the therapy sessions is useful and a necessary part of the therapeutic process.

• • •

We suggest some additional recommendations regarding ethics:

- Practice within your area of expertise and competency even with the use of out-of-session activities and exercises.
- Therapeutic homework exercises should be described to clients as supplementary to counseling, and not a substitute for counseling.
- As a part of the informed consent process, discuss fully with your clients how the activities and exercises will be utilized in counseling and how they can benefit from out-of-session tasks.
- Allow clients to opt out of using exercises should they so desire.
- Discuss possible adverse reactions to completing the activities and exercises. Reflecting on stressful or upsetting themes may trigger some clients (e.g., those who have not processed their trauma), so

use your best clinical judgment in evaluating which exercises to assign and whether or not to modify them for any particular client. Be on the lookout for adverse reactions (e.g., stress, anxiety, depression, repressed memories) and intervene accordingly.

- Empower clients to determine whether or not they want to complete an exercise if they start working on one and become overwhelmed or triggered. If they report back to you that they stopped working on the exercise because it increased their distress, be sure to praise them for exercising good judgment and for taking care of themselves. Processing this experience may be more therapeutic and valuable than the exercise itself.
- The written responses are the property of the client. Clients have the right to share their responses with whomever they choose (remember, you are bound by confidentiality—clients are not). However, it may not be in their best interest to discuss their out-of-session work with others. Discuss with clients the pros and cons of sharing such information with others before this homework is assigned.
- Discuss with clients how their written responses will be maintained to protect their privacy. Would the client prefer that they be returned to you for safekeeping? Kept at home or stored on their computer or in the Cloud? Where will they be most secure? These are all issues to discuss with the client.
- For more on legal and ethical issues including those of informed consent, see Wheeler and Bertram (2019).

It is essential to keep all relevant ethical issues in mind throughout the counseling process and ensure that activities and exercises are only used in the best interests of the client.

Instructions and Suggestions for Using Workbook Exercises and Activities

Richardson, Richards, and Barkham (2010) found that self-help materials have the potential to provide a valuable aid to counseling but that they should be used in conjunction with guidance and support from mental health workers. We agree wholeheartedly. To practice responsibly and ethically, practitioners must make a concerted effort to match the intervention strategies they use, including therapeutic homework assignments, to the unique needs and characteristics of the client. It is also important to strive for coherence between the goals of treatment and therapeutic homework tasks (Lenehan et al., 2019). We anticipate that clients will benefit most from doing selected activities if they have the space and time to process their reactions to them within the context of a supportive and healing therapeutic relationship. Some of these exercises may evoke powerful emotions and reactions that need to be worked through in therapy.

Most of the exercises require clients to write down or record their answers and bring them back to counseling to process, so ask clients to purchase a notebook or journal. (As you will see, there is insufficient space after each question, exercise, or activity to provide in-depth responses.) If you prefer, you could keep a stack of blank journals in your office to give to clients as needed. If clients prefer to record their thoughts on a computer, remind them to print a copy to bring to session. We encourage you to use the exercises in this workbook in a flexible and creative manner. Most clients would benefit from keeping a journal and writing their reactions to selected exercises in it; however, we are aware that some clients may not have the writing skills, motivation, or interest to keep a journal. Some clients may be ready for exercises that will promote deep introspection or catharsis, and others may not be ready. Some exercises are more appropriate for clients who have a greater capacity for insight or abstract thinking. Again, use your best clinical judgment when assigning these exercises. The key question to ask is, "Which therapeutic activities will be most helpful for my client at this specific point in her or his therapeutic journey?"

Julius A. Austin, a clinical therapist and coordinator of the Office of Substance Abuse and Recovery at Tulane University, describes his use of out-of-session exercises to guide clients in building on their existing skills.

Drawing Upon Clients' Skills to Cocreate Productive Therapeutic Homework Exercises

Julius A. Austin

To help clients build coping skills, I try to use the tools the client organically possesses and then move forward with cocreating coping skills unique to that client. To best illustrate what I mean, here is a case example in which I empowered my client to generate solutions to his own problems.

I worked with a client who was disabled, and he told me that he played video games at a high level against individuals from all over the world when he was not in school. He said he enjoyed doing so because his disability was never a topic of discussion. At one point, this client expressed that he wanted to make a change from making friends in the virtual world to making friends in the physical world. After a lengthy discussion revolving around his fear of rejection, self-esteem issues, and self-talk distortions, he seemed ready to experiment with creating relationships in the physical world.

Building on his experiences with creating relationships in the virtual world, we worked together to develop scripts of possible conversation starters, small talk options, and disengagement strategies that he could use when meeting people. After tweaking the scripts, practicing them in session, and committing the scripts to memory, this client felt ready for his first attempt at creating a relationship in the physical world. After his first attempt, we came together and discussed the experience and the usefulness of the scripts. He continued to use the scripts, and over time he was able to be more flexible and fit the words to the particular situation.

To maintain a foothold in both worlds, the virtual and the physical, we cocreated the following homework assignment: For every two friends he made while playing video games, he had to attempt to make one friend in the physical world. My client enjoyed this assignment because (a) the goal was attainable; (b) he could build on skills he already possessed to stretch himself and take interpersonal risks; and (c) he was an active participant in creating the therapeutic homework assignment, which enabled him to buy-in to the process.

When creating therapeutic assignments with clients, I recommend the following:

- Draw upon skills your clients already possess.
- Empower clients by actively involving them in the process of designing homework assignments.
- Do not give homework assignments with a pass or fail option. An "attempt" is also a viable, attainable option for some clients.
- Always be open to feedback from the client with regard to adjusting or changing aspects of the homework assignment.

● ● ●

Dobson and Dobson (2017) provide additional suggestions for the use of out-of-session activities with clients, which are highlighted here:

- It is essential that the use of out-of-session exercises is a collaborative and mutual effort between client and counselor.
- Be sure the client has a clear understanding of the task and the time frame. Identify page numbers and item numbers you wish the client to work on.
- Explain how the out-of-session work will enhance the client's experience and progress in therapy.
- Follow up on the assignment(s) at the next session, and compliment the client for working on the task(s).
- Consider asking the client in session what her or his response might be for one of the activities assigned. This may inspire the client to begin thinking about the task and may whet her or his appetite to continue working on the task outside of counseling.
- The process of the client's work on a given task may be as important as the content of the client's response to an exercise. Both content and process should be discussed in the next counseling session.

We reiterate that you have our permission to photocopy any of the For Clients materials to give to your clients or even to design exercises of your own inspired by the activities in this workbook. Use your best clinical judgment in assigning out-of-session activities that meet clients where they are and that will not push them beyond their ability to cope. Neither the authors nor the American Counseling Association (ACA) is responsible for the impact of the workbook activities on individuals or their possible therapeutic outcomes.

Conclusion

As we contemplated this project, the very notion of addressing such distressing and wide-ranging topics as natural disasters, tribalism, cyberbullying, mass shootings, social injustice, and terrorism, just to name a few, in *one* book, seemed daunting. After much introspection, we recognized that our objective in creating this resource for counselors was not to solve society's problems but to provide clients with exercises and activities that would help them process their reactions to stressors. As much as we would love to be able to solve society's problems, we are well aware of what is and what is not within our ability to control! Clarifying our goals definitely helped us move forward with this workbook. These activities were designed to help clients clarify their thinking about stressors and focus on what they can control—even if they cannot change the facts or actual events that triggered their stress or crisis—and we hope clients will feel that a weight has been lifted from their shoulders.

Chapter 2

Cultivating Client Resilience

In a time when mass gun violence has become normalized, severe weather patterns threaten livelihoods and force migration from communities, and sociocultural and political climates are tense, the need for resilience has never been greater.

—Simone Lambert
President, American Counseling Association
2018–2019

• • •

For Counselors

The word *resilience* is variously described as "hardiness," "resourcefulness," or "mental toughness" (Corey & Corey, 2021). Stories abound of individuals who excel beyond what anyone might normally expect in times of crisis. Others collapse under the pressure of similar crises. What is it that enables some to thrive but leads others to become immobilized, paralyzed with self-doubt and unable to react or adapt?

On May 8, 2019, 35-year-old Amanda Eller set out on a 3-mile hike in a forest reserve in Maui. She became lost, and her ordeal turned into a 17-day fight for her life, during which she fell 20 feet off a steep cliff, fracturing her leg and tearing the meniscus in her knee, and subsisting on whatever she could salvage, including plants she could not identify and moths that landed on her body. When rescued and in the hospital, she commented, "I wanted to give up. . . . But the only option I had was life or death" (Kerr, 2019). Many people would not be able to withstand the pain and the environmental conditions that Amanda endured. So what are the ingredients for success that we can teach our clients?

Many individuals who cope successfully with a disastrous event develop new strength and self-confidence in their ability to cope. Oftentimes people not only cope with the traumatic event but thrive, discovering strengths and skills they didn't know they had (Collier, 2016; Stebnicki, 2017). This positive result is called *posttraumatic growth* (PTG), and it can mark an individual's struggle throughout a crisis event. PTG was first described by psychologists Richard Tedeschi and Lawrence Calhoun (1995) and was ascribed to people who had difficulty bouncing back from a traumatic event and whose core beliefs were challenged or shaken. Through PTG they ultimately found strength and experienced personal growth (Collier, 2016). Resilient individuals may not experience PTG because they are not rocked to their core; these people respond fairly quickly and effectively to any event. The emergent strengths from PTG might include survival skills, self-acceptance, and a greater appreciation and understanding of life in general. Mancini (2016b) views the concept of PTG as problematic on the basis that one's *perception* of growth and change may be unrelated to *actual* growth and change. However, he does acknowledge that people tend to have a robust and innate capacity to cope effectively with trauma and that exposure to tragedy can improve psychological health for some people (Mancini, 2016a).

I (Bob) consulted with a mother whose 21-year-old daughter, Alicia, was present at the Route 91 Harvest Music Festival shooting in Las Vegas on October 1, 2017. At that shooting, a lone gunman fired more than 1,100 rounds from the 32nd floor of a Las Vegas hotel, killing 58 and injuring 869 from gunshot wounds or in the frantic escape. It was the deadliest mass shooting ever by an individual in the United States (Montero & Tchekmedyian, 2017). Alicia had been in the front row and witnessed individuals next to her being shot. She and her friend escaped the carnage of the dead and wounded and found refuge outside the arena. Needless to say, the trauma was horrifying and overwhelming. Alicia felt guilty for not stopping to aid those who had been shot but knows now that it would have been a deadly decision and she would not have survived. Her mother was at a loss as to how to help her daughter deal with the trauma of this event. I explained that the brain of a trauma victim is like a house in an earthquake; everything is turned upside down and out of place, and it takes time to get all of that back in order. It would take patience, support, love, and understanding from her family, her support network, for Alicia to recover. A communal trauma event is highly complex and many personal attributes and clinical interventions are required during recovery. This event rocked many of those involved to the core of their being and will be life-changing. I know Alicia to be bright, determined, goal-oriented, and a problem solver. I was confident that she was an inherently resilient person who would recover and become stronger and more determined to do something with her life to make a difference with others. In essence, this life-changing event will leave deep scars on this young woman, but her ability to find strengths she did not know she had and to do something with her life that is positive and dramatic are assets that will encourage personal growth.

As you approach your work with clients on the topic of resilience, take a moment to think about your own level of resilience and how that has affected your work as a counselor and in your personal life.

- Are you able to maintain your composure and react to situations and crises effectively?
- Are you able to bounce back from the low points and crises in your life?
- Have you always been a resilient person, or has that evolved and developed through your experience, education, support, and having a connection with others?

Think about your reaction and response to the difficult life situations your clients face as you work with them to cope with adverse life events. Your own development and current level of resilience can provide clues for helping clients develop resilience in their lives. Resilience is one of the key components of living a stable, satisfying, and productive life and being able to cope with the stresses of life events and crises (Meyers, 2019). Our job as counselors is to help our clients become as resilient as possible.

A resilient lifestyle can help us endure through these difficult times. The political and personal rhetoric and divisiveness we see today is exhausting, demoralizing, depressing, and sometimes downright sad for us. It erodes our optimistic and hopeful outlook for the future and the future of those we care about (e.g., Bob's children and grandchildren and Michelle's nephews and great nephew). Counselors must be sensitive to the increasing stress that is affecting clients who are marginalized, oppressed, or living in poverty. Life is tough enough when everything else is relatively stable. Coping with discrimination, bankruptcy, and the threat of homelessness in addition to the tension, hatred, and anger permeating our world today makes life's journey exponentially more difficult. Resilience helps us bounce back, recover, maintain hope for the future, and endure through these conflicting times. It is resilience and hope that support and foster our clients' survival under the most difficult circumstances.

We may think hardiness and mental toughness are inherent in the personality and enable some folks to be resilient when faced with a crisis, but resilience is a set of skills that can be learned and developed. In many cases, resilience is the result of learning a set of behaviors that gives the person confidence in his or her ability to cope with the crisis. The training of airline pilots, for example, includes learning how to respond when things go wrong in the air. Resilience training is also widely used in the U.S. Army. For several years, the U.S. Army has implemented a large-scale Master Resilience Training program for soldiers, their family members, and Army civilians. "More than 55,000 U.S. Army Soldiers have attended this train-the-trainer program and gone on to teach the resilience skills to hundreds of thousands of Soldiers" (University of Pennsylvania, 2019). Research on resilience has focused on the process that occurs when individuals react to stressful situations (Meichenbaum, 2012). Resilience is more what you do in a situation than it is who you are as a person. Resilient people also experience sadness, difficulty, and distress, but their ability to use coping skills and bounce back leads them to a positive outcome in a crisis.

A number of factors are known to be associated with resilience. Turk Nolty, Rensberger, Bosch, Hennig, and Buckwalter (2018) state that one major and often overlooked dimension of resilience is religion, a person's beliefs and spirituality. As they state so well, "spirituality may provide a safety anchor that allows more of a sense of control, even in dire and helpless situations" (p. 56). Another critical factor that contributes to bolstering psychological resilience as well as PTG is social support. In a study of people living in the Gulf of Mexico region who had survived two major disasters—Hurricane Katrina in 2005 and the Deepwater Horizon oil spill in 2010—investigators discovered a significant and inverse relationship between PTG and loneliness (Lee, Blackmon, Lee, Cochran, & Rehner, 2019). In addition to the power of social support, studies of resilience generally point out the beneficial effects of optimism, positive affect (e.g., joy, ebullience, and excitement), and coping, all of which protect against the development of psychiatric disorders (Schaefer, Howell, Schwartz, Bottomley, & Crossnine, 2018; Shrestha et al., 2018).

Another factor in resilience is the role of brain chemistry in handling difficult situations. Cortisol promotes survival by mobilizing the body's fight or flight response. DHEA is another hormone that works in conjunction with cortisol and protects the brain from the negative effects of cortisol (Turk Nolty et al., 2018). In a discussion of "infusing hope amid despair," Laura Meyers (2018) found that a person who has lost a job can be experiencing significant stress and is likely flooded with cortisol in the same way as someone who has experienced a violent and aggressive act. Exposure to unrelenting stress and trauma, such as soldiers in wartime, can change brain chemistry permanently (Stebnicki, 2017). We are just beginning to scratch the surface in understanding the role of brain chemicals in the development of resilience.

Ordinary People Do Extraordinary Things and Demonstrate Resilience

What is it that makes some people so resilient when others are simply unable to cope with stressful events? We have examples all around us of individuals reacting to life events with resilience, and still others who are shaken to their core but are able to recover and experience PTG or improve their psychological functioning. Here are three examples.

- Twelve members and the coach of a boys' youth soccer team lost in a cave in Thailand were found alive and rescued through a heroic effort that included hundreds of rescue personnel diving through dangerous channels to reach the boys (Suhartono & Paddock, 2018). Even after being lost for 9 days and enduring an additional 9 days in an exceedingly dangerous rescue operation, the boys and their coach demonstrated surprising hope, optimism, and resilience. How were these boys and their coach able to maintain these feelings throughout this ordeal?
- Pakistani activist Malala Yousafzai, the youngest Nobel Peace Prize winner, is championing the education of girls after being shot in the head as a teenager by Taliban militants in 2012 (Norwegian Nobel Committee, 2014). Her survival, recovery, and return to become a national hero in Pakistan and around the world fosters hope and optimism for the education and freedom of women everywhere and for the defeat of extremism. How did this young teenager muster the courage and determination to recover and lead such an international movement?

- Jayme Lynn Closs was 13 years old when her parents were murdered and she was abducted from her home. She was held captive for 88 days in a cabin located 70 miles away. While in captivity, she was often forced to hide underneath her kidnapper's bed to ensure that no one would find her. On January 10, 2019, Closs bravely escaped and had the presence of mind to seek assistance and report this horrific crime. In sentencing her abductor and her parents' murderer, Closs's statement was read aloud in court: "I was smarter. . . . I watched his routine and I took back my freedom. I will always have my freedom, and he will not. Jake Patterson can never take my courage. He thought he could control me, but he couldn't" (Shapiro, 2019). Where did this 13-year-old find the strength to survive the tragedy of losing both parents and plan her escape from her kidnapper?

Cultural Issues and Resilience

In helping a client develop resilience, it is essential that counselors are cognizant of differences between counselor and client and are mindful of the impact of the client's culture on the client's beliefs, attitudes, and behavior in regard to understanding and developing resilience. This applies to gender, race, sexual orientation, spiritual beliefs, disabilities, and any way in which individuals might define themselves (Stebnicki, 2017). Counselors also need to be aware of their own cultural stereotypes in understanding a particular client and that individual's culture. In addition to one's own knowledge and awareness of cultural differences, the best source for understanding the client's culture and cultural definitions of resilience is *the client*.

Counselors need a broad knowledge of the cultural context, the value of resilience, and the cultural resources available for recovery. Resilient cultures and communities cultivate natural support systems, have leadership and organizational resources, can restore safety and security, are tolerant and respectful of individuals, progressively move forward after a crisis, and often use cultural healing rituals (Stebnicki, 2017). Healers in many cultures embody the idea of balancing one's physical, mental, emotional, and spiritual dimensions. When assisting clients as they examine and develop resilience in their lives, counselors should be mindful of their cultural and individual context. Stebnicki (2017) sums it up best by stating, "the path to resiliency within a cultural context transcends the individual's experience of loss, trauma, and disaster . . . to an understanding of how the critical event impacted the culture as a whole" (p. 280).

What We Have Learned About Helping Others Therapeutically

Whether recounting the drive of the Thai soccer team, the perseverance of Malala Yousafzai, or the strength and determination of Jayme Lynn Closs, each of these remarkable people showed great resilience in the face of seemingly insurmountable odds. Here are some questions to discuss with your clients to evaluate their own reserves of resilience:

- Would you be able to maintain your composure and implement a plan of action in a time of crisis? If not, are you motivated to develop a plan of action so you will feel more prepared should a crisis arise?
- When I hear these stories, I often wonder what I would have done in that situation. Do I have what it takes to persevere and survive? To maintain a positive attitude? To recover quickly after the crisis? How about you?
- Were you born with resilience, or do you think you have learned this skill with age and experience? How resilient are your loved ones (e.g., your partner, parents, or children)?

We cannot predict with certainty how any individual will react in a crisis. We do know that the success clients have had when coping with past events predicts a greater likelihood of succeeding in future events. We also know that individuals with the ability to adapt to adversity, cope successfully with stressful events, recover quickly, endure stress without lasting harm, and adapt to the new situation are more likely to be resilient (Meichenbaum, 2012; Stebnicki, 2017).

The Counselor's Task With Clients

A number of evidence-based treatment approaches and interventions can promote the development of resilience and help clients recover from trauma. Whether one specializes in cognitive behavior therapy, relational psychotherapy, mind-body therapies, or any other approach, it is essential to look for opportunities to strengthen the client's resilience. Indeed, regardless of the specific treatment goals, following a crisis a primary task is to assist the client in developing the characteristics and skills of resilience. The exercises and activities provided in this chapter are designed to assist clients in thinking about previous experiences and determining what they can learn about their level of resilience and ways to strengthen it. Resilience can be learned, and it involves the following factors:

- A set of attitudes and beliefs in one's ability to cope with life's situations
- Practice implementing those attitudes in action
- Support from friends and family in being a strong and resourceful individual
- Connectedness to others through family and community organizations
- Spiritual development

Resilience is a set of life skills, strategies, beliefs, behaviors, and connections that bolster the individual and reinforce her or his ability to manage, master, and succeed in the face of trauma.

Notes

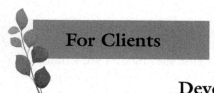

Developing Resilience in One's Life

Most of us hope life will be fun, uncomplicated, predictable, and easy to navigate. In reality, life is often full of twists and turns and has high points as well as disappointments. As licensed professional counselor Cynthia Miller says, "Life is a traumatizing experience. It's full of challenges, unexpected and uncontrollable events, and losses. I don't think anyone of us gets through it unscathed" (as cited in Meyers, 2018, p. 21). It is critical that you develop a resilient and resourceful approach so you can cope with the stresses and crises you encounter.

What is resilience? Simply stated, resilience is your ability to cope with and bounce back from stressful and adverse events while maintaining a positive outlook. Recent studies have explored resilience as one of the key factors that help people cope in a crisis. *Optimism*, often considered an inherent trait, is a positive disposition that leads to having a hopeful outlook on life. It plays an important role in resilience. If you tend to be more pessimistic—that is, you tend to have a negative view of events and expectations for the future—don't despair (even if that comes naturally to you). Optimism can be learned and cultivated, just like resilience.

Posttraumatic growth is the life-changing strength and growth that can result from your struggle to recover from a deeply traumatizing event or disaster. Exposure to traumatic events can result in a "steeling or inoculating effect," which helps you manage future traumatic events.

Key Thought

Resilience is more what you do in a situation than it is who you are as a person. If you experience sadness, difficulty, and distress, but you are able to roll with the punches—to cope and bounce back—you will have a positive outcome in a crisis.

How Does Resilience Work in Your Life?

Resilience helps you make realistic plans and develop the steps to carry out those plans to resolve a crisis. It also helps you maintain a positive expectation for the outcome of the situation and gives you confidence in your strengths and abilities. In addition, resilience can help you recover from the effects of a crisis more quickly.

What is it that makes some people so resilient when others are simply unable to cope with stressful events? Resilient individuals tend to be goal-oriented, self-directed and self-motivated, open to learning new ways to handle stress and crisis in their lives, grounded in family and community, have a sense of spirituality, bounce back from adversities that life provides, take good emotional and physical care of themselves, and have a sense of belonging, purpose, and strength. We have examples all around us of individuals reacting to life events with resilience.

Hell in Paradise: A Case Illustration

Nichole Jolly, 34, a nurse at Feather River Hospital in Paradise, California, described what it was like trying to escape from the 2018 Camp Fire, the deadliest and most destructive fire in California history. At one point, Nichole called her husband and said, "I think I'm going to die. Tell the kids I love them. I'm not gonna make it home" (Rosenblatt, 2018). After rapidly and successfully evacuating patients from the hospital, she was fleeing from the rampage, driving her car out of the tornado-like inferno in Paradise. The line of traffic on the road came to a halt, then she was hit from behind. Her car was pushed into a ravine, smoke began to enter the car, and she could feel the heat of the flames. That's when she called her husband and told him she thought she was about to die. He told her not to die, to fight for her life, to get out of the car and run for her life. She ran to the next car, but the door handle was melted. She found another car and got inside. By this time, Nichole's pant leg was on fire, and it set the front seat on fire.

She quickly extinguished that fire. As the heat and the flames intensified, she heard her husband's voice telling her to fight for her life, to run out of it if she could. She got out of the hot and smoky car and began to feel her way ahead, but the smoke and flames and ash were so intense she couldn't see a thing. Nichole said she breathed in the hottest air she has ever breathed, and she could feel her shoes melting on the hot pavement. Suddenly her hand touched the back of what turned out to be a fire truck, and the firemen took her inside and covered her with a fire rescue blanket. They all thought they were doomed, but a bulldozer suddenly appeared and cleared the road so the fire truck could escape.

After she was free of the fire area, she got a ride from the firemen back to her hospital. She spent the next several hours treating walk-in patients until they were forced once again to evacuate the hospital. When she thought she would die, her husband became the voice that motivated her and directed her through a near death experience. That voice became her voice, driving her to survive and to help save others on that horrible and deadly day. She is just an ordinary person who found the inner resources to not give up, to bounce back, and to succeed in her drive to live. That is true resilience.

• • •

What Are the Characteristics of Resilient Individuals?

Mark A. Stebnicki (2017) is a licensed professional counselor who works with clients who have chronic medical/physical health conditions and who have experienced traumatic stress (both civilian and military trauma). He describes resilient individuals as those who

- are positive thinkers and believe in themselves and their abilities;
- are self-directed and self-motivated and confident they will succeed in challenging situations;
- choose healthy emotions, behaviors, and thoughts;
- demonstrate a persistence with tasks;
- take self-responsibility, own their shortcomings, and strive to improve themselves;
- are willing to take risks, are realistic and flexible, and do not avoid new activities or experiences that might benefit them; and
- exhibit tolerance and a sense of openness in looking at different ways to resolve situations. (pp. 278–279)

The exercises and activities that follow will help you examine ways to develop a more resilient approach to life.

Workbook Material for the Client

The following questions and exercises are designed to help you examine the topic of resilience in your life between therapy sessions. There are no right or wrong answers. This is an opportunity for you to spend some time thinking about how well you cope and bounce back from tough situations in your own life. Some questions and exercises may be easy for you, and others may require more time and thought on your part. We hope you will take plenty of time to consider each topic or question that your counselor has asked you to complete. The value of these activities and questions comes from your careful consideration about your position on the topic. The goal is for you to learn as much as you can outside the counseling setting. If you are better prepared to explore these issues, your session time will be more productive. We suggest that you keep a journal as you contemplate your resilience. Purchase a notebook or journal or record your responses to selected questions and activities on your computer. Remember to print your responses and bring them with you to your next counseling session.

Exercises and Activities

The following are some exercises to help you understand resilience in your own life.

1. Describe a situation you encountered that was stressful for you. How did you handle the situation? On a scale of 1 to 10, rate how well you rebounded or recovered from that experience.

   Scale: 1   2   3   4   5   6   7   8   9   10

   Not at all   *Complete recovery*

   Explain your response.

   _____

2. In thinking about the situation you described in question 1, what helped you get through the experience that worked especially well?

   _____

   _____

3. What would you like to learn to help you better handle those kinds of situations?

   _____

   _____

4. Overall, how well are you able to bounce back from difficult situations and events when life challenges you?

   _____

   _____

5. Describe another stressful situation you experienced. Were you able to learn and gain strength from your handling of that situation, or did the experience get you down? Did it make you doubt your ability to cope with stress or adversity?

   _____

   _____

6. Resilience is the ability of an individual to cope with and bounce back from stressful and adverse events while maintaining a positive outlook. Do you think people are born resilient, or is it something we learn with age and experience? How about for you personally?

   _____

   _____

7. If applicable, how would you describe your significant other/partner in terms of being a resilient individual?

   _____

   _____

8. If applicable, how would you describe your children in terms of being resilient individuals?

   _____

   _____

How Can You Become More Resilient?

The list that follows is adapted from "The Road to Resilience" (APA, 2018b). Each item states a factor that builds resilience and suggests activities to help you build your own resilience. Review the list and consider one or two items you might try each week. See what works for you and what doesn't, and create ways for the resilience-increasing activities to be enjoyable and specific to your needs and wishes.

1. Build connections with people. These include connections with family and friends, as well as organizations and groups that will enable you to interact with others who share your interests (e.g., faith-based groups, community groups, sports).

   a. Would you like to spend more time with one family member or friend? Think of a few ways you could spend more time with that person (or group). You could go to coffee, lunch, dinner, a movie, the gym, fishing, or some other activity. Identify the person you have chosen to initiate more contact with and what you will invite them to do.

   _____

   _____

   b. Come back to item (a) one month from now and describe how that has worked out for you and whether you think this is a positive experience for you. Select another person with whom you would like to spend more time, and describe what you will invite that individual to do with you.

   _____

   _____

   c. Think about a group you might like to find out more about or join: a faith-based organization, volunteer group, or another community organization. Make plans to contact that group and learn more about it, and arrange for a trial visit. Identify the group you contacted and describe how the initial inquiry went for you.

   _____

   _____

   d. Come back to item (c) 6 weeks from now and describe what you have done with this group and whether you are encouraged to continue. Have you met some individuals you hope to get to know better?

   _____

   _____

2. Try not to see crises as insurmountable. You can't change events, but you can change the way you perceive and respond to those events. As Jaycee Dugard stated regarding the three young women kidnapped in Cleveland and enslaved for 10 years, "This isn't who they are. It is only what happened to them. The human spirit is resilient. More than ever this reaffirms we should never give up hope" (as cited in Mather, 2013).

   a. When you encounter a crisis do you generally respond by:
      • Looking to others for help and direction?
      • Hoping the situation resolves itself?
      • Looking at potential solutions?
      • Believing that you will be able to resolve the situation?
      • Thinking things will end poorly?

   b. Describe how you approach difficult/stressful situations. Do you see the glass as half empty or half full?

   _____

   _____

c. Do you hope to become a more positive problem solver? What skills would you like to develop for resolving stressful situations?

_____

_____

3. Work to accept circumstances that can't be changed and put your energy into situations that you do have control over. By acknowledging that change happens whether we like it or not, we are more empowered to accept it and embrace change.

Select the number that most accurately describes the frequency with which you experience the following situations:

Scale: 1   2   3   4   5

         Rarely/never   _Always_

_____ I relish the challenges that life's various stages offer.

_____ I spend too much time worrying about things I can't change.

_____ I feel irritated at work when I see things that could be improved and function more efficiently but don't change.

_____ I am comfortable with the rapid pace of change I see happening in society and the world today.

_____ I tend to look back in time and wish things were like they used to be.

_____ I typically embrace changes in my personal life and get bored when things remain the same.

_____ I often feel that others don't appreciate the changes I make in my life.

_____ I have difficulty appreciating or accepting changes I observe in others (e.g., family members, friends).

_____ I tend to feel helpless when I cannot control what is happening around me.

_____ I become angry or frustrated when I cannot control what is happening around me.

a. Please take this opportunity to write in your journal about any of the previous statements that elicited a strong reaction.

_____

_____

b. List three to five words or phrases that best describe how you typically handle change in your life.

_____

_____

c. List three to five words or phrases that best describe how you would ideally like to handle change in your life.

_____

_____

4. Develop realistic goals, and work toward accomplishing one or more of your goals, no matter how small they might seem.
   a. Ask yourself, "What is one thing I can do today to move toward accomplishing my goals?"

_____

_____

   b. What are three goals you would like to achieve in the next year?

_____

_____

c. What will it take to reach each of those goals? What will be needed? What might get in the way? What are realistic time frames?

_____

_____

d. What would your life look like if you accomplished each of these three goals?

_____

_____

e. Summarize your plan for meeting each goal using the following template.

Goal:

_____

_____

Resources needed:

_____

_____

Potential obstacles:

_____

_____

Goal accomplished:

_____

_____

Time frame:

_____

_____

5. Instead of hoping a crisis or stressful situation just won't happen, act on the situation and do the best you can to resolve it. Keep a log of each stressful situation that occurs in your life for the next 2 weeks. Describe each situation and your reaction to it (i.e., what you thought and felt, what you said to yourself about the situation, what actions you took to resolve the crisis, and how effective those actions were for you). Then describe what you learned from your response to the situation and what you hope to do differently next time.

_____

_____

6. Learn as much as you can about yourself from every adverse situation. Tragedy and hardship can be learning experiences from which you improve self-confidence and reorder your priorities about life. What tragedies and hardships have you encountered in life? What have you learned about yourself from those experiences? In what ways have you grown as a result of these difficult experiences?

_____

_____

7. Develop an ability to trust your instincts when responding to a crisis. Use what you do know and have learned to help you respond rather than focus on what you don't know about responding in the situation.

   a. As you think about how you have handled crises and what you have learned from those experiences, do you feel better prepared to handle future crises? Explain.

      _____

      _____

   b. What remains for you to learn? How can you build on what you already know to acquire new skills and knowledge?

      _____

      _____

   c. Do you believe you possess an inherent ability to rely on your instincts in a crisis? If so, say more about this.

      _____

      _____

8. Maintain an optimistic outlook on life and focus on what you want to accomplish rather than on what you fear or don't have. How would you describe your basic outlook on life? Are you more inclined to be a negative or a positive thinker? Do you tend to think of life as a glass being half full or half empty?

   _____

   _____

9. Pay attention to your self-talk. Keep a journal of your self-talk dialogue, and change the way you view and react to crisis situations. What you perceive and tell yourself about your ability to cope with crises is essential to becoming a resilient person. Resilient individuals believe in their ability to take charge of situations rather than feeling powerless, hopeless, and overwhelmed. Does your self-talk work for you or undermine your self-confidence?

   _____

   _____

10. Successfully navigating crises and stressful situations often entails flexibility and adaptability, and paying attention to what you need in any given moment. When faced with a crisis, how often do you:

   Scale: 1   2   3   4   5   6   7   8   9   10
             Never   *Always*

   _____ Allow yourself to get in touch with your deep emotions and express them.

   _____ Give yourself permission to avoid delving into deep emotions when it would be counter-productive to get in touch with them.

   _____ Mobilize into action and take care of tasks that need to be completed.

   _____ Honor your limits and know when you need to take a break and get some rest or relaxation.

   _____ Identify what you need to do to nurture yourself.

   _____ Seek support and encouragement from people who love and care about you.

   _____ Know when you need to spend time alone to recharge yourself and your energy.

   _____ Know when to reach out to others and rely on them versus trying to handle everything on your own.

   _____ Know when it would be more appropriate or empowering to rely on yourself to accomplish certain tasks.

Take the opportunity now to write in your journal about any of these statements that elicited a strong reaction:

_____

_____

11. Resilience helps us cope with and bounce back from a crisis. Some of us seem to be born with a resilient personality, but all of us can improve our resilience with help and support from family and community. If you do not possess a certain resiliency in responding to life's crises, you can learn and develop it. You can endure horrific situations and experiences and not only survive but thrive with a new sense of hope, purpose, and optimism. That is the essence of resilience. Answer the following questions based on what you have learned about your own resilience.

a. What three things can you begin to do right away to increase your level of resilience?

_____

_____

b. What one item do you believe is the most important to you?

_____

_____

c. Who can you turn to for support and encouragement as you work on strengthening your resilience

_____

_____

d. To maintain your inspiration, identify three to five individuals who embody resilience and can serve as positive role models for you. They may be individuals you know personally or individuals you have read about or seen in the media. Describe what you admire most about them. In what ways would you like to emulate them?

_____

_____

Part II

Addressing Common Mental Health Issues

In Part II you will find discussion of some issues for which people often seek counseling—anxiety and stress, depression and loneliness, anger, low self-esteem, and grief and loss—and how these issues may be intensified by emerging stressors in our rapidly changing world. Each chapter provides an overview of one of these problem areas, discusses the concerns clients typically report, provides brief insights into working therapeutically with clients, and reviews the counselor's key tasks. The exercises and activities included in the chapters are designed to facilitate the therapeutic process and are not a substitute for effective counseling or psychotherapy.

Additional therapeutic exercises for clients are provided in Appendix A. See Appendix B for an annotated list of useful websites and online resources.

Scope of the Problem

People are stressed, anxious, angry, depressed, lonely, and filled with self-doubts in ways they haven't been since the nuclear threats of the cold war in the 1960s. The pace of life has accelerated with the advent of social media and digital communication, and the rapid dissemination of news about world events and natural disasters can be exhausting. Collective anxiety has increased in the wake of myriad uncertainties about the environment and global warming, financial instability, and the upswing in terrorism (Bourne, 2015). Today our children practice active-shooter drills in school, and public places where people gather have become targets for violence. Cyberbullying is increasingly toxic and seemingly without solution. We have struggled with racial and gender discrimination from the beginning of this republic, and despite concerted efforts by activists, each step forward toward social justice seems to be followed by two steps back. In this stress-filled world, people are likely to be in greater need of counseling and to seek it more frequently. We cannot predict the long-term effects of the stress of living in today's world, but it does not seem to bode well for the mental health of America.

In 2018, I (Bob) learned of a stabbing that occurred at a local CVS Pharmacy as a result of road rage over a parking spot. Two people were vying for the same parking spot; when one took the space, both drivers exited their cars and began pepper spraying each other. Then one stabbed the other with a knife. I read about a similar incident in which one man was arguing with a woman who had taken a handicapped parking spot at a mini-mart. When the woman's boyfriend came out of the store and saw what was occurring, he walked over to the man and shoved him to the ground. The man on the ground pulled a gun from his waist and shot the boyfriend dead. Both incidents occurred over a parking spot, and the net result was a stabbing and a killing! More recently, I (Michelle) learned that carjacking crimes were increasing in the city where I work. On October 9, 2019, the *Baltimore Sun* reported that there were 433 carjackings across Baltimore from the beginning of the year through September 28, up 30% from the previous year. This crime instills anxiety, fear, stress, and trauma (Oxenden & Zhang, 2019).

When fundamental norms of civilized society are constantly violated and people's rights are not respected, we feel more stress and so do many of our family members, colleagues, and friends, most of whom are fairly steady solid individuals who competently cope with life's ups and downs. We are aware of our privilege as individuals with a high level of education and income security, and we know daily living is much more difficult for low-income families and single parents who lack a financial safety net and face each day with a multitude of stressors.

The most common sources of stress reported in an APA (2017b) survey were concerns about the future of our nation, money, work, the current political climate, and violence and crime. Stress levels among women and among adults 72 years of age and older are on the rise, and both Hispanic and Black adults report higher levels of stress. The American Psychiatric Association (2018) poll demonstrated a sharp increase in American's anxiety levels from 2017 to 2018.

According to Bourne (2015), anxiety is the number one mental health issue among women and number two among men, second only to substance abuse. He contends that anxiety, including panic attacks and phobias, increases with the cumulative effects of stress over a period of time. Meyers (2017) refers to an increasing sense of "global anxiety" among Americans, and loneliness is at epidemic levels and is becoming a major threat to public health ("America's Loneliness Epidemic," 2018). In a survey of 20,000 adults in 2018, health insurer Cigna learned that nearly 50% of adults sometimes feel alone and left out and 43% feel that their relationships are not meaningful. A systematic review of the scientific literature revealed that "loneliness has been investigated much less than perceived social support, but there is some evidence that greater loneliness predicts poorer depression outcomes" (Wang, Mann, Lloyd-Evans, Ma, & Johnson, 2018, p. 1). Major depression is on the rise among Americans, and young adults and teenagers have had a more rapid increase in rates of depression than adults (Molina, 2018). Some research suggests that social media may play a role in the increasing rates of depression and other mental health concerns such as post-traumatic stress disorder (PTSD; McHugh, Wisniewski, Rosson, & Carroll, 2018). Teens who spend many hours each day on their screens with social media report higher rates of social isolation, including sadness, hopelessness, and suicide ideation.

Some common reasons people seek counseling and therapy are depression, anxiety, addiction, PTSD, attention-deficit/hyperactivity disorder (ADHD), grief due to the loss of a significant other or injury/illness, and self-exploration to gain a better understanding of oneself (Howes, 2008). The severity of the issues causing a client's stress is largely in the eye of the beholder; that is, what is stressful and discouraging for one person may not be as discouraging or have a lasting impact on another individual. People vary on many dimensions, including their level of resilience. Some clients may develop addictions to video games or become depressed and increasingly isolated as their social media use spirals out of control. Other clients set limits for social media use and enjoy its benefits (e.g., reconnecting with old friends) but experience minimal negative effects.

Until we better understand the long-term effects of today's stressors, the bottom line is that we simply need to recognize that these are indeed difficult times for clients coming for therapy. Counselors must determine the level of distress of the individual and devise treatment approaches that best meet the needs of their client.

Chapter 3

Anxiety and Stress

Worrying is carrying tomorrow's load with today's strength—carrying two days at once. It is moving into tomorrow ahead of time. Worrying doesn't empty tomorrow of its sorrow, it empties today of its strength.

—Corrie Ten Boom

· · ·

For Counselors

Anxiety is a common mental health problem in the United States, and it is one of the most pervasive concerns counselors encounter with their clients (Anxiety and Depression Association of America, n.d.). Anxiety manifests as worry or fear over a range of personal and situational factors. We all feel anxious and worry about everyday events at times, but those with an anxiety disorder experience that worry and fear for a prolonged period and may find that it becomes worse and perhaps even unbearable over time. As anxiety intensifies, it can interfere with home life, one's job or school work, and relationships. Symptoms of anxiety include feeling restless or constantly on edge; having difficulty concentrating; experiencing fatigue, irritability, or tension; feeling a sense of uncontrollable worry; and experiencing sleep and eating disturbances. More extreme anxiety may result in a panic disorder or social anxiety disorder (National Institute of Mental Health [NIMH], 2018a).

Bourne (2005, 2015) indicates that nearly 40 million Americans suffer from a variety of anxiety disorders each year, and nearly 25% will suffer some form of anxiety disorder in their lifetime. In fact, Bourne claims that panic and anxiety disorders have reached epidemic proportions and that unrelieved stress that continues over a period of time results in anxiety disorders. Bourne (2015) points to changes in our environment, social order, pace of modern living, technological advances, and the proliferation of nuclear weapons as leading to a collective increase in anxiety. People are challenged to find a sense of stability and consistency in their lives as they continually adjust to these rapid changes. These are difficult times laden with uncertainty, and this more stressful era affects all of us in the United States.

Anxiety and fear are a part of life; they are part of the human condition. Anxiety can serve as a motivator to accomplish life goals. Fear warns us of impending danger and serves an essential function for survival. Anxiety and fear become problematic in a clinical sense when they are perceived as constant, excessive, persistent, and exceed what one would expect in normal situations (Clark & Beck, 2012). Fear and doubt associated with anxiety are at the root of many disorders, relationship dysfunctions, work-related difficulties, and low self-esteem. Freud contended that anxiety is an essential basis of neurosis (Kennard, 2008) and described neurotic anxiety as diffuse and free-floating, whereas focused and specific anxieties are commonly labeled as phobias today. Clark and Beck (2012) describe fear as an automatic response to a situation or object that is perceived as being dangerous. Anxiety is a much more extensive and complex emotional state typically triggered by fear. Anxiety is more enduring than the initial fear and involves the apprehension that one cannot control future adverse situations.

Several anxiety disorders are described in the *DSM-5* (American Psychiatric Association, 2013; NIMH, 2018a), and we briefly review some of them here. *Generalized anxiety disorder* is characterized by excessive and chronic anxiety, worry, and tension even when there is little or nothing to elicit the anxiety. *Agoraphobia* involves fear of being in open places, using public transportation, being in enclosed buildings with others such as a movie theater, being in a crowd, and being outside one's home alone. *Panic disorder* is characterized by panic attacks and episodes of intense fear along with physical symptoms that may lead the individual to feel as though he or she is dying. *Social anxiety disorder* is characterized by overwhelming anxiety and self-consciousness in social situations in which the individual fears scrutiny by others. *Phobias* are fear or anxiety about a specific object or situation such as heights, flying, or public speaking.

What We Have Learned About Helping Others Therapeutically

Counselors begin by conducting a thorough assessment of the life situation, history, and development of the disorder; factors involved in clients' current situation; and clients' goals for counseling. A critical curative factor in counseling begins when clients put what they are experiencing into words. Clients may have a pervasive sense of fear and anxiety that they have been unable to pinpoint, describe, or understand. Having clients describe what has occurred, what they have done to try to fix the problem, what has worked and what has not, and what they would like to accomplish in counseling is a significant first step in the healing process. Bourne (2005) notes that many clients with anxiety disorders lack a sense of direction in life and are frequently in a state of chronic hyperarousal. Recovery involves lifestyle changes that promote a more relaxed and balanced approach to life's challenges.

The Counselor's Task With Clients

Social relationships provide a buffer against stress, and Meyers (2019) points out that one of the basic services counselors can offer stressed and anxious clients is a refresher course on social skills in helping them build supportive relationships. A major part of the counselor's task in working with such clients is to help them identify exactly what is going on, when their anxiety occurs most often, what triggers that anxiety, what they have tried to ameliorate the symptoms, and what has worked and what hasn't. Detailing the triggers, symptoms, and length of time anxiety has been occurring will assist clients in understanding their situation. It is important to distinguish between everyday anxiety, which we all experience and is to be expected, and an anxiety disorder, which involves more intense anxiety over a continuous period. See the *DSM-5* (American Psychiatric Association, 2013) for additional details about anxiety disorders and stress.

One widely used treatment approach is cognitive behavior therapy (CBT). In CBT, counselors examine the cognitive processing of an activating event (Matu, 2018) and look for cognitive errors in the client's evaluation of the anxiety-eliciting event. Cognitive restructuring is often essential in bringing about stress reduction. Regardless of the counseling approach, establishing a supportive and trusting therapeutic relationship is essential and should be a primary task of counseling. The client will most likely be anxious about counseling, and every effort should be made to demystify the process to reduce the amount of anxiety associated with it. Out-of-session exercises and activities can aid the client in examining issues surrounding the anxiety reactions and life situation without the stress associated with being in the counselor's office and responding to questions on the spot. For the client burdened with anxiety, we believe out-of-session work is especially beneficial.

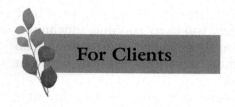

For Clients

Anxiety and Stress

Many of us find ourselves consumed by worries, fears, guilt, and grievances. And let's face it, stress and anxiety are a part of everyday living. A 2018 Gallup poll revealed that 55% of Americans feel stressed during much of their day, and 45% admit to feeling worried a lot (Ray, 2019). Whether you get your news on TV, your smartphone, or in a newspaper, you are bombarded with a range of serious and bothersome issues, most of which are beyond your control. The bad news may seem overwhelming and inescapable, but many reasonable and kind-hearted people are doing good things for one another, so be careful not to focus exclusively on the negative stories you hear or read about constantly. Be vigilant, and make a concerted effort to get a healthy dose of positive/happy news to offset the negative news cycle and ensure that you have some balance in your life.

Key Thought

Do you want to reduce your anxiety level? Look toward modifying your inner dialogue to focus less on fear and more on problem solving.

Defining Stress and Anxiety

Stress is a feeling of strain or pressure that we place on ourselves, such as wanting to be the perfect parent, employee, or student; the source of stress also can come from outside ourselves, such as feeling the crunch of making financial ends meet. Stress can result from a positive event, such as starting a new job or class or moving to a new house or apartment. It also can be triggered by a negative encounter or event, such as dealing with a critical coworker or boss, evacuating from a wildfire, or dealing with the threat of deportation. Stress, like beauty, is often in the eye of the beholder. Your perception of the situation plays a large part in how you react emotionally and how you act to resolve the situation.

Anxiety is best described as the worry or fear we experience in anticipation of those stressful events. It is one thing to be concerned about an event that will occur today or tomorrow (e.g., a final exam at school or an important meeting at work), but it is something else to be worried about all kinds of things over an extended period. When we move from worrying about one event to the next, the worry and anxiety never seem to go away. Clark and Beck (2012) believe that fear is at the heart of all anxiety and that anxiety is complex. If you are anxious, it affects you physically, emotionally, and behaviorally. Worrying about events that are very unlikely to happen can increase your anxiety. In fact, about 85% of the things we worry about never occur (Goewey, 2017). To clarify, anxiety over real events that are likely to occur soon (e.g., a tornado warning) is productive because it reflects a real threat and may prompt you to take necessary action; however, anxiety over events that are unlikely to occur is nonproductive and a waste of your energy and emotions. Fear is more specific to a situation or object, whereas anxiety tends to be vague or diffuse and results in a general state of apprehension. That state of apprehension can range from a vague uneasiness to a full-blown panic attack in which physical symptoms develop including heart palpitations, sweating, nausea or dizziness, and perhaps even a feeling that you could die.

Anxiety that is situation-specific and comes and goes with the event is very common. More intense anxiety that lasts much longer than the event that triggered it may lead to phobias (intense unrealistic fears) or other symptoms and can become disabling and require counseling.

What Can We Do About Our Stress and Anxiety?

If you are anxious about a work-related issue that you need to discuss with your boss, that anxiety can work in your favor and help you prepare for the discussion. Once the meeting has passed, the anxiety will subside. But if you have a vague, nonspecific worry about your standing on the job—even though you have received no negative feedback from your boss or coworkers—that anxiety will likely continue indefinitely without relief. It may even take an emotional and a physical toll on you. It is like being prepared to run from a dangerous situation all the time, with adrenaline flowing nonstop. Eventually you may wear out from that unrelieved anxiety and stress.

It is important to examine your perceptions of your life situations. Are you realistically assessing situations or are you blowing these things out of proportion? Ask yourself: Am I spending time and energy worrying about things I have no control over? What is my self-talk about these situations? Am I engaging in all-or-nothing thinking about my circumstances? Am I telling myself I can handle the situation? Or am I thinking, "I will likely fail to handle the situation? I am not good enough, bright enough, and don't have the self-confidence to do this?" What you tell yourself about a situation and your ability to handle it has a major impact on how you feel about the situation, yourself, and how you act to ameliorate the situation. To better cope with anxiety and stress in your life, it is essential to be kind to yourself and to avoid the trap of demanding perfection. Look to others for support, and take good care of yourself emotionally and physically.

Here are some ways to reduce the amount of stress and anxiety you experience.

- Avoid stressful situations or at least identify significant sources of stress and anxiety in your life and try to minimize them.
- Focus on those things you have control over and can change, and let go of things you cannot change.
- Modify your self-talk so you have a healthy and positive outlook on life. (Your self-talk affects your perceptions, emotions, and reactions to many things in life, including stress and anxiety.)
- Assess the accuracy of your beliefs about yourself.
- Work hard to dispute any irrational or inaccurate thoughts (e.g., "I must always be perfect. Anything less is failure.").
- Examine your automatic thinking when in stressful situations and evaluate whether your inner dialogue (self-talk) works for or against you.
- Enlist help and feedback from others you trust—perhaps friends and family members—to gain a clearer sense of how you are doing.
- Practice good self-care habits and get proper sleep, nutrition, exercise, and relaxation.
- Join a support group and surround yourself with others who are committed to become stronger and more able to handle stress and anxiety.
- Develop your social relationships. (Having a network of social relationships and a social support system can be a buffer against stress.)
- Give yourself permission to struggle with anxiety. If it were easy to fix this problem, all of us would be free of anxiety. Change is difficult and requires patience with yourself and much practice.
- Use the exercises that follow to your advantage. Try not to be overwhelmed by them, and have some fun learning how you can improve yourself. Try one or two exercises, and be prepared to discuss your responses with your counselor.

Workbook Material for the Client

The following questions and exercises are designed to help you examine stress and anxiety in your life. There are no right or wrong answers. This is an opportunity for you to spend some time thinking about how well you manage stress and anxiety. Some exercises may be easy for you, and others may require more time and thought on your part. We hope you will take plenty of time to consider each topic or question that your counselor has asked you to complete. The value of the activities and questions comes from your careful consideration about your position on the topic. The goal is to learn as much as you can about yourself outside the counseling setting. If you are better prepared to explore these issues, your session time will be more productive. We suggest that you keep a journal as you contemplate making changes in your life to reduce your stress and anxiety. Purchase a notebook or journal or record your responses on a computer. Remember to print your responses and bring them with you to your next counseling session.

Exercises and Activities

Assessing the Situation and Your Reaction

1. Let's take a look at what causes stress and anxiety for you. How would you rate your general level of anxiety on a daily basis?

Scale: 1   2   3   4   5   6   7   8   9   10
            Low/   *Extremely*
            none   *high*

Explain your response.

_____

2. What are the most powerful sources of stress and anxiety in your life?

_____

_____

3. What is toxic in your life? What would your life look like without that toxic element?

_____

_____

4. How would a close family member or a friend describe your level of stress and anxiety?

_____

_____

5. Do you have what you would consider anxiety attacks or panic attacks?

_____

_____

   a. Describe what happens to you when you have those attacks.

_____

_____

   b. Do you experience physical symptoms such as dizziness, shortness of breath, nausea, chest pain, sleep disturbances, or fatigue? Please describe those and rate their severity.

Scale: 1   2   3   4   5   6   7   8   9   10
            Not   *Extremely*
            at all   *severe*

Explain your response.

   c. Do you have an experience that makes you feel detached from the situation (e.g., looking at yourself and the situation from afar)? Please describe and rate the severity.

Scale: 1   2   3   4   5   6   7   8   9   10
            Not detached   *Extremely*
            at all   *detached*

Explain your response.

_____

6. Are there any particular objects (e.g., spiders, clowns) or situations (e.g., social gatherings, heights) that you are particularly fearful of to the extent that you avoid them completely? What feelings do you experience when reacting to those stressful situations or objects?

_____

_____

7. What are some thoughts you have or tell yourself (self-talk) when you are feeling seriously anxious? Do those thoughts and inner dialogue help you or make you more anxious in those situations?

_____

_____

8. Describe a recent situation, object, or event that led you to become seriously anxious. What was it like for you? How did you feel? What did you say to yourself? How did you react? Were you satisfied with the way you handled the situation? If so, describe what worked well. What would you hope to do differently next time? For each situation, create a chart like Chart 3.1 to log your responses.

Chart 3.1 Assessing the Anxiety Event and What Is Behind It

Situation, object, or event	
What was it like for me?	
How did I feel?	
What was the fear that something bad would happen?	
What did I say to myself?	
How did I react? Was I satisfied with my action?	
What would I do differently next time?	

Learning to Manage Your Anxiety

1. A good place to begin is to examine your inner thoughts and beliefs about yourself and your ability to cope with anxiety. For example, do you say to yourself, "I am just a mess, I can't handle anything! What a failure I am!" That kind of self-talk is likely to be devastating for you and may lead to failure in a kind of self-fulfilling prophecy. But if you say "I am anxious, but I can handle this. My response may not be perfect, but I will give this a try and see if I can improve from the last time," you are more likely to handle the anxiety successfully. What are your inner thoughts and beliefs about anxiety?

_____

_____

What could you change about those beliefs to help you better manage?

_____

_____

Key Thought

Give yourself permission to struggle with anxiety. If it were easy to fix this problem, all of us would be free of anxiety. Change is difficult and requires patience with yourself and much practice.

2. One of the major ways to reduce your anxiety is to combat catastrophic thinking—imagining the worst outcome in a situation. Are you a catastrophic thinker? Check the statements that you find yourself thinking in a stressful situation:

   ❏ "This is the worst thing that could happen to me."
   ❏ "I'm sure I will fail this test."
   ❏ "I am afraid that people will finally see me for who I really am."
   ❏ "This is just too hard, I can't do it."
   ❏ "Damn, I'm stupid."
   ❏ "I just want out of here."

   What are some other catastrophic thoughts you have had in stressful situations? How could you challenge those thoughts?

   _____

   _____

3. Cognitive therapy is a common counseling approach used for the treatment of anxiety. With this therapy, you are instructed to assess your thoughts and beliefs, your inner dialogue about these anxiety-producing situations, and begin to modify them so your thoughts can assist you in dealing with the situation. What helpful thoughts could you practice in stressful situations?

   _____

   _____

4. Making significant change requires focus and practice. For the next week, keep track of situations that make you anxious, and log your automatic thoughts. As you log those thoughts, try to come up with other more helpful and productive thoughts that you can practice in these situations. For example, suppose you are afraid that you offended a coworker. You might log your automatic thought like this: "I am in trouble now. I am sure that everyone in the office thinks I am terrible. I don't have a clue about how to fix this. What a disaster!" Then offer yourself some more productive thoughts: "I may not know immediately how to fix my mistake, but maybe I should ask for feedback before I assume that everyone thinks the worst of me. Even if others give me the feedback that I fear, I can choose to grow from it. It doesn't have to be a disaster." For each automatic thought, create a chart like Chart 3.2.

Chart 3.2 Automatic Thoughts

Anxiety-provoking situation	
Automatic thought	
Productive/helpful thought	

5. Can you think of ways to respond more effectively in anxiety-provoking situations? List some of the things you could say or do to have a better outcome for each situation. Try some ideas out in low-stakes situations to see what works for you and what doesn't. When you discover what works, use that solution in less stressful situations to practice for more consequential or high-stakes situations that may eventually come along.

   _____

   _____

6. What have you learned about yourself and about coping with anxiety in your life? Do you have a plan to become more effective in coping with anxiety? If so, describe your plan. What else would you like to learn and accomplish in this regard?

_____

_____

7. Relaxation training has been proven to be essential in overcoming anxiety. Taking 15 to 20 minutes to practice relaxation several times a week can help you combat stress and instill a more relaxed approach to life in general. The basic idea is that you cannot be both stressed and relaxed at the same time. If you increase your ability to relax, especially when under stress, you should be able to reduce the intensity of your anxiety response. Relaxation involves a release of tension. It is more than the absence or minimization of stress. True relaxation requires an inward focus and a deep awareness of your body and mind. Relaxation is not simply kicking back on the sofa, putting your feet up, and watching a movie or a sporting event on TV. It is more than just doing nothing for a while. One way to practice relaxation is to focus on your breathing. As you inhale and exhale, say a phrase that relaxes you. For example, you might say something like, "I can picture being at the beach and seeing and hearing the waves crashing on the sand. As I inhale, the waves recede and the tide goes out, as I exhale the waves come crashing back in on the beach." Set aside 15 minutes and give this a try. Describe how this attempt at relaxing was for you. Is this something you could do when feeling stressed and anxious in future situations?

_____

8. Relaxation can be found in many forms and activities. You can focus on your breathing and relax your muscles, or you can hike, fish, garden, meditate, read a book, do yoga, or socialize with friends, to name a few. Find the form of relaxation that provides relief and restores you, and do more of that. What forms of relaxation work for you? What forms of relaxation would you like to do more of to help you combat stress and anxiety? Specify the relaxation activities that you might try. Rate how likely you are to actually put these into practice?

Scale: 1   2   3   4   5   6   7   8   9   10
        I will definitely   *I will definitely*
         not do this   *do this*

Explain your response.

_____

9. Another common form of relaxation is visualizing a relaxing scene. As a counselor in private practice, I (Bob) often used relaxation and visualization with clients who were experiencing stress and anxiety. My goal was to teach them how to de-stress through breathing techniques and visualization. I led them through the procedures with the goal that they would learn to do it on their own. I asked them to focus on their breathing, then their heart rate, then their muscles in the neck, arms, shoulders, and legs. I asked them to try to put everything out of their mind except the scene I described. I described a pleasant and peaceful scene (one they had identified as restful and serene such as the beach, a pasture of flowers, a mountain stream) and asked them to imagine the scene—the smells, the sounds, and the feelings they had in that setting. After staying with the scene and enjoying it for a few minutes, I slowly and gently brought them back to the sights and sounds in the office. Clients nearly always reported a sense of well-being and peacefulness from the experience.

You can practice this on your own, and you may find it quite refreshing. Achieving a relaxed state takes practice, and you may wish to ask your counselor to practice this with you in session. Be sure that you are not rushed, and set aside 15 to 20 minutes in a setting where you will not be disturbed.

As you gain experience and skill, you will find that you can relax in various settings for short periods of time most anywhere. Set aside time to do the deep breathing, muscle relaxation, and visualization of a pleasant scene. Focus on that and enjoy that scene, then slowly bring yourself back to the present time. Reflect on this experience: How was that for you? To what extent were you able to relax? Could you see yourself doing this on a regular basis?

_____

_____

10. Mindfulness is another way to manage stress. Mindfulness is similar to meditation in that it involves a state of actively focusing on what you are doing. For example, if I am anxious about a presentation I have to make at work tomorrow, I can either focus on the task or on all the fears I have about how it might go, what people might think of me, and what might happen if I forget what I am talking about. By focusing on my fears, I ramp up my anxiety about the presentation and increase the likelihood that I will fail. By being mindful, I am better able to focus on the task at hand and work on preparing for the presentation, all the while telling myself (self-talk) that I can do this, that I will succeed, and that my coworkers will be supportive and forgiving if I make a mistake. With mindfulness, I focus on the task and on succeeding, and that keeps the fears about my performance at bay.

    Describe a situation where you were deterred by focusing on your fears and how being mindful of what you were doing might have helped. Can you see yourself being more mindful in future situations?

_____

_____

11. Engaging in physical exercise is an important way to reduce anxiety. Incorporating some physical activity into your lifestyle will help you manage stress. How often do you exercise? Do you find yourself avoiding it, or is it something you look forward to doing?

_____

_____

12. Solution-focused approaches concentrate less on the problems you bring to counseling and more on solutions to those problems. Instead of spending a lot of time examining what's wrong (the origin of the problem, how it developed, etc.), solution-focused practitioners prefer to talk about what has worked well for you when the problem (e.g., anxiety) didn't exist. In this exercise, you are going to apply solution-focused strategies to your own life. Identify an issue that causes you stress and anxiety, and write it down. Then answer the following questions:

    a. Can you think of times when the anxiety-provoking issue/problem did not exist? What was different about that time, situation, or circumstance? How did you act, think, or feel differently?

_____

_____

    b. Can you think of a time when the problem did exist but you didn't experience the same level of stress or anxiety as you typically do? Again, what was different about the situation and your reaction?

_____

_____

c. Solution-focused practitioners often pose the miracle question: If a miracle happened and the problem was solved overnight, how would your life be different? What can you do to move in the direction of achieving that?

_____

_____

d. Another strategy is to use scaling questions. You might ask yourself each day, "On a scale of 1 to 10, how severe is the problem?"

Scale: 1   2   3   4   5   6   7   8   9   10

Problem is   *Worst the*
solved   *problem has been*

Chapter 4

Depression and Loneliness

Depression is a prison where you are both the suffering prisoner and the cruel jailer.
—Dorothy Rowe
. . .

For Counselors

Depression is a persistent and extensive low with sadness, emptiness, pessimism, irritability, loss of pleasure, decreased energy, and frequently an overwhelming feeling of dread. Those who suffer from clinical depression may experience difficulty concentrating, sleeping, eating, working, and making decisions. In addition, they may experience physical symptoms such as headaches, digestive problems, and a range of other ailments as well as suicidal ideation. Depression can be described as a deep, dark sense of hopelessness and dread, and it is caused by a combination of biological, genetic, environmental, and psychological factors.

Unfortunately, rates of depression and suicide are rising nationwide (Mental Health America, 2019; Preidt, 2019). NIMH (2018c) estimated that nearly 7% of U.S. adults had at least one major depressive episode in 2016. About 1 in 6 Americans will experience depression in their lifetimes. In 2017, 47,000 people committed suicide in the United States, a rate of 14 per 100,000 people, and that rate has increased on average by 16% each year since 2014 (Bacon, 2018). It seems that more people are feeling hopeless, and many of the issues affecting us are simply beyond our control.

An especially alarming trend is the increase in suicide among young people. In the United States, suicide is the second-leading cause of death among youth ages 10 to 19 (Brownlee, 2019). Over the past two decades, suicide rates among younger people have gradual increased. Brownlee notes that "untreated or undertreated clinical depression, impulsive aggressive traits, ready access to firearms, social disconnection, and violence in the home or community have all been linked with youth suicide" (p. 28). In analyzing a nationally representative data set, Twenge, Cooper, Joiner, Duffy, and Binau (2019) discovered that rates of past-year major depressive episodes and suicide-related outcomes, as well as recent serious psychological distress, have increased among youth ages 12 to 17 and young adults ages 18 to 25 from the mid-2000s to 2017.

One issue especially relevant to suicide is the growing sense of loneliness and social disconnection that often accompanies depression. Cigna surveyed 20,000 American adults using the UCLA Loneliness Scale, and they learned that nearly 50% of respondents felt alone and left out either sometimes or always, 54% claimed they sometimes or always felt that no one knew them well, and 2 in 5 reported that they lacked companionship and meaningful relationships (Chatterjee, 2018).

Scores on the UCLA Loneliness Scale range from 20 to 80, with scores of 43 and above indicating loneliness. Here are some generational comparisons:

> Members of Generation Z, born between the mid-1990s and the early 2000s, had an overall loneliness score of 48.3. Millennials, just a little bit older, scored 45.3. By comparison, baby boomers scored 42.4. The Greatest Generation, people ages 72 and above, had a score of 38.6 on the loneliness scale. (Chatterjee, 2018)

Undeniably, loneliness has become an epidemic, and it seems to be taking the greatest toll on the younger members of society. Although helping professionals must be concerned about identifying and treating depression and loneliness in younger clients and remain attuned to societal trends that may exacerbate their mental health issues, we must not lose sight of the affects of depression and loneliness on older adults. Research has shown a relationship between loneliness, depression, and cognitive decline in older adults (Donovan et al., 2017). The Cigna study did not find social media use to be a major factor in predicting loneliness, but one's level of in-person interactions, physical and mental wellness, and life balance were predictors. Some have argued that the widespread use of social media and more time spent "on screen" is linked to depression and loneliness. Researchers at the University of Pennsylvania discovered a causal link between decreasing social media use and improvements in depression and loneliness (Hunt, Marx, Lipson, & Young, 2018). For more on the effects of social media, see Chapter 13.

Rates of depression and suicide are on the upswing, and the incidence of loneliness is increasing in the face of improved technology and electronic communication. A causal effect is difficult to determine, but as divisiveness, hatred, and social injustice increase, so do rates of depression and suicide. We can expect that many of those seeking counseling services will be experiencing increased depression and loneliness.

What We Have Learned About Helping Others Therapeutically

Many counseling approaches can be effective in the treatment of depression, but some argue that current treatments are far from satisfactory (Kong, Fang, Park, Li, & Rong, 2018). Despite a clinician's best efforts, some cases of depression are treatment-resistant, which can be a source of stress and concern for practitioners who desperately want their clients to experience relief. Just as it is important for clients to be instilled with hope that they will eventually find relief from their depressive symptoms, we believe clinicians also need to hold onto hope that promising treatments are on the horizon, if not already available. The good news is that advances are being made on this front. Some argue that depression improves faster with electroconvulsive treatment (ECT) than with antidepressant medications (Jagtiani, Khurana, & Malhotra, 2019). In fact, Mathew, Wilkinson, Altinay, Asghar-Ali, and Anand (2019) suggest that ECT is the most effective treatment for major depressive disorders and is the gold standard therapy for treatment-resistant depression, even though it continues to be underutilized. This may be due to stigma and other factors, such as limited availability in certain locales and concerns about cognitive side effects. Nevertheless, "the overwhelming majority of trials comparing ECT directly to a standard antidepressant have shown superior efficacy for ECT" (p. 20). New promising forms of treatment for clinical depression are being explored. Ketamine, a rapid-acting antidepressant, is showing robust short-term efficacy in clinical trials (Mathew et al., 2019), and transcutaneous auricular vagus nerve stimulation (taVNS) is also showing promise (Kong et al., 2018).

There is no one-size-fits-all approach in the treatment of depression, but a caring and empathic relationship between counselor and client is a common denominator. The role of hope is another critical factor in counseling those who are depressed. Helping individuals who are feeling hopeless and helpless about their life situation to identify and work toward a more hopeful outlook can be a major breakthrough. For those who are depressed, hope of a brighter future can be lifesaving.

We cannot overemphasize the importance of proper assessment in the diagnosis and treatment of depressive disorders. A thorough assessment of the causes and precipitating factors is essential because depression may be caused by a combination of genetic, biological, environmental, and psychological factors (NIMH, 2018c). All aspects of an individual's functioning, including physiological and medical causes, must be evaluated. The Beck Depression Inventory–II is a brief self-report inventory that measures the attitudes and symptoms of depression, and it is widely used and useful for assessment (Beck, Steer, & Brown, 1996; Steer, Rissmiller, & Beck, 2000; von Glischinski, von Brachel, & Hirschfeld, 2019).

Conducting a lethality assessment is also of the utmost importance when serving depressed clients. Corey et al. (2019) describe the value of a written safety plan designed collaboratively with clients who are a danger to self. Clients are asked to list their reasons for living as a resource for assessing risk. Those considered high risk are asked to list the names and phone numbers of two people they can call for assistance or just to talk. Clients are provided with phone numbers for emergency suicide prevention resources (suicide hotlines, mobile crisis intervention teams) and are advised to go to the nearest emergency room if they try everything on the safety plan and still feel suicidal.

The Counselor's Task With Clients

Treating someone suffering from a severe depressive disorder requires extensive evaluation for medical and psychological issues as well as consideration for medication. Depression often involves suicidal ideation and thoughts of dying as a solution, so counselors must be adept at evaluating for suicide potential. Although it is not possible for counselors to predict with perfect accuracy what a client will do, we must do everything we can to recognize the suicide indicators and intervene appropriately. Here are some common signs of suicide risk:

- Depression
- Writing suicide notes
- Talk of suicide or death
- Loss of a relationship or job
- Feelings of hopelessness and helplessness
- Dramatic change in appearance, behavior, or mood
- Giving belongings away or putting things in order
- Changes in appetite or sleep patterns
- Sudden euphoria
- Physical illness
- History of suicide attempts
- Having a specific plan and a lethal means of completing the act (Haynes, Corey, & Moulton, 2003, p. 233)

The presence of any one or even a few of these indicators does not necessarily constitute suicide risk, but when taken together with the client's current life situation, a thorough assessment of risk should be made.

Clients who talk about suicide must be taken seriously. Women attempt suicide more often than men, but men are more likely to complete the act than women. As mentioned, suicides rates are on the upswing, especially among young people. Rely on your resources and your colleagues as you assess depression and suicide risk and devise a treatment plan. Become familiar with resources such as the National Suicide Prevention Lifeline, not only for your clients in distress but for their family members and loved ones as well. Appendix B provides additional internet resources.

Notes

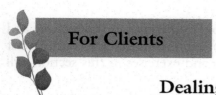

For Clients

Dealing With Depression and Loneliness

"I was so down on myself. I didn't have any self-love and quite honestly, I just didn't want to be alive. It was a really, really, really crazy time for me and I didn't want to see anybody. I saw myself as letting so many people down—and myself in particular. That's hard to carry" (as cited in Konow, 2018). The person recounting this is Michael Phelps, winner of 28 Olympic swimming medals. No one is immune from depression, not even someone who appears to have everything going right for him. Something finally clicked when Michael Phelps reached bottom. He realized he could ask for help, although he had never done that in his life. He said, "I was basically on my knees, crying for help" (cited in Alltucker, 2018).

Depression and loneliness are two major reasons individuals seek counseling and therapy. The fear of loneliness can be powerful and overwhelming. One in 5 Americans will struggle with a major depression in their lifetime. If you are experiencing depression, you may perceive it as a dark, lonely, and empty place that few understand unless they have been there. It can consume your life and alter your motivation to be involved with friends and family, a significant other, colleagues, coworkers, or the community. A loss of pleasure and enjoyment in life is common in depression, and thinking about what you need to do to overcome this unhappy and lonely state of mind may feel overwhelming. At times you may feel depressed even though it seems as if nothing in your life situation has changed for the worse. Depression is a common and serious mood disorder that may leave you feeling like you are drowning in despair. It can affect how you think and feel and can alter your actions in everyday living.

What causes depression and that painful and isolating feeling? Many factors play a role, including genetics, medical conditions and illnesses, life situation, your own physiology, specific events, and even things we see on the news and on social media. People experience and are affected by depression in different ways, and no one treatment best fits everyone. With the support of an empathic helping professional, you can find what works for you and your personal situation. Depression has a physiological element, and whether the physiological changes in your brain and body cause or are a result of depression is a complex question. Some people are more prone to depression than others. If you are depressed, take it seriously and work with your counselor to do everything you can to get the depression under control so it does not continue to diminish your quality of life.

Typical symptoms of depression can include the following:

- Sadness and pessimism about the future
- Psychological numbness
- Irritability
- A sense of anxious distress
- Feelings of guilt and worthlessness
- Exhaustion and fatigue
- Loss of interest or pleasure in things you normally enjoy
- A sense of dread and doom
- Difficulty with sleep, appetite, and concentration
- Physical illnesses and conditions
- Thoughts of death or suicide

If you are in a depressed state, just getting out of bed in the morning may be difficult. People may say it is all in your mind and you just need to focus on the positive, but it is not that simple. Combating depression requires a systematic effort to analyze the causes and sources of your feelings and thoughts and devise a variety of psychological and possibly medical efforts to remedy the situation. One symptom of depression is lacking motivation or a drive to change. Do everything you can to follow your counselor's direction, and force yourself to do as much as you can in complying with the course of treatment. Sometimes the most difficult part of change is simply getting started. We hope the activities and exercises in this section will help you in this journey.

What Are Some Things I Can Do Today?

Here are some things you can do to combat depression right away, as suggested by the NIMH (2018c):

- Commit to get some physical exercise and be active.
- Develop realistic goals for yourself.
- Spend time with people and confide in a relative or friend you trust.
- Avoid the temptation to isolate yourself, and allow others to help you.
- Expect your mood to improve gradually, not instantly.
- Postpone consequential decisions, such as getting married or divorced or changing jobs, until your depression lifts and you feel better.
- Consult with people who know you well and may have a more objective view of your situation before making decisions.
- Educate yourself about depression on an ongoing basis.

You are working on the exercises in this section because your counselor thinks these activities and exercises can be of value to your therapy. You have taken a bold and courageous step. Even though you may not feel up to working on these activities, doing so will help you. An important step in the healing process is putting into words what is happening within you. Then you can begin to look at ways to improve your situation.

Workbook Material for the Client

The following questions and exercises are designed to help you examine the topic of depression and loneliness in your life. There are no right or wrong answers. This is an opportunity for you to spend time thinking about how well you are managing your depression. Some questions and exercises may be easy for you, and others may require more time and thought on your part. We hope you will take plenty of time to consider each topic or question that your counselor has asked you to complete. The value of these activities and questions comes from your careful consideration about your position on the topic. The goal is for you to learn as much as you can outside of the counseling setting. If you are better prepared to explore the issues, your session time will be more productive. We suggest that you keep a journal as you contemplate making changes in your life to decrease your loneliness and depression. Purchase a notebook or journal or record your responses to these questions and activities on your computer. Remember to print your responses and bring them to your next counseling session.

Exercises and Activities

Depression Affects Thoughts, Attitudes, and Actions

1. Each of us has a predisposition to feeling more "cheerful and optimistic" or more "negative and pessimistic" and expecting the worst to occur. How would you describe your general outlook on life? What are you most optimistic about? Most pessimistic about?

   _____

   _____

2. Some people find it useful to describe their emotional state using metaphors. For example, a person might liken depression to the sensation of being weighed down by a heavy gray blanket or to sinking into the depths of the ocean without anyone knowing he fell off the boat. Can you think of a metaphor that captures your experience with depression? Be sure to journal about it, and record any emotions that come up for you as you think of the metaphor.

   _____

   _____

3. I am feeling depressed currently because of the following life situations or people in my life:

   _____

   _____

4. When I feel depressed I also feel:

   _____

   _____

5. When I am depressed, I typically respond by thinking _____ and doing _____. (Use as much additional space as you need to fill in these blanks.)

   _____

   _____

6. What has worked for me in the past when I am depressed is to:

   _____

   _____

7. What I hope to gain from counseling to help me when I am depressed is:

   _____

   _____

8. Make a list of the things you think would make you happier.

   _____

   _____

9. Does the current situation in our world contribute to your feelings of depression? How does the social climate of divisiveness affect you? Does it affect your relationships with family? Friends? Co-workers? If so, describe this feeling.

   _____

   _____

Measuring Sadness and Depression

Depression can lead from feeling "mildly down" to feeling outright "hopeless and helpless." Sonja Lyumbomirsky (2007) suggests that 50% of our happiness is determined by genes, 10% by circumstances, and 40% by our thoughts, actions, and attitudes. As you can see, your circumstances play a relatively small role in influencing your level of happiness. If you have been the victim of a disaster, a crime, a divorce, or a death in the family, the percentage that the circumstance plays in worsening your depression and decreasing your happiness will be much higher. In normal day-to-day routines, you have control over your thoughts, actions, and attitudes, and they play a larger role than you may have assumed in how you feel. The following exercises can help you focus on your thoughts, actions, and attitudes as they pertain to depression and loneliness.

1. To get a handle on your level of sadness and depression, indicate how much each of the items in Chart 4.1 applies to you and how you feel.

Chart 4.1 Levels of Sadness and Depression[1]

Scale: 1   2   3   4

     Never/rarely   *Sometimes*   *Often*   *Most of the time*

Dimensions of depression:

_____ I feel sad or blue.

_____ I feel lonely and isolated.

_____ I lack any real enjoyment or pleasure in my life.

_____ I am optimistic about my future.

_____ I feel a sense of dread or impending doom.

_____ I am happy with my life.

_____ I am happy with the person I am.

_____ I feel constantly overwhelmed.

_____ I feel a pervasive sense of anxiety.

_____ I have trouble sleeping at night.

_____ I have to contend with physical/medical issues.

_____ I feel that life is no longer worth living.

_____ I have thought about suicide as a solution.

Please expand on and describe in more detail any of the items from the chart that are of concern to you.

_____

_____

Which items from the chart trouble you most?

_____

_____

2. Review Chart 4.1 and describe in your own words where you would like to be with respect to each of the items.

_____

_____

3. What would it take for you to get from where you are now to where you would like to be?

_____

_____

4. What is preventing you from getting to where you would like to be?

_____

_____

5. List two painful experiences in your life that have led to you feeling sad or depressed. How do your values (e.g., personal, cultural, religious) affect your feelings about those experiences?

_____

_____

_____

[1] *Source:* Adapted from Burns, 1999, pp. 20–21.

6. What would your life be like if you were happy? What would you be doing? Who would you be with? What would be your situation in terms of family? Children? Friends? Work? School? Leisure activities? How far are you from living that life? What would need to happen for you to make progress toward living that life? What one step are you able and willing to take now toward achieving a happier life?

_____

_____

7. Loneliness is a common feeling that many people experience. When do you feel most lonely? Where and with whom do you feel the loneliest?

_____

_____

8. Are you a member of a marginalized group (e.g., LGBTQ+, an ethnic or racial minority, a woman, a person with a disability)? If so, how have your experiences as a member of a marginalized population contributed to your feelings of loneliness? What is it about your situation that makes it feel so lonely

_____

_____

9. What have you tried to do to combat that loneliness? How has that worked for you?

_____

_____

10. Can you think of something else you might try to reverse that feeling of loneliness? What would it take for you to do more of that?

_____

_____

11. If a miracle happened and your depression or loneliness suddenly disappeared, how would your life be different? In what ways might you live your life differently? Would you make different choices in any areas of your life? Describe.

_____

_____

12. Examine the role of social media in your life. Keep a log of how much time you spend on social media each day, and track your mood and level of loneliness on a chart like Chart 4.2. Complete these entries each night before you go to sleep for 1 to 2 weeks. Include a "Notes/Comments" column to record any observations you've made.

Chart 4.2 Social Media and Mood

Use the scale to record your level of depressed mood or loneliness. At week's end, reflect on what you've learned about the impact of your social media use on your mood and loneliness.

Scale: 1   2   3   4   5   6   7   8   9   10
       None   *Extreme*
                                            depression/loneliness

Social Media Platform	Date/Day of Week	Hours Per Day Online	Level of Depression	Level of Loneliness	Notes/ Comments
Twitter					
Facebook					
Instagram					
Other platform					

Chapter 5

Anger

Holding on to anger is like grasping a hot coal
with the intent of throwing it at someone else;
you are the one who gets burned.

—Buddha

. . .

For Counselors

Clients who seek counseling frequently have an underlying issue with anger, which may be externalized and directed at others or internalized and directed at themselves. Suppressed anger and resentment can have a negative impact on emotional and physical well-being. When feelings of anger and frustration become intense, the individual is likely to feel out of control and overwhelmed and may experience guilt, low self-esteem, and self-blame, and possibly become suicidal. *Emotional regulation* is an individual's ability to effectively manage and respond to an emotional experience and to reduce his or her emotional suffering (Linehan, 2015; Rolston & Lloyd-Richardson, 2019). As Linehan (2015) points out, "emotion regulation skills help you to change emotions that you (not other people) want to change, or to reduce the intensity of your emotions" (p. 197). Individuals might cope by talking with others, taking a walk, modifying their self-talk, writing in a journal, taking a time-out from the emotionally charged situation, taking slow deep breaths, or meditating. Linehan emphasizes the use of mindfulness skills in regulating emotions, especially nonjudgmental observation and description of current emotions. Those who handle emotionally charged situations poorly experience *emotional dysregulation* and may try to cope by blaming others, becoming enraged, sulking, overeating, self-medicating with alcohol or other substances, self-injuring, or withdrawing from the situation.

Anger is an emotional and physiological response to a perceived provocation, threat, or hostile act. It is "an emotional state that varies in intensity from mild irritation to intense fury and rage" (APA, 2019). *Hostility* is emotionally charged aggressive behavior, and *rage* is a more intense feeling of violent or growing anger. Some people react to situations with outbursts of anger and frustration, some react with calm resolve and manage their anger effectively, and others suppress any notion of anger and may take their anger out on themselves. To illustrate the latter, I (Michelle) learned growing up that anger and conflict were unacceptable. My role in my family was that of peacemaker, and I internalized my anger and essentially "imploded" by directing any unpleasant feelings inward toward myself. Inevitably, my well-being and my self-esteem were negatively affected. Through my own therapy and introspective work, I learned to express my anger appropriately and not to "stuff it" down as I had done in my youth. We all receive *implicit* (unspoken) and *explicit* (spoken) messages in childhood and adolescence about how conflict and anger are to be handled. Many of these messages are transmitted through our family of origin; however, they are also conveyed to us through various media, on the school grounds, and through other sources. Unless we examine these early patterns and engage in meaningful reflection about them, we are likely to repeat them (or unconsciously react against them) as we become adults.

Lashing out, name-calling, bullying, seeking revenge, and divisiveness have been portrayed in the behavior of our political leaders, and media coverage eagerly disseminates this disturbing behavior. "Being immersed in a news feed with a different ideological bent has the potential to create conflict between friends and family" (Hunt, Robertson, & Pow, 2018, p. 411). Today we never seem to get a break from "breaking news," which tends to highlight shocking behaviors that capture the public's attention and boost ratings.

> Regardless of political ideation, negativity in the media is more effective in getting attention, eliciting a higher arousal response, and is often remembered longer than positive or neutral information. It also has the effect of evoking more cautious and suspicious attitudes in people. (p. 408)

Given today's toxic political climate, anger and hostile feelings are expanding at an unprecedented pace in our culture. To make matters worse, Hunt, Robertson, and Pow point out that ideas once considered extreme have found their way into the mainstream. White nationalist groups easily disseminate their propaganda online today, and the numbers and visibility of these groups has increased dramatically. By weaponizing online communities and using them as a key recruiting tool, these groups stoke anger and fear in people by spreading the dangerous and misguided "notion that White people are at risk of racial violence at the hands of multiple groups . . . with the power and desire to commit White genocide" (p. 410). Issues related to divisiveness, tribalism, and identity politics are examined further in Part IV.

Anger is largely a matter of one's perception of a situation or threat. Some people don't take things as "personally" as others do and don't see the same set of circumstances as a personal threat as much as others do. What enrages and elicits the desire for revenge for one may result in another person feeling mildly irritated and frustrated. Some people harbor their angry and resentful feelings for years, and others move on with a more optimistic and hopeful outlook on life. Some people have a shorter fuse than others and are more likely to "go off" at the drop of a hat. We do not want to convey the idea that anger is merely a matter of one's temperament or perceptions. Some people, particularly those who have experienced oppression or marginalization in society, understandably have much to feel angry about, and helping professionals must consider contextual factors when assisting a client who is experiencing anger.

It is important to distinguish anger from aggression. Anger is a strong emotion, and aggression is a behavior that expresses this angry feeling. Anger does not necessarily lead to aggression, but uncontrolled anger can provoke another to react with aggression, alienate others, put the person in harm's way, and create rifts in relationships. Intense anger places a strain on the body, and without relief anger can kill through high blood pressure, stroke, or heart attack.

Anger is a common emotion found among a majority of the population. When it becomes extreme, counselors may see clients with oppositional defiant disorder or intermittent explosive disorder (American Psychiatric Association, 2013). Oppositional defiant disorder is characterized as a pattern of angry mood, defiant behavior, or vindictiveness lasting at least 6 months and often characterized by loss of temper, constant anger, being argumentative, defiance toward authority, a pattern of blaming others, and being vindictive. Intermittent explosive disorder is characterized by a failure to control aggressive impulses and recurrent behavioral outbursts out of proportion to the precipitating event or person that interfere with interpersonal or occupational functioning.

Reilly and Shopshire (2002) have identified four common myths about anger:

Myth 1: *Anger is inherited.* Some people say, "I express my anger just like my mother (or father) did." Expressing anger is a learned behavior, and we can learn more appropriate ways of responding when angry.

Myth 2: *Anger always leads to aggression.* We can learn to our control anger and respond assertively in a way that does not escalate the situation.

Myth 3: *People must be aggressive to get what they want.* We are more likely to get what we want by being assertive and firm, but kind and caring, when expressing anger.

Myth 4: *Venting anger is a desirable thing to do.* We may say, "I am just blowing off a little steam" or "I just need to get it off my chest." Anger begets anger, and venting the raw feelings of anger may make us feel more angry and worked up.

What We Have Learned About Helping Others Therapeutically

When serving clients who struggle to control their anger, remember that their perception is their reality. These clients may feel unloved and misunderstood. Their perceptions of situations are likely to lean toward seeing others as being against them, so they are prepared to react strongly to others. These clients lack the skill to de-escalate upsetting situations and respond in a more effective and rational manner. Counselors must be vigilant about their own triggers in relation to anger and avoid becoming defensive. Clients' self-talk, beliefs about others and the world, and values about what's right and wrong often underlie their reaction to perceived threats.

Progress with clients who lose control of their anger and act out violently may be hampered by the effects of neurological or neurochemical factors. One team of researchers discovered that violent offenders who make more risky decisions appear to profit less from CBT (Kuin, Masthoff, Kramer, & Scherder, 2015). Speculating on possible reasons for this, they noted that "neurological and/or neurochemical factors might explain the relationship between risky decision-making and aggression . . . lesions in the orbitofrontal cortex have been related to problems with (reactive) aggression as well as to increased risk taking while making decisions" (p. 165). Moreover, they suggest that lower autonomic arousal (as detected by decreased activity in the right rostral anterior cingulate cortex on functional magnetic resonance imaging [fMRI] measures) may lead some violent offenders to have a reduced capacity to emotionally experience uncertainty about potential gains and losses and thus have a decreased capacity to anticipate and avoid punishment. Kuin and colleagues suggest that "another potential neurobiological cause for the co-occurrence of risky decision-making tendencies and aggression might be attributed to hormones, such as testosterone and cortisol, since these are both related to aggression" (p. 165). Although this information does not offer solutions, it may provide an explanation for why some violent offenders appear to be treatment-resistant to CBT. Working with clients' anger issues involves consideration of all relevant factors, not only the cognitive, emotional, behavioral, and cultural dimensions of a client's presenting issue but the neurological and physiological ones as well.

The Counselor's Task With Clients

The task of the counselor is to guide clients through a complete and thorough assessment of their concerns about anger. With your assistance, clients can be encouraged to explore the following questions:

- What happens when their anger surfaces?
- How do they react internally and externally?
- Who are their role models for managing or coping with anger?
- What did they learn about managing conflict and anger in their family of origin?
- What is their self-talk when they are reacting with anger?
- What situations or people are most likely to trigger their anger?
- How have they handled anger in the past, and how has that worked for them?
- What have they learned from their previous responses with anger?
- What do they hope to accomplish in counseling and in what time frame?

In addition to posing these questions, the Novaco Anger Scale and Provocation Inventory (Novaco, 2003) is a practical self-report questionnaire that can be used to quickly assess the client's level of anger.

Notes

Dealing With Anger in Your Life

Do you get angry or frustrated when standing in a long line at the supermarket, at a sporting event, or at the movie theater? Do you find yourself becoming increasingly frustrated when your internet or TV service fails? Do you become angry when a car pulls right in front of you and nearly forces you off the highway? Do you react with anger when someone accuses you of saying something you know you did not say? If you answered yes to any or all of these questions, don't jump to the conclusion that you have an anger problem. Feeling angry is a part of the human condition. No one is immune from feeling angry at times; however, problems arise when anger is not managed well and escalates out of control. When anger leads to aggression or violence directed toward others or toward yourself, it is fair to say that it has become problematic and is interfering in your life.

In reflecting on situations that trigger your anger, consider the following questions:

- Do you feel guilty when you get angry?
- Do you become overwhelmed and immobilized?
- Do you tend to lash out and blame others?
- How often do you become angry? On a weekly basis? A daily basis?
- What would you like to change about how you handle your anger?

What Is Anger?

Anger is a completely normal and common human emotion. We all get angry, but some of us handle our anger more effectively than others. Some of us instantly blow up, some of us remain calm and assertively deal with the situation, and some of us "sit on the anger" and let it build until we explode or take it out on ourselves. *Anger* is a strong emotional and physiological response to a perceived provocation, threat, or hostile act. It ranges from feeling irritated to intense feelings of rage accompanied by the desire for revenge. You can get angry about anything, but the source is usually an external situation, person, or event, or an internal thought or memory (APA, 2018b). The body typically responds to the emotion of anger with increased blood pressure, heart rate, energy, and adrenaline.

Anger serves a survival function when it motivates us to react aggressively or fight when we encounter danger. However, in our modern world, reacting aggressively is often counterproductive and can get us in trouble. We have to learn better ways to manage our anger than by reacting aggressively and lashing out. When managed ineffectively, anger can lead to uncontrollable rage, abusiveness, violence, and destruction. Some individuals remain calm, cool, and collected in even the most aggravating situations. Others experience their anger like a pressure cooker, and the hotter it gets, the more likely they are to explode.

Key Thought

It is a myth that a "just get it off your chest" approach to anger relieves the pressure of an upsetting situation. Instead, this can escalate rather than reduce the feelings of anger you and others involved in the situation already have.

Early Messages About Anger and Conflict

Early in life we received messages in our family of origin about how to think, behave, and feel. Some of these messages were unspoken (or *implicit*), and others were spoken (or *explicit*). They help us understand what is acceptable and unacceptable. Most of us learned lessons in childhood and adolescence about how to handle anger and conflict. Some of us received direct messages from adults (e.g., our parents and teachers) about restraining our feelings, particularly negative ones such as anger. Our parents might have said, "Children are to be seen and not heard. Keep your feelings to yourself!" or they might have modeled that behavior themselves and never expressed anger in front of us. Others of us may have witnessed violent expressions of anger in our family, resulting in trauma. Depending on your family circumstances, you most likely learned healthy or unhealthy strategies for coping with anger and conflict.

Depending on your socialization, you also may have received messages growing up about how you should (or should not) express anger based on factors such as your gender, social class, or cultural background. In families that subscribe to traditional gender roles, it may be deemed acceptable for a boy to become angry and aggressive in a sporting activity but improper for a girl to do the same. For those from marginalized populations who have less power in society—ethnic, racial, sexual, and religious minorities; immigrants; and refugees—expressing anger can have severe and unjust consequences. Growing up, these individuals may receive explicit advice from parents and others about how to navigate difficult situations in which they might find themselves simply because of their marginalized status (e.g., how to interact if pulled over by a police officer). Unfortunately, some people who are in positions of authority and power have misused or abused that power and treated those with less power oppressively. In those cases, the combination of power and unbridled anger can lead to devastating circumstances (e.g., instances of police brutality against Black males or sexual violence against women and LGBTQ+ persons).

How Can You Better Manage Your Anger?

Here are some suggestions for managing stressful or upsetting situations that tend to provoke an angry response:

1. *Avoid or alter the situation.* When I (Bob) encounter someone who is driving erratically, it makes me angry because I know that driver is making me and others unsafe on the road. In this case, the best thing for me to do is to slow down and get away from that driver. I might have to pull over for a few minutes to get far away from the situation, but I will do whatever it takes to get away from the source of what is making me angry.

2. *Analyze the situation and assertively express anger in a rational and caring fashion.* Learning to calm down enough to rationally look at the situation and figure out a way to express concern without further exacerbating matters takes practice. Reacting aggressively and verbally lashing out rarely helps resolve the situation; it usually intensifies the feelings and the anger. Typically, "blowing off steam" escalates our own feelings of anger and makes those around us madder than they were. When encountering rude drivers, for instance, flashing my lights, honking the horn, and giving hand gestures may make me feel better in the moment, but it will escalate the tension.

3. *Practice calming your internal response system.* What you tell yourself about the situation as you try to make sense of it can help you calm down so your body's physiological response is less intense. Experiment with practice, patience, and trial and error to discover what helps you calm yourself. Taking time out and getting away from the situation before you respond can help you calm down and gather your thoughts.

4. *When ready to let go of your anger and bitterness, consider forgiveness as an option for healing.* It is difficult to forgive someone if you remain angry with them. You have to decide to move on to release this anger. Forgiveness simply means that you are ready to put the situation aside and stop harboring anger that can eat away at you. Forgiveness does not mean admitting you are wrong or that another is right. It does not mean you are necessarily ready to reconcile with the person who angers you.

Unexpressed anger, if left to simmer inside, can lead to all kinds of psychological and physiological effects. It is important to find ways to express anger, avoid anger-provoking situations, and learn to calm yourself in intense situations. Identify what you have control over, and work on your reactions to those issues.

Workbook Material for the Client

The following questions and exercises are designed to help you examine the topic of managing anger in your life. There are no right or wrong answers. This is an opportunity for you to spend time thinking about how well you manage your anger. Some activities may be easy for you, and others may require more time and thought on your part. We hope you will take plenty of time to consider each topic or question that your counselor has asked you to complete. The value of the activities and questions comes from your careful consideration about your position on the topic. The goal is for you to learn as much as you can outside of the counseling setting. If you are better prepared to explore these issues, your session time will be more productive. We suggest that you keep a journal as you contemplate making changes in your life to manage your anger more effectively. Purchase a notebook or journal or record your responses to these questions and activities on your computer. Remember to print your responses and bring them with you to your next counseling session.

Exercises and Activities

We hope the following exercises will help you:

- Identify the triggers of your anger.
- Examine the thoughts, emotions, and behaviors associated with anger.
- Challenge distorted thinking in experiencing anger.
- Develop helpful techniques in coping with anger.

1. In the following scenarios, describe how you might react:

   a. You have asked a family member (partner or child) to take out the trash, and that person ignores you.

   _____

   _____

   b. You are trying to watch a good movie at the theater, and the person behind you keeps talking loudly.

   _____

   _____

   c. You are at lunch with a friend who dominates the conversation and won't give you a chance to get in a word.

   _____

   _____

   d. You are in line at the grocery store and in a hurry. The person checking out in front of you keeps asking for a price check and is taking *forever* to pay for the groceries and leave.

   _____

   _____

   e. A coworker challenges you and questions your judgment.

   _____

   _____

   f. Your partner/spouse wants to know if you want to go to dinner but never asks where you would like to go.

   _____

   _____

g. You are on a cross-country flight, and the baby in the row behind you has been screaming for the last hour.

_____

_____

h. You just learned that your partner/spouse has been cheating on you.

_____

_____

2. Anger seems to happen spontaneously. Some of us become mildly irritated and others become furious when faced with the same situation. When you become angry, in general how would you describe your level of anger?
   - ❏ No/minimal reaction
   - ❏ Somewhat irritated
   - ❏ Moderately irritated
   - ❏ Angry but able to manage
   - ❏ Angry and feeling like I would like to lash out
   - ❏ Furious with "smoke coming out of my ears"
   - ❏ Furious with rage and likely to react with a verbal or physical confrontation

3. Are you satisfied with the way you react when you are angry? How would you like your reaction to be different?

_____

_____

4. What types of situations or events make you most angry? Why do you think that is the case?

_____

_____

5. What types of people make you most angry? Why do you think that is the case?

_____

_____

6. Describe your physical reaction when you are angry (e.g., heart racing, sweaty palms, dry mouth).

_____

_____

7. Describe your emotional reaction and what you might say out loud when you are angry.

_____

_____

8. What might you be saying silently to yourself?

_____

_____

9. What one issue almost always gets you riled up and angry?

_____

_____

10. Families handle anger in different ways. For some, emotions are "worn on their sleeve," and anger is expressed openly and often. For other families, expressing anger may be seen as a sign of weakness or vulnerability, or even as an act of betrayal, and anger is rarely expressed. Growing up in your family, what expectations or limitations were you taught about expressing anger?

_____

_____

11. How does your family currently handle anger and conflict?

_____

_____

12. How does your family experience influence how you handle anger today in relationships?

_____

_____

13. Social, political, and economic issues can add to your frustration and anger today. How do you experience today's world? Have you witnessed or directly experienced more hatred, anger, and divisiveness in recent years? Do family members hold different views? How optimistic or pessimistic are you about America's future? About your own?

_____

_____

14. Recall a recent situation in which you became angry:
    a. What was the situation?

    _____

    _____

    b. How did you initially react?

    _____

    _____

    c. What was your inner monologue about the situation? What were you saying to yourself? Did that self-talk help or hinder your reaction to the situation?

    _____

    _____

    d. What did you do to manage and de-escalate the situation? Were you satisfied with the outcome?

    _____

    _____

    e. What would you do differently next time?

    _____

    _____

15. You learned how to experience and express anger at least in part as a product of your culture, ethnicity, gender, religion, and socioeconomic class, and the way you were socialized growing up. How do these factors currently affect your experience and response to frustration and anger? How did they affect you when you were growing up?

_____

_____

16. One good way to manage your anger is to build in a "cooling off period." When you are furious, your rational self goes out the window, and you may do and say all kinds of hurtful and destructive things. Pick a few of these "cooling off" techniques, and try one or two the next time you are angry:

    - Walk away from the situation and take a walk.
    - Do deep breathing or mindfulness exercises.
    - Talk to someone not involved in the situation.
    - Wait to talk to the other person involved until you have had a cooling off period.
    - Seek others to help remedy the situation.
    - Other_____

17. Managing your inner dialogue (self-talk) is another important and powerful way to manage anger. What you tell yourself about a situation can have a major impact on how you react and respond. Check the following self-statements that represent your self-talk when you are angry:

    - ❏ "This makes me so mad I can't even see straight!"
    - ❏ "Is this really anger I am feeling, or am I more sad and hurt?"
    - ❏ "Payback will be sweet!"
    - ❏ "I wonder what the other person meant by that? Maybe I misunderstood the message and should ask for clarification."
    - ❏ "This just makes me furious. Everything makes me furious. I am out of control."
    - ❏ "This is just awful, horrible, the worst thing that could possibly happen."
    - ❏ "This is frustrating, but it isn't the end of the world; I will work to get this resolved."

Key Thought

The words "always" and "never" are rarely helpful in your inner dialogue regarding anger; in fact, they can increase your level of anger.

18. Examine your inner dialogue in situations that make you angry. What could you say to yourself that would help you manage your anger and resolve the situation?

    _____

    _____

19. Envision a person you know who handles anger well. If you cannot identify someone you know personally, identify a character in a film, TV series, or novel who manages anger effectively. How does that person react? What does the person say? What would it take for you to react more like that person when you are angry?

    _____

    _____

Key Thought

In developing plans to better handle anger in your life, it is important to create short-term and long-term goals. Create a plan for managing anger in situations that arise with some frequency in your life. Then consider developing a longer term "prevention plan" that redefines your relationship with anger, resentment, and forgiveness and addresses how you can modify your self-talk to achieve your anger management goals.

20. Visualize yourself reacting like the person you want to be more like when angry. Take a few moments and picture a situation where you would react like that person. How does that feel? What does that look like?

    _____

    _____

21. If you sit on your anger or, conversely, readily express anger and alienate and anger others, it is time to look at other ways of managing your anger. Check the following options that seem like realistic ways you could better handle your anger:

    ❑ Have a built-in "cooling off period" to deter you from reacting immediately and allow you to process your thoughts and reactions.

    ❑ Make a concerted effort to improve your thinking and self-talk about people, situations, and life. Pay attention to how shifts in your thoughts and self-talk affect your feelings and emotions.

    ❑ Examine your beliefs and values about life (e.g., "Everyone should see things the way I do"), and modify those beliefs and values to work better for you.

    ❑ Work on your problem-solving skills to help you resolve situations without getting so emotional or angry.

    ❑ Develop better relaxation techniques and implement them when you become angry.

    ❑ Improve your communication skills so you can have rational and productive conversations with people when you are angry.

    ❑ Spend more time with leisure activities or hobbies or exercise to increase your level of relief and satisfaction with life.

    ❑ Other _____

22. Pick one of the options from the previous list and develop a plan for how you will use that to manage your anger: when, where, who is involved, time frame, and desired outcome.

    _____

    _____

23. Anger can be expressed as passive aggression. Getting back at someone indirectly or talking sarcastically are indicators of hidden anger. People who harbor anger develop a lifestyle that is cynical, bitter, and hostile. Anger saturates everything they say and do. To what degree, if any, does this apply to you and your style of dealing with anger?

    _____

    _____

24. Are you unable to let things go? Does something that someone said just eat away at you and make you even angrier? Forgiveness is a concept that we hear a lot about when learning about managing anger. We see examples of people who forgive others who have committed unspeakable acts. How do they do that? Forgiveness means that you will let go of the resentment you harbor—that pent up anger and desire for revenge—and it is a value that you can develop. Where are you in terms of your ability to forgive? Check the one statement that best reflects your thinking:

    ❑ I will never let this go. It is just too much.

    ❑ I guess with time I will get over it.

    ❑ I think I can forgive, but I know I won't forget.

    ❑ Once I get some distance from the situation, I think I can forgive and forget.

    ❑ Forgiveness is part of the human fabric and simply the right thing to do.

    What steps could you take to work toward being a more forgiving person?

    _____

    _____

25. Do you have greater difficulty forgiving yourself or others when things don't work out (e.g., relationships, jobs)? Reflect on how that affects your life. How would your life be different if you could forgive yourself or others?

    _____

    _____

26. Now that you have a better understanding of your anger and what triggers it, how will you better manage anger in the future?

_____

_____

Chapter 6

Self-Esteem

The worst loneliness is to not be comfortable with yourself.

—Mark Twain

...

For Counselors

You may recall the fairy tale *Goldilocks and the Three Bears*, in which a little girl named Goldilocks samples three bowls of porridge and discovers she prefers porridge that is neither too hot nor too cold, but is just the right temperature. This Goldilocks principle—the notion of achieving just the right balance—seems especially relevant to a discussion of self-regard and self-esteem. Possessing too little self-esteem can lead to *feelings of inferiority* and a lack of self-confidence and self-worth. Paradoxically, low self-esteem also may lead to developing an overly inflated sense of self and *feelings of superiority*, which can pave the path to a sense of entitlement and narcissism. We can all think of individuals who struggle with self-esteem issues and either present with feelings of inferiority and inadequacy or with feelings of superiority and grandiosity. These conditions often involve a great deal of suffering for the person and those around him or her. How does one achieve just the right balance of self-regard—neither a deep sense of inadequacy nor feelings of superiority?

Counseling can help an individual strike a proper balance of self-confidence, humility, and a willingness to turn to others when one's abilities are exceeded. Helping a client develop a more positive and realistic evaluation of self is one of the more difficult challenges counselors face. One widely held value is that one should not think too highly of oneself. Boasting, bragging, and touting one's accomplishments is generally seen as a negative trait, so many people have learned to downplay or even disregard their strengths and accomplishments for fear of being "too full of themselves." The burgeoning technology and social media platforms have led many people to create YouTube videos of themselves, and posting "selfies" has become a part of daily life for others. Researchers have studied the relationship between taking selfies and self-esteem, and March and McBean (2018) found that higher levels of grandiose-exhibitionism narcissism and lower levels of self-esteem were associated with posting more selfies. They also discovered that the relationship between grandiose narcissism and posting selfies on social media was only significant when self-esteem was low or average.

It is easy to mistake narcissism for high self-esteem, but there are a number of reasons to draw a distinction between these two concepts. As Markman (2018) explains, measures of self-esteem and narcissism are not highly correlated. Although some narcissists have relatively low self-esteem, many people with high self-esteem do not achieve high scores on measures of narcissism. Moreover, narcissists feel that their abilities are superior to those of others, and feeling superior necessitates unremitting comparison between one's self and others. Narcissists are compelled to denigrate people if they sense their abilities are being matched and their superior position is threatened. As Markman points out, superiority requires that if one individual is better, then another person is worse. In contrast, people with high self-esteem are satisfied with their abilities and feel worthy as individuals independent of the characteristics of others. They want to connect with others and to help other people advance. In their view, excellence is not a zero-sum game.

So what is self-esteem? Self-esteem is an individual's overall self-evaluation, and it is a central concept in counseling and psychology theory, research, and clinical practice. Self-esteem has been studied and discussed for more than a century (Abel-Khalek, 2016). Sedikides and Gress (2003) defined it as an individual's perception or appraisal of one's self-worth, one's feelings of self-respect and self-confidence, and one's negative or positive views of oneself. Some theorists have viewed self-esteem as a trait that is a stable and consistent part of the personality, whereas others have viewed self-esteem as a state dependent on events and circumstances. Kang (2019) investigated the relationship between trait self-esteem and contingent self-esteem. When a person's self-esteem is more contingent on evaluations, it tends to exhibit instability and fluctuation. High self-esteem is associated with achievement; success in relationships, work, and school; overall emotional well-being; and a resilient and hopeful outlook on life. Low self-esteem is associated with feelings of inferiority and worthlessness and often accompanies psychological disorders such as depression and aggressive behavior.

A discussion of self-esteem would be incomplete without mentioning the importance of its counterpart: *other-esteem*. Corey, Corey, and Muratori (2018) address the topic of other-esteem and the notion that healthy self-esteem entails respect, acceptance, and valuing others without reservation. Philip Hwang (2000) also makes a strong case for promoting personal and social responsibility as an essential element of one's self-esteem. Corey, Corey, and Muratori (2018) conclude that it is not a matter of choosing between self-esteem and esteem for others but rather striking a balance between the two.

What We Have Learned About Helping Others Therapeutically

When I (Bob) was in private practice and managing a clinical training program, self-esteem issues played a central role. I would guess that 75% of clients I worked with in counseling for a variety of issues and problems were dealing with low self-esteem (or at least questioned their self-confidence in resolving their issue). Moreover, the most common issue with graduate psychology interns was their self-doubts about becoming competent and respected psychologists. Many of them lacked confidence in their abilities and were reluctant to reveal the authentic person they were behind their professional role. On a similar note, as a faculty associate in a master's degree program in counseling, I (Michelle) observed many counselor trainees struggling with self-doubts about their clinical skills and their ability to succeed as helping professionals. So we both can attest to the fact that self-esteem issues are common, not only in client populations but also among helping professionals. Helpers who are wrestling with their own unresolved self-esteem issues must be vigilant to the emergence of countertransference toward clients struggling with low self-esteem.

Working with clients on the topic of self-esteem is one of the most challenging and potentially rewarding tasks we take on as counselors. Low self-esteem seems to be rooted in one's values and beliefs and is resistant to change. Somehow people tend to feel guilty about feeling good about themselves. Modesty is a virtue, and self-confidence is rife with braggadocio. Clinical work with clients on self-esteem and self-acceptance issues is typically a slow process. The work that needs to be done can seem obvious to the counselor, but it is difficult and challenging for the client. Clients must find their own way to better self-acceptance consistent with their beliefs and values and at a pace that works for them. Counselors who struggle with impatience at the slow pace of their clients' progress must be careful not to impose their own agenda on clients and are advised to engage in self-reflection about their reaction. Clients who detect the counselor's impatience may feel they are disappointing or frustrating their counselor, which could intensify their sense of inadequacy. Clearly this would be counterproductive.

The Counselor's Task With Clients

The cognitive behavior approach is widely used in the treatment of self-esteem issues, and the tasks we propose are based largely on CBT principles. The first task with clients is to help them examine their beliefs about their self-confidence and self-esteem and help them look at the messages they have adopted from family and other sources. The next step is to help clients examine common thinking distortions that affect low self-esteem. Challenging those thinking distortions may prove to be a challenge for the counselor. Those thinking distortions are heavily ingrained, and it is difficult to move the needle toward more positive and realistic thinking patterns and self-talk. Counselors should also help clients eliminate the "yes, but" of self-esteem. Clients often move toward negating self-statements of affirmation by adding qualifiers that discount their strengths and value as an individual. Another task is to work toward positive affirmations in self-talk. We know that one's internal self-talk can have a major impact on how one's value, significance, and self-image are viewed. Modifying that self-talk to make it more positive and affirming can be a helpful goal for clients. Finally, counselors should collaborate with clients to define the road to improved self-esteem that endures. This includes self-affirmation, accurate self-evaluation, solid relationships, defining and implementing strategies for success, a strong sense of resilience and the ability to recover from setbacks, an ability to receive joy and satisfaction from life, a commitment to contributing to the community through involvement in various organizations, and an examination of the spiritual realm of life as it affects their self-esteem.

Notes

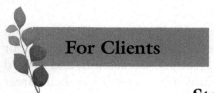

For Clients

Strengthening Your Self-Esteem

If you were totally honest and forthcoming, how much would you say you like yourself? Do you respect yourself? Do you accept your faults and shortcomings and forgive yourself for mistakes and failures in life? Or do you torture yourself with second-guessing and self-doubt about decisions made in the past? Do you feel optimistic about your future, or do you feel burdened with a sense of doom about what lies ahead for you? The answers to these questions form the essence of self-esteem.

Beatles Wisdom

"I think people worry about things. And it doesn't matter how elevated you get, or your reputation gets, you still worry about things" (Alfonsi, 2019). These words, spoken by Sir Paul McCartney, a 77-year-old billionaire and one of the most acclaimed musicians of all time, expressed his continuing worries and self-doubt. No one is immune from the worries, doubts, and anxieties of everyday living, not even one of the legendary Beatles! Research has shown that it is not the poor decisions and mistakes that people tend to regret most in their lives; rather, it is what people want to do or accomplish and do not that weighs on them more heavily (Bruk, 2018). Our self-esteem is tied to making the most of our lives and not being afraid to pursue those lofty goals for ourselves. As McCartney's bandmate and iconic peace activist, the late John Lennon, was quoted as saying:

> We need to learn to love ourselves first, in all our glory and our imperfections. If we cannot love ourselves, we cannot fully open to our ability to love others or our potential to create. Evolution and all hopes for a better world rest in the fearlessness and open-hearted vision of people who embrace life. (Lennon, 2017)

What Is Self-Esteem?

Self-esteem can be defined simply as your opinion of yourself, the value you place in yourself as a human being, and your self-confidence and self-respect. When people have too little self-regard or self-esteem, they can become depressed, achieve less in life, and may have unsatisfactory relationships because they do not think they deserve better. Those who have an overinflated sense of self-regard may become narcissistic and feel a sense of entitlement. To get a better handle on this concept, answer the following questions:

- How would you describe yourself in five words?
- What is your evaluation of the person you are? The accomplishments in your life? Your abilities and limitations?
- Do you feel good about who you are and what you are doing, or are you dissatisfied with yourself, your accomplishments, your values, and your relationships?

Your degree of self-respect is a major part of your sense of self-esteem. Factors that tend to influence self-esteem include how others see you as well as your thoughts and perceptions of yourself; your experiences in your family, at school, in the workplace, and in social situations; and your experience with illness, adversity, injury, or trauma. In many cases, your relationships with others and their reactions to you are likely to play a major role in your development of self-esteem. Messages that you have received either explicitly or implicitly about your culture, race/ethnicity, gender, sexual orientation, socioeconomic status, education level, ability/disability, or other dimension of who you are will most likely affect your self-esteem. Promoting personal and social responsibility, along with having "other-esteem" (valuing and respecting others), is another essential element of your self-esteem. You do not choose between self-esteem or esteem for others but strike a balance between the two.

Some people find a goldmine of self-worth in work, parenting, a hobby, or volunteer work. You would expect that to be the case, but if you put all of your eggs in that one basket and that basket goes away, your self-esteem can be shaken. Some put all their stock in a career and find great joy, satisfaction, and reward from that career, but these people may feel lost and depressed and lack direction in life when their career comes to an end. The old adage to become a well-rounded person is not a bad idea. If you can find satisfaction, self-respect, and confidence in a variety of things you do in your life—parenting, family, career, education, friends, hobbies, community, religion/spirituality, volunteering—the loss of any one of them is not likely to put a huge dent in your self-esteem.

Self-esteem fluctuates depending on your life circumstances and your response to those circumstances. If you focus on your weaknesses and are unhappy with the way you are handling situations, your self-esteem may suffer. When life is going splendidly and you are managing well, your self-esteem will be higher. Ups and downs are common, but a chronically negative view of yourself or an unrealistic and overinflated view of yourself can work against you. With healthy and balanced self-esteem, you have an accurate and realistic view of yourself that is generally favorable and confident.

One of the true enemies of healthy self-esteem is *self-doubt*. Most of us experience self-doubt from time to time. In fact, it can be in our own best interest to occasionally question whether we are taking the right course of action. However, too many of us suffer from self-doubt, lacking confidence in ourselves and our abilities and choices. I (Bob) recall a recent conversation with my two teenage grandsons who are both bright, kindhearted, and concerned about others and are making productive and moral choices in life. The only thing that might get in the way of accomplishing what they desire is self-doubt. If they can overcome that and believe in themselves and their abilities, they can succeed in whatever lies ahead in their lives. I believe that is true for all of us—self-doubt is our greatest enemy, and we should do whatever we can to forge ahead with hope, persistence, and the belief that we will prevail and be successful. Of course, you can have too much confidence and be unable to realistically look at yourself and examine how you might improve. That is the essence of narcissism—believing unrealistically that you are the best, the smartest, the best looking, the best at making decisions and the most deserving in the face of facts to the contrary. All you have to do is look at politicians to see how narcissism works as a protective shield to keep them insulated from any negative feedback.

Key Thought

One of the true enemies of healthy self-esteem is self-doubt, which is one of your greatest enemies in life. Do whatever you can to forge ahead with hope, persistence, and the belief that you will prevail and be successful.

In summary, individuals with healthy self-esteem are confident, realistic about their strengths and shortcomings, able to express themselves effectively, grounded in healthy and honest relationships, and resilient and able to bounce back from failures and setbacks (Mayo Clinic, 2017).

Enhancing Your Self-Esteem One Choice at a Time

Robert E. Wubbolding, director of the Center for Reality Therapy, uses the metaphor of a train to describe the relationship between choice theory and reality therapy. He explains how the WDEP system of reality therapy can bolster your sense of self and satisfy essential needs that increase your life satisfaction.

Using Reality Therapy to Bolster Your Self-Esteem

Robert E. Wubbolding

Choice theory is the train track. Reality therapy is the train. Both are needed. Each is useless without the other. The track directs the train. The train delivers the product. Choice theory directs the human mind to find ways to satisfy its inner motivations: to survive, to make connections with other people (belonging), to be in charge of self (power), to make choices (freedom), to enjoy life (fun), and most fundamentally to maintain a sense of meaning and purpose.

The failure to satisfy these needs results in feelings, thinking, and actions. Negative feelings include stress, anxiety, loneliness, malaise, and many others. Negative thinking involves "The world sucks," "My supervisor is not fair," "Even though what I'm doing is not working, I'll keep doing it." Unsatisfied needs can also result in an unlimited range of actions: complaining, doing minimal or mediocre work, and even drug abuse.

Catching fire about your job or anything you care about—the opposite of burnout—can be facilitated by employing the WDEP system of reality therapy. Each letter represents a cluster of reflections.

> **W – Reflection I:** As soon as possible, write down your ***wants***: a better relationship with your spouse, your friend, a promotion at work, a successful career, a new car, getting in better physical condition, more self-confidence, or a thousand other things. Keep in mind that it is not sufficient to merely think about your wants or goals. Write them down; this means you are serious about fulfilling them. Next, pick one and decide how committed you are to achieving it. There are three levels of commitment: (1) "I don't really want it." (2) "I'll try to get it." (3) "I'll do whatever it takes." Reflect on your level of commitment. Only one level is effective: level (3).
>
> **W – Reflection II:** The W also represents ***perception***—how you see the world. Do you see yourself as powerless, as put-upon by society, as in need of a safe space, or as stressed out by your job, your marriage and family, and other elements in your environment? Which one of these is the easiest to work on? (If you would rather choose the hardest, go for it.) Try to connect this perception with your actions, and ask yourself whether or not you indulge these perceptions and allow them to overflow into your conversations.
>
> **D – Reflection III:** The D represents ***doing***, which refers primarily to actions and secondarily to self-talk and feelings. Pause here and spend a few minutes thinking about your actions today, especially your conversation. Has it focused on complaints or criticism accompanied by "they won't let me" or "the world is unfair"? Then ask yourself whether you have focused your conversation on the joys of life, such as your successes and those of the people around you. Which focus is better for you? More than likely it is the second set of conversations. A practical suggestion is to force a smile rather than a frown. John Arden (2010), in his book *Rewire Your Brain*, states that "by smiling or frowning you send messages to your subcortical or cortical areas (of your brain) that resonate with happy or sad feelings. So, put on a happy face—it helps you to feel better" (p. 52). I have suggested to many people who state that they are shy to pretend they are outgoing with one person for 60 seconds. Keep in mind that it is easier to change your actions than to change your thinking and feelings. In 12-step programs, a common axiom is, "You can act your way to a new way of thinking (and feeling) easier than you can think your way to a new way of acting."
>
> **E – Reflection IV:** E represents the heart and soul of reality therapy. It stands for ***self-evaluation***. After reflecting on the above principles, ask yourself, "Does it help me to see the world the way I've been interpreting it? Is what I want realistically attainable? Are my current actions effective for achieving my goals?" (Wubbolding, 2017). Writing down the self-evaluations, especially the positive ones, constitutes the most important component of your inner search for purpose and meaning.
>
> **P – Reflection V:** These ***reflections*** culminate in a plan of action. Effective self-care and lessening stress require that you make a positive plan that replaces negative and limiting feelings and thoughts that we all experience at times. Reality therapy embraces the axiom, "To fail to plan is to plan to fail." So be sure to develop a helpful, realistic, and doable plan of action.

• • •

Although there is so much in the world that we cannot control, Wubbolding reminds us that we can make choices that will enhance our lives and help us feel more empowered and in control of our lives. As you weather life's countless stressors, it is crucial to reflect on whether your decisions are strengthening or eroding your self-esteem. How would you answer that question at this point in time? As you look to the future, what choices do you want to make?

Workbook Material for the Client

The following questions and exercises are designed to help you examine the topic of increasing your self-esteem and improving your life satisfaction. There are no right or wrong answers. This is an opportunity for you to spend some time thinking about your self-regard. Some questions and exercises may be easy for you, and others may require more time and thought. We hope you will take plenty of time to consider each topic or question that your counselor has asked you to complete. The value of these activities and questions comes from your careful consideration about your position on the topic. The goal is for you to learn as much as you can outside the counseling setting. If you are better prepared to explore these issues, your session time will be more productive. We suggest that you keep a journal as you contemplate making changes in your life to increase your happiness and sense of self-esteem. Purchase a notebook or journal or record your responses to selected questions and activities on your computer. Remember to print your responses and bring them with you to your next counseling session.

Exercises and Activities

1. First, let's revisit the questions we posed at the beginning of this section on self-esteem. We'll take them one at a time.

   a. How well do you like yourself and respect yourself? Please rate yourself and then explain your rating.

   Scale: 1   2   3   4   5   6   7   8   9   10
              Not at all   *A great deal*

   Explain your response.

   _____

   b. Which characteristics, beliefs, values, and actions do you like *most* about yourself?

   _____

   _____

   c. Which characteristics, beliefs, values, and actions do you *least* like about yourself?

   _____

   _____

   d. Which characteristics, beliefs, values, or actions would you like to be different, and how would you like them to be different?

   _____

   _____

   e. What emotions are you experiencing when you think about your beliefs, values, and actions? What disturbs or pains you the most?

   _____

   _____

2. How would you describe yourself in five words?

   _____

   _____

3. Do you accept your faults and shortcomings and forgive yourself for mistakes and failures in life, or do you torture yourself with second-guessing and self-doubt about decisions you have made?

_____

_____

   a. We all have made decisions we regret, but have you made decisions that you believe are truly unforgiveable? If so, explain.

   _____

   _____

   b. What would it take for you to be able to forgive yourself for those decisions or actions?

   _____

   _____

4. Your own thoughts about yourself (self-talk) have a major effect on how you see yourself and the self-respect and self-esteem you have today. Examples of thoughts that can work against us are:

   • "I never know the right thing to do. I am just a failure in every case."
   • "If I don't do things perfectly, others will think that I am a failure."
   • "Nobody likes me, and no one ever will."
   • "This is too overwhelming, it's too hard, and I just can't do it."
   • "Why do I always screw things up? Why am I so stupid?"
   • "Yes, but . . ."

   Examples of thoughts that work for us and we can stand to increase are:

   • "This seems overwhelming, but if I work hard, I can figure this out."
   • "Some people will like me, and others won't. The key is to like myself more."
   • "I will do the best I can; and if people don't like it, that's just the way it is."
   • "I will try to make the most of my strengths and minimize my deficits while keeping a positive and hopeful outlook throughout."

   You have to train your brain to change your thinking patterns. It takes practice and effort to change those automatic messages you give yourself. Write down your negative messages, and see if you can come up with more positive messages that work for you rather than against you. Write down those positive messages and practice them, say them out loud. The more you say them, the more likely it is that they will become the new messages that guide your daily life. After writing a few of these, reflect on how this exercise was for you.

   _____

   _____

5. Self-appreciation is the respect you have for your own value in life (Leutenberg & Liptak, 2014, p. 44). Say a few words about what you appreciate in life:

   Your life _____

   Your family _____

   Your relationships _____

   Your strengths _____

   Your goals _____

   Your actions _____

6. In *Authentic Happiness*, Martin Seligman (2002) describes a number of positive traits that contribute to happiness and well-being. A few of these are gratitude, optimism, altruism, humor, wisdom, courage, love, humanity, justice, temperance (self-restraint), spirituality, and transcendence. In your journal, describe which of these traits are strengths of yours and how they enhance your well-being. Also, describe which traits you would like to possess (or strengthen) and how you envision your life satisfaction might improve as a result.

_____

_____

7. An important part of improving your quality of life is to increase happiness. The next set of questions focuses on this concept. Rate your overall happiness. Explain your rating.

Scale: 1   2   3   4   5   6   7   8   9   10
            Not happy   Very happy

Explain your response.

_____

a. If your subjective experience of being happy fluctuates, describe what's different between the times when you are happy and less happy.

_____

_____

b. To what extent do you think you have control over your level of happiness?

Scale: 1   2   3   4   5   6   7   8   9   10
            No control   Complete control

Explain your response.

_____

c. I think I would be a lot happier if: (check all that apply)
❏ I had more money.
❏ I had a better relationship with my significant other.
❏ I was better at parenting.
❏ I had a job I like or was on a clear path to achieving my desired job/career goals.
❏ I was kinder to and more forgiving of myself.
❏ I could identify what will make me happier with my life.
❏ I had better eating and exercise habits.
❏ I didn't worry about the world so much (e.g., global warming, nasty politics, and so much divisiveness).
❏ I spent less time comparing myself to others on social media.
❏ Other: _____

d. I think I would be a lot happier if: (check all that apply)
❏ The world was a kinder place to live.
❏ People were more supportive of me.
❏ People would just leave me alone.
❏ My friends and family were more supportive.
❏ My health was better.
❏ My faith-based community was more supportive and encouraging.
❏ Other: _____

Additional comments about this exercise:

_____

8. If a miracle happened and your self-esteem instantly became what you would like it to be, what would that look like? What would be different?

_____

_____

9. Do you feel optimistic about your future, or do you feel trapped and have a sense of doom about what lies ahead for you?

_____

_____

   a. If applicable, what about your life makes you feel trapped or feel a sense of doom?

_____

_____

   b. What will it take for you to overcome those negative feelings and be less pessimistic?

_____

_____

   c. What is your specific plan for improving your outlook on life? How long do you think it will take? Who else needs to be involved to help you actualize your plan?

_____

_____

10. Describe three early childhood memories that really began to shape your self-concept and self-esteem. Include details such as what happened and how that made you feel.

_____

_____

11. Relationships are an important factor in having sound self-esteem.
   a. What are the messages about yourself you received from other people (family and friends) as you grew up, and how have those messages affected how you see yourself?

_____

_____

   b. What messages do you receive from others today, and do they have a bearing on your self-respect and self-esteem?

_____

_____

   c. How are those messages different from the messages you received from others when you were growing up?

_____

_____

12. Locate a small cardboard box—approximately 6×6 inches—and gather some old magazines. Cut pictures from your old magazines and paste them onto your box to represent who you are. On the outside, paste pictures that represent how you think people see you. On the inside of the box, paste pictures you think represent who you really are. How different is the overall image of the person on the outside from the person on the inside of the box? How easy or difficult was it for you to do this activity? Were you surprised by your result?

_____

_____

Be sure to bring your completed box to the next counseling session for discussion with your counselor.

13. What self-talk (inner dialogue) affects how you see yourself today? Is your self-talk more positive or negative?

_____

_____

14. Keep track of your self-talk (your inner dialogue) for the next week, and see what you can learn about the messages you give yourself and how that affects how you feel and what you do. Keep a journal of those thoughts. When you have a good sense of the themes of your inner dialogue, begin to slowly modify it. It may not be easy because that dialogue is automatic. It takes awareness and practice trying a new dialogue and then more and more practice until you can turn those thoughts around to work for you. Describe your experience and what you learned from this activity.

_____

_____

15. Create a chart with the headings in Chart 6.1. Describe an inner dialogue you typically have in the first column, and in the second column describe what it would be if you could successfully modify it to work for you rather than against you:

Chart 6.1 Inner Dialogue

Current Self-Talk	Desired Self-Talk
"Like my father told me years ago, I will never be good enough to go to college, so why should I even try to get decent grades."	"My father's discouragement and negativity don't have to limit me. He was not always right about things. If I work hard, I will be better off and will improve my chances of going to college."

16. Imagine you have learned that you have only one month to live.
    a. How would you like to live your life in that last month?

    _____

    _____

    b. Who would you want to spend more time with? Who would you want to spend less time with? What activities would be most important for you?

    _____

    _____

c. What clues does that exercise give you about how you would like to live your life today? What would you like to do more of? Less of?

_____

_____

17. How would your significant others describe you today? How would you like to be described? How about in 5 years? In 10 years? How would you like to be remembered by those who care about you?

_____

_____

18. Neff and Germer (2018) describe the importance of self-compassion, which is treating yourself with the same kindness that you would treat a friend who is in trouble or having a hard time. Our culture places value on treating our friends with kindness and respect, but when it comes to treating ourselves with compassion, those ideas are not valued. Neff and Germer believe that self-compassion entails learning to treat yourself as a friend and becoming an inner ally and not an inner enemy.

a. Describe a time when a friend was in need of help and support and how you helped that person.

_____

_____

b. Now think about a time when you were in need of help and support. How did you treat yourself

_____

_____

c. What would it take for you to treat yourself more like you would treat a friend?

_____

_____

19. Write a letter *to* your younger self and include whatever "life lessons" you would want "younger you" to know to make life easier to navigate over the years.

_____

_____

20. Write a letter *from* your older self to your present self and include whatever life lessons "older you" would want you to know. In other words, write a letter from the future that expresses what you would like to be able to say about how you lived your life.

_____

_____

21. Write a letter to your self-doubt as if "self-doubt" were a person. Imagine that you are writing a "breakup letter" to this part of yourself that has sabotaged your well-being and happiness. What would you most want to say to self-doubt? If self-doubt were no longer in your life, how would it be different?

_____

_____

22. To challenge self-limiting assumptions, *act as if* you are the person you want to be. Catch yourself in the process of repeating old patterns that have led to ineffective or self-defeating behavior. For one week, *catch yourself* in unproductive patterns that have eroded your self-esteem. Then pause briefly to consider how you would like to respond differently. Allow yourself to assume that you have made a desired change in your behavior. Write about this experience in your journal. At your next session, discuss with your counselor how *acting as if* worked out for you.

_____

_____

Key Thought
Individuals with healthy self-esteem are confident, realistic about their strengths and shortcomings, express themselves effectively, grounded in healthy and honest relationships, and resilient and able to bounce back from failures and setbacks (Mayo Clinic, 2017).

Chapter 7

Grief and Loss

Only people who are capable of loving strongly can also suffer great sorrow,
but this same necessity of loving serves to counteract their grief and heals them.
—Leo Tolstoy

• • •

For Counselors

Everyone experiences the loss of a significant other through death at some point. We celebrate birth, marriage, and accomplishments in life, but we are less able to openly address death and cope with the grief that accompanies it. In fact, we seem to be surprised when someone dies, as if we didn't think it could happen. As a society, we do not spend much time preparing ourselves for death and the grief that accompanies that loss. Grieving is no longer widely viewed as a predictable and measurable linear process as described by Elisabeth Kübler-Ross in 1969. She had convinced the professional community that grieving entails going through a series of predictable stages: denial, anger, bargaining, depression, and acceptance. We have since come to understand that grief is a unique experience and that no two people experience and adapt to it in the same way. Counseling professionals have largely adopted nonlinear grief models over the universal stage approach to understanding grief (Humphrey, 2009), and clinicians rely on a range of counseling and psychotherapy models in their work with grieving clients.

Grief is a heavy emotional burden brought about by loss and characterized by distress and sadness. The loss can be "the real or perceived deprivation of something" (Humphrey, 2009, p. 5). Grief is also our way of healing from the loss. *Loss adaptation* refers to the adjustment we make in life to both the loss and the grief. Humphrey points out that *coping* is misleading in this context because it implies a time-limited event from which the individual will return to the previous state. An individual suffering from grief and loss does adapt but is unlikely to return to the state he or she was in prior to the loss. *Mourning* is the expression of grief for both death and non-death-related losses (Humphrey, 2009).

Grief is often associated with death, but it can result from any real or perceived loss. It is a normal re-action to the loss or death of a friend, family member, pet, house, or job. It can also be a response to the loss of wellness or the onset of chronic illness. In general, the more significant the loss (e.g., a child or spouse), the more intense the reaction and often the longer the recovery period. Grief reactions to loss include similar elements, but individual responses vary tremendously. It is essential for the counselor to make a thorough assessment of the client's response to the loss and the expected course of recovery. People are resilient and are able to adapt, adjust, and move through these emotions, and some develop newfound strengths as they work through their grief. Some individuals struggle with the loss and their grief and need professional help to move through the recovery process. Others become stuck in their grief, preoccupied with and consumed by the loss, and are immobilized and unable to move forward toward recovery.

Most individuals grieving the loss of a loved one do not develop a major depressive disorder. Howev-er, the *DSM-5* identifies persistent complex bereavement disorder, characterized by severe and persistent mourning and grief, under the category of other specified trauma-stressor–related disorder (American Psychiatric Association, 2013). Sadness and depression are typical components of the grieving process, but they tend to come in waves. Persistent and extended grief can become a major depressive disorder, or a major depressive disorder could coexist with and be exacerbated by the grieving process. Refer to *DSM-5* guidelines for assistance in distinguishing grief from major depression.

Multicultural Issues and Grief

Culture, ethnicity, gender, socioeconomic status, age, religion, and many other aspects of diversity may play a significant role in clients' lives. When working therapeutically with the grieving, we must consider what the loss means in the context of their life setting and culture. American Indians, for example, have suffered considerable losses over the decades, and their grief over the loss of a loved one may be intensi-fied by the cultural oppression they have experienced. Skilled clinicians working with grief and loss blend traditional counseling and psychotherapy approaches within the multicultural context in which clients live and experience the grieving process. Counselors should make a concerted effort to seek knowledge about culturally sensitive interventions from other sources and should not place the burden on clients to teach us basic information about their cultural context.

What We Have Learned About Helping Others Therapeutically

Most people proceed through identifiable stages of the grieving process, but the individuality and the variations in their responses can be striking. No one fits the grieving model perfectly, and the range of reactions is expansive. To illustrate this, I (Michelle) knew a woman who went back to work the day after her husband died because she desperately needed to feel a sense of normalcy, structure, and control in her life at a moment in time when her world had just been shattered. Others simply want the world to stop after the death of a loved one, and they may "check out" of life for a long period of time. No one model or approach to grieving fits all of us. We have found that the best approach is to learn where the client currently is in the grieving process and go from there. Clients need to tell their story and oftentimes tell their story repeatedly. With support and guidance from the counselor, some clients recover in a relatively short time, and others may never reach a satisfactory resolution and acceptance of the loss. The key is to follow the client's lead throughout this unique journey of grieving.

The loss of a loved one is frequently profoundly traumatic, but other losses can affect clients as much or even more, such as the loss of a job or career, a markedly lower standard of living, or a significant change in their health and wellness. People can experience grief over the loss of their culture, feeling that their beliefs and values have been shattered or their civil rights trampled, or simply be grieving the aging process. We cannot know how these kinds of losses will affect an individual, so we have to rely on the client to lead the way in providing that information.

In the case example that follows, Crissa S. Markow, a social worker for a hospice service, describes some activities she and her team found helpful for working with hospice clients and their family members. These activities could easily be adapted for many clients suffering from a chronic or terminal physical condition.

Creative Activities With Hospice Clients and Families

Crissa S. Markow

We worked with a young single mom in the final stages of cancer. She was very concerned about the future well-being of her children and how they might remember her. In addition to working tirelessly to arrange for the children to be raised in a stable, secure, and loving home, the hospice staff suggested several options this woman could take to ensure her connection with the children over time. She chose to write birthday cards for each child for every birthday up to their 18th year. The staff checked in at each visit to see how she was coming along with the cards and helped her put it all together. This activity gave the client confidence that she was doing something for her children that would continue her legacy with them long after she was gone. This activity was successful in offering the dying client something concrete she could do for her children, and it gave her a sense of control over a seemingly helpless and hopeless situation. She was able to say what she needed to say to her children in a way that would continue for many years to come.

Another activity involved helping clients make videos for their significant others in which they expressed whatever they wanted to say, including topics they had never discussed with anyone. Clients shared their life story, reminisced about meaningful life events, said goodbye, or offered thoughts about life lessons learned. The videos could be shared with others whenever clients so desired, either before or after death. This activity encouraged clients to talk freely with their significant others and not to leave things unsaid. Clients also felt they had a sense of control over this terminal event.

Clients also practiced relaxation and breathing exercises between sessions. Aware that diaphragmatic breathing triggers body relaxation responses that benefit physical and mental health (e.g., Ma et al., 2017), the team made use of Square Breathing (see Figure 7.1). This technique, sometimes referred to as *box breathing*, consists of (a) breathing in for 4 seconds, (b) holding one's breath for 4 seconds, (c) breathing out for 4 seconds, and (d) holding for 4 seconds before repeating the cycle (Becker-Phelps, 2013). This is essentially mindful breathing; it can be done anywhere, but it is often done sitting in a chair with feet flat on the floor. Meditation and visualization exercises could be added to the Square Breathing exercise for additional relaxation and to help clients focus on the present. Staff would then do *synchronized breathing* (breathing in unison with the client) to aid in connecting with the client and to model breathing and relaxation techniques. These methods are frequently taught to family members and significant others so they too can model them for and connect with the client. Goals for this exercise are to help the client gain some control over any anxiety being experienced and to connect with family members and significant others.

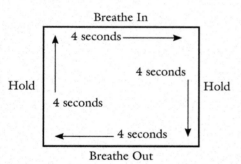

Figure 7.1 Square Breathing

Hospice also supports the grieving process of family members. I worked with the distraught daughter of a mother who was dying. The daughter was depressed and feeling hopeless and helpless about the future loss of her mom and was becoming immobilized. I provided step-by-step concrete tasks for the daughter to carry out between our meetings, such as scheduling an individual counseling appointment, arranging to procure medication, and making menus and shopping lists for herself. At each meeting, we would follow up on the previous week's assignments and prepare for the next week. Although these may seem like simple and easy tasks, the daughter needed direction in small, definable, and concrete steps to begin to get her life in order.

• • •

The Counselor's Task With Clients

Humphrey (2009) identified three essential roles for the counselor when working with grief and loss: the witness role, the facilitator role, and the collaborator role. In the role of *witness*, the counselor's task is to observe and listen with empathy to the narrative presented by the grieving client. To be fully present with the client can have a major healing effect in itself. In the *facilitator* role, the counselor provides focus and structure for the client to participate in the procedures and strategies that will best fit with the client's unique needs for dealing with grief. In the *collaborator* role, the counselor works together with the client, recognizing the client as the expert regarding this experience of grief and loss. Humphrey recommends homework for clients and suggests that homework activities be discussed and selected as a collaborative effort between client and counselor.

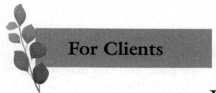

Dealing With Grief and Loss

It often begins with a phone call. Sometimes we are at the bedside, comforting our loved ones as they take their last breath. Death is predictable even though its timing may startle us. My (Bob) first encounter with death occurred when I was 14 years old and my grandfather, Frank, died from the ravages of leukemia. I was stunned, disbelieving that such a strong and supportive hero in my life could leave this world, leave me. For some reason, I just never expected that he would die. I knew intellectually that dying happens to each of us—I just didn't think it would happen to him. I was in a fog of disbelief and confusion. I missed him, especially on holidays and special occasions when I was so accustomed to his presence. Over time I began to come out of the fog and my shock and returned to my normal routine. But I have never forgotten Frank and the wonderful times we had with him.

The experience of grief and loss following the death of a spouse, child, friend, or family member is universally difficult and challenging for each of us. Although we know that death will touch us all at some point in our lives, it seems we are rarely prepared for the experience of loss. Feelings of loss can be devastating, depressing, inconvenient, and completely unexpected. The grief that follows the loss of a loved one is one of the worst experiences we will have in our lives, and that grief can be all-consuming, especially at first. The range of emotions we experience following the death of a loved one is extensive. It can range from shock and disbelief to anger and guilt. Through this roller coaster of emotions, we have a pervasive sense of loss and sadness that we often fear will never go away.

Grief is a heavy emotional burden that is our reaction to the loss (S. Hayes, 2018). It is typically characterized by sadness and distress, and grieving is our way of healing from the loss (Jose, 2016). The loss of a loved one or of anything significant in our life is truly a heavy burden that we may carry with us for the rest of our lives. Loss turns our world upside down and challenges our sense of what matters most in life. After a significant loss, we often reexamine whether what we are doing with our life is, in fact, at the top of our priority list.

Grief can also follow the loss of your physical abilities or good health, loss of a job, a divorce, or loss of any significant relationship. However, nothing is quite like the pain you experience when someone close to you dies. Accept the feelings of sadness and distress, and recognize that the pain and sadness may last for some time. People do recover from the loss of a loved one, and the time it takes to recover is different for each of us. In addition, you will recover in your own way at your own pace, and it is important to give yourself permission to do so. This is not to say that you will forget the person or that you will ever stop feeling the loss, but the grief and sadness does seem to diminish with time and help from friends, family members and getting back into the activities of daily living.

Most of us remain preoccupied with the event for a period of time. We may have a vivid visual image of the deceased, and we may go over the details and the time frame of the event repeatedly. We usually talk about the event with others, and there is something healing about telling this story over and over. With time, the event begins to fade from our mind, and we move on to thinking more about routine living. My (Bob) mom died at age 97. She lived a long and productive life and was a role model for our family. She lived life to the fullest and adapted to every curve ball she encountered. She had been ill for some time, so her passing was not a surprise. Nonetheless, it was a significant loss. My wife and I visited her on Monday and Tuesday, and my brother called on Wednesday to tell us she had died that day. For several weeks, I replayed in my mind what I was doing on the Monday and Tuesday before my mom died. I talked with many people about the events surrounding her death and how we were all feeling and adapting to her loss. As the weeks passed, I relived those days and hours less and less, talked about her death less and less, until finally I stopped replaying those tapes about mom in my mind. Mondays and Tuesdays became just days in the week, no longer with a special significance. This is a normal reaction to and recovery from the crisis of loss of a loved one. Sometimes, however, that process is short-circuited or takes longer than we expect or isn't addressed at all. We know that holidays, birthdays, and anniversaries may be especially difficult because they bring with them many cherished memories.

Key Thought

People do recover from the loss of a loved one, and the time it takes to recover varies from one individual to the next. You will recover in your own way and at your own pace, and you may not go through a set of predictable stages of grief. Give yourself permission to feel the pain, the loss, and the sadness; allow yourself time to recover; and accept the comfort and support of others.

Licensed psychologist Sherry Cormier (2018) shared her insights following several deaths in her family, including that of her husband. She experienced the presence and spirit of her loved ones and noted that it is common for survivors to experience the image of the deceased in a variety of forms and places, including in dreams. *Visitation dreams* are commonplace, and the deceased appears to provide guidance, reassurance, or in some cases, even a warning. Cormier had read and studied the concepts of grief and loss as a psychologist, but the actual experiences of loss were so much different and in many ways richer. She expressed surprise over how many of those experiencing loss developed new strengths as a result of this experience. In fact, Cormier recognized firsthand how these major events could lead to positive change and adaptation. Experts refer to this as *posttraumatic growth*. The basic idea is that the net result of such a loss is the development of newfound abilities, relationships, activities, and contributions to the community and even beliefs and values that were not present before the loss. These changes result from your struggle to make sense of the loss and to examine how to move forward. This doesn't mean that life will be easy or even better, but you may live life on a deeper level with new priorities and balance. Cormier's message is that through the loss, depression, and pain, we should be hopeful that things will get better and that we will adapt effectively.

You cannot make the pain and the grief disappear by not thinking about it. In fact, the more you try to squash or suppress those feelings and reactions, the more of a problem those emotions become, and you will find yourself working harder and harder to keep them in check. So what can you do about loss in your life and the grief that follows? Steven Hayes (2018) suggests that one of the best things you can do is to treat yourself with kindness and compassion throughout the grieving period. You will probably beat yourself up emotionally with guilt about what you could have or should have said or done, but accept the fact that you cannot go back and change things. The best you can do for yourself is to let go of those ruminations of what might or should have been and refocus on the future and what you can do to ensure that your loved one's spirit and memories are not forgotten. To continue the healing process, Hayes suggests the following:

1. Acknowledge the loss and pain, and know that sometimes it feels uncomfortable and even unbearable. Don't fight it or try to suppress the feelings; give yourself permission to feel the intense sadness.
2. Embrace the feelings of loss. If you focus all of your energy on trying to eliminate the pain, it will likely get worse. Instead, open yourself up to allow these feelings to occur.
3. Expand your scope of vision. Other emotions or remembrances may come into your mind that you might think shouldn't be there—allow those in. That is perfectly normal.
4. Prepare to be overwhelmed. It is normal for the emotions to come in surges like waves. Some days seem better, and others may seem miserable. Measure your progress toward recovery over a period of weeks or months, not from hour to hour or day to day.
5. Watch out for unhelpful thoughts such as "this should be over by now" or "life isn't fair" or "I will never get over this." These are perfectly normal thoughts and emotions to have, but look at them for what they are—normal reactions and not directions to be followed.
6. Connect with what matters with the people and activities that give your life meaning.
7. Take committed action to following what you feel in your heart—reaching out to others, getting back to work, or taking on a desired volunteer activity.

Key Thought

One of the best things you can do is to treat yourself with kindness and compassion throughout the grieving period.

Workbook Material for the Client

The following questions and exercises are designed to help you examine the topic of loss and grief in your life. There are no right or wrong answers. This is an opportunity for you to spend some time thinking about how well you are healing from losses. Some questions and activities may be easy for you, and others may require more time and thought on your part. We hope you will take plenty of time to consider each topic or question that your counselor has asked you to complete. The value of the activities and questions comes from your careful consideration about your position on the topic. The goal is for you to learn as much as you can outside of the counseling setting. If you are better prepared to explore these issues, your session time will be more productive. We suggest that you keep a journal as you contemplate making changes in your life to move forward with the grieving process. Purchase a notebook or journal or record your responses to selected questions and activities on your computer. Remember to print your responses and bring them with you to your next counseling session.

Exercises and Activities

You may have experienced one or more losses that you need to process. If you are grieving multiple losses, it may be overwhelming to focus on them all at the same time, so choose the one that seems to preoccupy you most when you respond to these questions. You can repeat these exercises with a different loss in mind to explore your feelings about it too.

1. Describe the loss that has occurred in your life with as much detail as possible. What was the loss? How did it occur, and who was involved? What was your initial response? Detail your thoughts and emotional reaction at the time it occurred or when you learned about it. What has been your physical reaction; that is, how has this event affected you physically?

   _____

   _____

2. How has this loss changed your life? How do you anticipate it will change your life in the future?

   _____

   _____

3. Did this event cause any earlier similar memories of loss to reemerge? Did it suddenly bring back all those emotions and thoughts? If so, describe.

   _____

   _____

4. Express your feelings of pain and sadness using words, images, drawings, or other artistic mediums. One idea is to keep an art journal as you process your grief. It is your journal, so you decide what to include: drawings, paintings, photographs, or some combination of materials and words. Let your creativity soar!

   _____

   _____

5. Imagine that your grief process is like going on a road trip. You'll definitely need some tunes to keep you company as you make the journey. Create a playlist of songs that will provide you with an emotional outlet for your sadness and pain and accompany you through your grief process. What is it about each song you chose that led you to include it on your playlist?

   _____

   _____

6. What have you done to try to relieve the pain the loss has caused you? How well has this worked for you?

_____

_____

7. What was the last conversation you had with the person who died or who left? Was it a positive or negative conversation? What did you say? What did you wish you had said?

_____

_____

8. Share your most vivid and cherished memory of the deceased. What emotions come up for you as you think about this memory?

_____

_____

9. Do you find yourself being flooded with thoughts of the person or the event? What is that like for you? What seems to trigger strong and vivid emotions and thoughts? Are you ever able to shut those floodgates so you are not consumed with painful thoughts and emotions? (If not, move on to the next part of the exercise on refocusing.)

_____

_____

Refocusing is one way to stop that flood of thoughts and change the subject in your mind. Think about or focus on something else, such as working in the garden, baking some cookies, watching a TV program, or talking to someone in person or on the phone. Come up with three thoughts or activities you could focus on or do to get your mind off the flood of thoughts about the loss. What are those?

_____

_____

Refocusing will take some practice, so give yourself some time to work on this. It may not be easy, especially at first. Describe how well this activity worked for you.

_____

_____

10. What were your initial emotions, and which of the emotions are you still experiencing today regarding the loss? Which emotions concern you most? Circle all of the emotions that apply to your experience right after the loss, your current emotions, and emotions you continue to experience that concern you most.

Initial Emotions	Current Emotions	Emotions That Concern Me Most
Anger	Anger	Anger
Disbelief	Disbelief	Disbelief
Fear	Fear	Fear
Sadness	Sadness	Sadness
Guilt	Guilt	Guilt
Depression	Depression	Depression
Confusion	Confusion	Confusion
Overwhelmed	Overwhelmed	Overwhelmed
Relieved	Relieved	Relieved
Motivated	Motivated	Motivated
Other _____	Other _____	Other _____

Say more about the emotions that concern you most. Why do they concern you? Describe how intense or severe these emotions are when they surface. How often do you experience them, and how long do you last?

_____

_____

11. Therapeutic writing has been found to be useful and often healing for people suffering from the grief of loss (Humphrey, 2009). Begin by writing about the thoughts, feelings, and actions you associate with the loss you have experienced. Feel free to add whatever you like to express yourself about the loss and your grief. Set aside some private time, and write something every day about your reactions and recovery from the loss. Do this as often as you can, but at least once each day, and summarize how you are feeling and doing. Describe how this activity has been for you.

_____

_____

12. One means of aiding the grieving process is for you to write a letter to the deceased or to the significant loss in your life. Express whatever you wish to the person or about the loss. This will give you a way to organize your thoughts and feelings about the person or situation. If the person is still alive, **do not send the letter!** The letter is for your use only; it is simply another way of expressing yourself. We want you to feel free of any judgment that might occur if you sent the letter, so we strongly encourage you to keep the letter in a secure place or destroy it when you have finished writing it and processing it with your counselor. Describe generally what you did and how that was for you.

_____

_____

13. What role does religion or spirituality play in your way of dealing with loss? (Has religion been a source of strength and support for you, or has it been a source of oppression and stress in your life? Has it had any influence on you at all?) What role would you like religion or spirituality to play in your life and in this healing process?

_____

_____

14. How does your culture or ethnicity affect how you view death and grief? What values and beliefs does that background and history provide in helping you understand your loss? Are symbolic rituals or practices part of your family's mourning or grieving process?

_____

_____

15. Do you have the friends, family, and other support you need to help you get through this rough period in your life? Is there something missing that would be helpful and healing if you had that available?

_____

_____

16. Some days will be better than others, and other days will be worse.
    a. Describe those days that are better for you and what it is about those days that make them better.

_____

_____

b. What are some things you could do to try to have more of those good days?

_____

_____

17. Describe strengths you have discovered that you didn't realize you had as a result of this loss.

_____

_____

18. If you woke up one morning and felt that you were back to normal, what would that look like? What would you be doing? What would you be feeling?

_____

_____

19. Metaphors can be powerful tools in the healing process. Is there a metaphor that comes to mind that aptly captures your loss, grieving process, or posttraumatic growth? For instance, someone might say, "My grief feels like an avalanche that is burying me alive at times, but then the sunshine melts the snow and gives me hope." Feel free to draw your own metaphor if it will help you clarify your emotions.

_____

_____

20. Cormier (2018) claims that it is common for survivors to experience the image of the deceased in a variety of forms and places, including in visitation dreams. Describe any dreams you have had that may be related to your loss. Keep a notebook by your bed so you can jot down notes upon awakening before you forget the details. Try to recall your emotions in the dream. Be sure to discuss your dreams with your counselor.

_____

_____

Part III

Coping With Trauma, Disaster, and Adversity

In Part III you will find discussions regarding clients' reactions and responses to natural and human-caused disasters and to the trauma, fear, and anxiety associated with chronic illness and other health issues. Our focus is on clients' reactions to adverse events in their lives; how they can enhance their response to and recover from adversity; and how they can build strength, confidence, and a sense of mastery in their lives as they work toward developing resilience and posttraumatic growth. Disasters are debilitating and devastating, but many people develop an inner strength as they struggle toward a positive outcome after these difficult and traumatic situations.

In Chapter 8, we discuss how people typically react to both natural and human-caused disasters. In Chapter 9, we explore what is involved in recovery from disasters and crises and how people develop posttraumatic growth. We recommend that counselors receive education and supervised training in the specialty of Disaster Mental Health and Disaster Mental Health Counseling prior to working with clients who have experienced such ordeals. Finally, in Chapter 10, we address the crisis of coping with chronic illness and other medical issues. In each chapter, we provide a range of exercises and activities for you to use with your client, either in session or out of session. These activities are designed to facilitate the therapeutic process and are not a substitute for effective counseling and psychotherapy.

Additional therapeutic exercises for clients are provided in Appendix A. See Appendix B for an annotated list of useful websites and online resources.

Scope of the Problem

In one day in 2018, we experienced a school shooting with 10 students and teachers killed and a dozen more wounded in the United States, a deadly volcanic eruption and lava flow to the sea that destroyed hundreds of homes in Hawaii, torrential rains and flooding in the Carolinas, and a breakdown in U.S.–North Korea negotiations to denuclearize our world. All this in just one day! Unfortunately, there have been far too many days like this.

Adversity and trauma are becoming part of our everyday lives at an alarming rate. Webber and Mascari (2018b) chillingly state that "an atmosphere of dread pervades American daily routines at athletic events, concerts, schools, and universities" (p. 4). Historically, counselors helped clients work through stressors that affected their personal functioning, but in today's world, events occurring miles and even continents away are affecting clients due to the rapid dissemination of news via social media and other media outlets. We expect counselors to see an increasing number of clients suffering from "global anxiety" resulting from the real time around-the-clock broadcast of human-caused, natural, and technological disasters. It begins to feel like one can never escape it, which is likely to increase fear and anxiety. Helping professionals are now much more attuned to trauma and its effects on people, and clients are more willing to seek counseling to help them learn to live with the constant fear, anxiety, trauma, PTSD, and concern for their family and friends. As counselors, we have to be prepared to assist these clients in need.

Natural disasters such as hurricanes, bomb cyclones, volcanoes, severe droughts, wildfires, earthquakes, and floods are devastating communities. In fact, while writing this material, over a 2-day period two massive earthquakes struck southern California, where many of my (Michelle's) family members and friends live. *Human-caused disasters* such as gun violence and mass shootings, kidnappings, acts of sexual violence and rape, the mistreatment or abuse of marginalized individuals at the hands of people in positions of authority, terrorist bombings and attacks, and more are taking a toll on human lives and touching the lives of everyone in the larger community. In 2015 in the United States, 36,252 people were reportedly shot and killed by firearms and another 85,000 were shot and survived (Centers for Disease Control and Prevention [CDC], 2017). The family and friends of those killed as well as those who were injured will likely suffer from the trauma for many years to come.

A clinical psychologist in Mill Valley, California, recalls treating a client who came for counseling following the 2017 Las Vegas shooting, which left 59 dead (including the gunman) and several hundred wounded. The client was not present nor was she connected to the event in any way. Nonetheless, she felt generally frightened and unsafe. This reaction is not uncommon; many people feel that they can't control what might happen to them, and they simply don't feel safe anymore. Gerald Brown, a licensed professional counselor in North Carolina, remarked that he doesn't need a survey to tell him that people are more stressed. He noted that "anxiety levels have increased tenfold" among his clients (as cited in Meyers, 2017, p. 39). A sense of general fear and apprehension as well as global anxiety are more commonplace as disasters and trauma become pervasive in our lives.

We are learning that trauma in childhood often leads to higher physical and mental health risks later in life (Mascari & Webber, 2018). The CDC-Kaiser Permanente Adverse Childhood Experiences (ACE) Study, which included more than 17,000 subjects and examined the impact of abuse, neglect, and household challenges, revealed that as the number of ACEs increases so does the risk for negative outcomes (CDC, 2019). Simply put, early adversity has a lasting impact. The bottom line is that a thorough assessment of crisis in the client's life must be conducted when working with clients experiencing crisis and suffering from trauma.

Health issues are another form of adversity that many clients may be facing. Advances in medicine, biomedical engineering, and related technologies have revolutionized health care and are nothing short of miraculous, but illnesses and disorders are increasing around the globe. Cancer, heart disease, lung disease, Parkinson's disease, Lyme disease, the Zika virus, HIV and STDs, obesity, opioid abuse, alcoholism and other substance abuse disorders, arthritis, dementia, Alzheimer's disease, diabetes, and influenza are taking an increasing toll on the health of our population. Our life expectancy has increased from 72.6 years in 1975 to 78.8 years in 2015 (National Center for Health Statistics, 2017), but as people are living longer, they are also experiencing an increasing number of health issues that can lead to additional trauma, fear, and anxiety, which detracts from their quality of life.

One factor that is undeniably contributing to recent natural disasters is climate change. The National Aeronautics and Space Administration (NASA, 2019) states that 97% or more of active climate scientists agree: Climate-warming trends over the past century are extremely likely due to human activities. In addition, most of the leading scientific organizations worldwide have issued public statements endorsing this position. Effects of climate change are expected to include rising sea levels and temperatures, more intense hurricanes and droughts, and changes in precipitation patterns (NASA, 2019; Whitmore-Williams, Manning, Krygsman, & Speiser, 2017). We must anticipate the impact that these changes may have on human beings, including on us, our loved ones, and our clients. Declining water supplies, health impacts in cities due to heat, reduced agricultural yields, and flooding and erosion in coastal regions are just a few of the challenges we will face (NASA, 2019). Sturm and Echterling (2017) conclude that climate change also poses enormous threats to our psychological well-being. Not only will we be coping with the stress resulting from disasters, but long-term fear and anxiety surrounding what lies ahead for ourselves, our families, and our communities will also affect our well-being.

In her impassioned message to world leaders at the United Nations Climate Action Summit on September 23, 2019, 16-year-old climate activist Greta Thunberg captured the range of emotions that many young people feel about the world they are inheriting. As Miss Thunberg stated most persuasively:

> You have stolen my dreams and my childhood with your empty words. And yet I'm one of the lucky ones. People are suffering. People are dying. Entire ecosystems are collapsing. We are in the beginning of a mass extinction, and all you can talk about is money and fairy tales of eternal economic growth. How dare you! . . . For more than 30 years, the science has been crystal clear. How dare you continue to look away and come here saying that you're doing enough, when the politics and solutions needed are still nowhere in sight. . . . You say you hear us and that you understand the urgency. But no matter how sad and angry I am, I do not want to believe that. Because if you really understood the situation and still kept on failing to act, then you would be evil. And that I refuse to believe. . . . You are failing us. But the young people are starting to understand your betrayal. The eyes of all future generations are upon you. And if you choose to fail us, I say: We will never forgive you. We will not let you get away with this. Right here, right now is where we draw the line. The world is waking up. And change is coming, whether you like it or not. ("Transcript," 2019)

Counselors should expect to see clients who are increasingly concerned about the potential dangers and the current effects of climate change.

The Specialty of Disaster Mental Health Counseling

The good news for the counseling community is that the field of disaster mental health counseling has evolved and developed rapidly in recent decades, providing us with an evidence-informed knowledge base and practice standards (Webber & Mascari, 2018a). Disaster recovery is a broad notion encompassing actions taken on the local, state, and federal levels and involving teams of counselors and psychologists. Stebnicki (2017) postulates that disaster mental health counseling is unique because of its cutting-edge research in areas of stress and trauma, interventions with emerging populations such as immigrants, its understanding of military versus civilian trauma, the impact of global terrorism, and the importance of resiliency and coping resources for disaster survivors. He notes that disaster counseling is intense work that requires a multifaceted and multicultural approach for which we should be ready at a moment's notice. Stebnicki emphasizes that disaster counseling "experiences can result in the counselor's own wounds that are continually revisited by their clients' life stories of chronic illness, disability, trauma, grief, loss, and extraordinary stressful events" (p. xi). He concludes by saying that it is imperative that counselors who provide disaster mental health counseling develop their own self-care program (see Chapter 14 for more on counselor self-care).

Research and intervention in disaster mental health (DMH) has become a specialty field in counseling and psychology. Since World War II, we have recognized the phenomenon of shell shock. In the 1950s, the American Psychiatric Association developed psychological first aid (PFA) guidelines for physicians (Webber & Mascari, 2018a). In the 1990s, attention was given to the emotional effects of first responder work, and critical incident stress debriefing (CISD) was developed. Ever since the catastrophic leveling of the World Trade Centers and the attack on the Pentagon September 11, 2001, mental health professionals have been developing and refining therapeutic approaches designed for work with victims of disasters. Short-term DMH counseling focuses on establishing presence and support, providing information, stabilizing of the individual, and helping the individual cope with normal reactions to an abnormal event and return to baseline functioning as soon as possible. Webber and Mascari describe Hobfol et al.'s (2007) five core factors that guide DMH counseling and trauma response: safety, calming, self-efficacy, connectedness, and hope. These core factors form the foundation for the practice of PFA (Brymer et al., 2006), a commonly utilized, evidence-informed, modular approach to help adults, children, and families in the aftermath of a disaster.

The need has never been greater for the development and refinement of trauma-informed and evidence-based practices and treatment that recognize that different skills are necessary for different types of disasters, stages of recovery, and various groups of people. Webber and Mascari (2018b) advocate for "trauma-informed treatment as an essential part of the continuum of care following disasters and mass violence" (p. 13). Even if DMH is not your specialty area, Webber and Mascari conclude that every counselor should have minimal training and be ready to respond to disasters and crises in their own communities.

Multiculturalism in Crisis and Disaster Counseling

Disaster mental health counselors must be adept at fostering empathy and be capable of fully hearing and understanding the traumatic stories of the events and reactions in a client's life. This involves both an understanding of the concept of *empathy* in counseling, which is the ability to put oneself in the shoes of another and experience what the client is seeing and feeling, and an understanding of the concept of *cultural empathy*, a skill that is pancultural (Stebnicki, 2017). Carl Rogers (1951) perhaps best described the components of empathy as attending, listening, understanding, and responding. Cultural empathy is a broader concept that involves a sensitivity to and understanding of the idiographic meaning of the client's story and experience within the context of their culture (Stebnicki, 2017). Merely having a general knowledge of the individual's culture and environment can lead to inaccurate stereotyping of the client. Developing cultural empathy requires that the counselor have knowledge, skills, and an intentional awareness of the totality of the cultural and personal environment of the individual client (Corey & Corey, 2021). Acknowledging racism and oppressive structures that influence trauma is crucial to building the therapeutic alliance (Raheem & Hart, 2019).

Trauma and Its Impact on the Brain

Trauma can have a lasting effect on brain chemistry and function. Bremner (2006) explains that the areas of the brain implicated in the stress response are the amygdala, hippocampus, and prefrontal cortex. Long-term exposure to constant trauma can lead to permanent changes in these areas. Traumatic stress is also associated with increased norepinephrine and cortisol levels in response to subsequent stressors. Integrating both hemispheres of the brain—the right, which controls the emotional center, and the left, which controls the verbal, rational, and analytical functions—is vital when helping an individual process his or her experience of the traumatic event (Perryman, Blisard, & Moss, 2019); however, those suffering from the effects of trauma may be challenged in this regard. Several studies have shown deficits in verbal declarative memory among those afflicted with PTSD (Bremner, 2006). Trauma, and especially long-term trauma, leads to the brain being "rewired." Although this discovery may seem to be of more use to neuroscientists than to counselors, it could lead to treatments that target certain neuropathways in the future (McRae, 2018). Today antidepressants or other medications may be effective in alleviating symptoms in certain clients, but this must be assessed in each case by a qualified medical professional.

Chapter 8

Individual Response to Trauma, Disaster, and Adversity

When written in Chinese, the word crisis *is composed of two characters—*
one represents danger, and the other represents opportunity.

—John F. Kennedy

• • •

For Counselors

Unfortunately, crises are becoming an increasing part of our daily lives, and it is important that counselors help clients learn to handle crises more effectively. Clients can then help their children and other loved ones learn to handle crises as well. This chapter provides resource materials, exercises, and activities for clients for use in session or out of session to enhance the therapeutic process. Our aim in this chapter is to assist clients in exploring and assessing how they react to trauma and adversity.

Take a moment to recall a crisis you experienced firsthand and how you handled that situation. How did you initially react? What were your first thoughts? What did you do in response? What did you learn about yourself from that experience? How might you have handled the situation differently? What was the emotional aftermath like for you, and how long did it take for you to really "get over" the event? As you approach your work with clients, think about your response to this event. Help clients examine how adverse events affect them and how they might improve their ability to handle new situations. People tend to react and respond in a crisis in some similar ways, but everyone's reaction is unique. It is quite common, for instance, to see two individuals reacting to the same event in dramatically different ways: one person struggles to cope and becomes overwhelmed and immobilized; the other person steps up to the challenge and handles the situation with calmness and mastery. What troubles one individual may be no more than a small bump in the road for another.

Cognitive, Emotional, and Behavioral Components of Reacting to a Crisis

Why is there so much variation in how people react in times of crisis? One way to answer this question is to point out that crisis reactions are multifaceted, involving cognitive, emotional, and behavioral components. The cognitive component in reacting to a disaster or adverse event involves individuals' perceptions, expectations, and self-talk monologue. What we tell ourselves about what is happening, how we are affected, and how we should react can have a major impact on how successfully we react. If we believe we cannot handle difficult and stressful situations, a self-fulfilling prophecy may be the result. If our expectation is that we are able to master whatever life throws at us, we have a greater chance of success in the situation. Emotions are difficult to control, and we may initially feel overwhelmed and immobilized by the event. Expectations about our ability to successfully cope with crises can help mitigate our emotional response to the situation. Our cognitions about the situation are also likely to play a major role in determining our behavioral response. The behavioral component of a person's reaction to crisis is not only the individual's immediate actions in response to the precipitating event but also the person's ability to develop and implement an action plan for recovering from the event.

What We Have Learned About Helping Clients Therapeutically

Countless scenarios come to mind in which counselors might need to help clients process their reactions to crises, disasters, or other adverse life events. The crisis event might be something that happened this morning, a month ago, or 10 years ago. The client may or may not have had time to process the event and his or her reaction to it. We have learned how essential it is to assess the crisis by exploring the *what, when, where, who*, and *how* of the event. It is important to allow clients to tell their story and their experience of the event. Even if you have knowledge of the event and the surrounding facts, clients need to be given the time and space to tell their story in a manner that suits them; they should not be interrupted or corrected. With that said, we have found that the following prompts help clients tell their stories: Ask when clients first became aware of the event. Where were they? When did it occur? What was their initial reaction? What were the thoughts and feelings associated with their reaction? What are they thinking and feeling now? Who else was affected by the event? A great deal of therapeutic progress can be made simply by encouraging and allowing clients to tell the full story of the incident through their unique lens. This approach can be useful in getting the counseling process started.

One point cannot be emphasized enough. In severely distressing situations, such as the two described next, helping professionals must be able to attend to and manage their own needs and reactions as they simultaneously juggle the demands of helping their clients cope with harrowing circumstances.

One Counselor's Experience as a Disaster Counselor

Susan Whitehead (2019), an assistant professor of counselor education at California State University, Stanislaus, served as a Red Cross volunteer during the height of the Camp Fire in Paradise, California, in 2018. This fire became a Level 7 disaster, the highest level the Red Cross can declare. She recalled that when she got to the shelter she found many of the survivors to be walking wounded in shock from what was happening. Many, she reported, talked of running along streets and through the forest to escape the raging inferno, barely escaping with their lives. When the survivors spoke of their experience, "their eyes lit up with fear, as if reliving the nightmare." She offered psychological first aid in the first few days and tried to keep track of who was coping relatively well, who was keeping it all inside, and who was clearly in distress. Yet, she said, "the stories of rescues and heroism made my heart skip, reveling at the strength of the human spirit; however, these are human lives you are working with, and to say it doesn't pull at your very soul would be a lie." Work with disaster victims can be challenging, rewarding, stressful, taxing, exhausting, and life-changing—all at the same time!

In 2018, Judy Van Der Wende, a clinical psychologist in private practice, also faced the arduous challenge of helping clients cope with a devastating California fire—only this time it was located in southern California. As astonishing as this may seem, when news of the Woolsey fire first broke, Van Der Wende and the residents in her community were still reeling from the pain of a mass shooting that had happened literally hours earlier at a local bar. Here is her harrowing story in her own words.

Surviving and Helping During Multiple Traumatic Events

Judy Van Der Wende

It has been 4 months since the simultaneous disasters of the Borderline Bar and Grill shooting and the Woolsey fire ravaged my community. It is only now that I am able to write about this terrible experience.

On the morning of November 8, 2018, I got up and automatically checked the phone. A text had come in at 4:00 a.m. "Oh my God, it's us, it's us—a mass shooting in Thousand Oaks, Oh, no, no, no, no, no." I immediately switched to a news site and saw the screaming red giant-font headlines. A mass shooting had taken place the night before at our local dance club, the Borderline. Twelve people had been murdered.

Then came the smoke. We were on fire. A fire had broken out at Rocketdyne, a facility on the hillside 3 miles from my house in Simi Valley on literally the same day. The Santa Ana winds whipped up at that exact moment, and the fire, fueled by a heavy rainy season the previous year that produced copious brush and tinder, took off with furious intensity.

As a therapist, you are constantly torn between taking care of yourself and being available to assist suffering clients. Every single person I spoke with at this point was going through the same panicked process. Everyone was desperately scanning for information. The desire to be at the vigil for the Borderline victims was rudely eclipsed by the desire to survive the fire. The pain and anguish of hearing about the dead only a few hours ago was abruptly replaced by personal fear. There was no time to find out about missing clients and friends and complete the mental checklist, "OK, this one is safe, who else is still missing?" For that is what immediately happened in my brain upon getting that early morning text—my mind began compulsively scanning to make a list of anyone I knew who might possibly have been out drinking and dancing on a Wednesday night. The overwhelming emotion was horror.

As with other disasters, the Woolsey fire seemed to go on forever, with layer after layer of suffering visited on local residents. The fire consumed 97,000 acres over 2 weeks, left three dead, and nearly 300,000 people had to be evacuated. As the fire was slowly contained and survivors returned to their lives, the slow work of processing and recovery began.

As a therapist with a full-time practice, I was inundated by stories of pain, loss, grief, and anger. Lots of anger. Our community is small, and the loss was enormous. Everyone had a story to tell, and the stories were raw, powerful, and anguished. It was exhausting. I had to manage my own fear and grief while helping others process theirs. It was impossible not to cry with clients, impossible to fight back feelings of helplessness and grief. It was also imperative to hold back as much personal grief as possible to help others through their own experiences.

I did not expect the degree of anger and even hatred clients began expressing. The desire to make "someone" pay for their pain and loss was expressed repeatedly. I did not expect the rage to generalize. Suddenly, people who had been previously rational and high functioning were agitated and pointing the finger. Politics and the media played a significant role in providing targets for people to hate. I did not expect long-term clients to suddenly quit therapy if I didn't join in their rage but stayed reasonable and calm. I imagine my calmness and refusal to rage was perceived as a great betrayal.

I did not expect how severely these multiple local disasters would affect people's ability to cope. Fight or flight was constant and interrupted everyone's ability to think rationally. Many folks resorted to more primitive coping behaviors—addictions are rampant. The overarching experience appears to be confusion. Nothing makes sense to people who run businesses, teach, or heal others. Parents are particularly frightened for their children's lives. I saw everything from primal anger to drug-seeking behavior from clients.

I did not expect the fight-or-flight response in clients to stay so elevated and result in so many dramatic life decisions. Countless clients are moving either out of the county or out of the state. I hear from many that they simply can't bear to look at the charred hills or the empty spaces where homes and businesses once were. We grieve the loss of local wildlife. Businesses have tanked, people are not getting insurance payouts to rebuild their lives, and illnesses are increasingly severe and difficult to manage. People are afraid of the wind now. They are afraid of another fire. They are simply afraid.

It was eerie to hear the stories from every point of view, from families who lost homes to the firefighters' wives who brought buckets of sandwiches to their unflinching husbands determined to save homes and lives as they worked around the clock. Similar to those who didn't go to their jobs at the Twin Towers on 9/11/01, it was unnerving to hear how many young people who are "regulars" at Borderline's Wednesday night "Campus Night" randomly stayed away that evening.

I heard other therapists were overwhelmed and experiencing burnout. It was unsettling to hear that therapists were struggling, even though I shared the struggle. Therapy became combined with funerals and grief counseling. The grief at times was unbearable. Highly respected physicians had homes burned to the ground. It was difficult to get appointments anywhere, just when you needed them most.

Another change is that many clients are now unable to do "normal" therapy due to their horrible trauma. I immediately took refresher CEU courses on trauma and grief. I explain over and over about the fight-or-flight response and about pausing and breathing. I am forcing myself to take my own medicine—exercise, breathe, meditate—and it does help. I work with clients on regaining a sense of normalcy. Boring, everyday routines do wonders to help frightened brains remember how to feel calm and soothed.

What I have learned, 4 months out, is that our community will never be the same. We are all exhausted from 2 years in a row of devastating fires. We hurt. We feel guilt. We feel sad. The shootings at Borderline brought indescribable pain to the community. We must learn from the past 4 months, learn what helps and what harms, and develop programs to help each other cope and survive. Factors that increase resiliency are important; finding out how to help others cope and return to normalcy is my primary goal. This is the reason I became a psychologist, and I'm honored to be part of the process of healing.

• • •

The Impact of Trauma on a Community

Van Der Wende describes both *primary trauma*, in which an individual or individuals are traumatized by an event, and *shared trauma*, in which an entire community shares the trauma directly, indirectly, or vicariously. Del Vecchio-Scully and Glaser (2018) discuss the complexity of *communal shared trauma* in which traumatic incidents can affect both clients and counselors as well as community residents and leaders. They emphasize that each community experiencing traumatic incidents is unique in its exposure to the incidents, culture, community structure, and characteristics. Del Vecchio-Scully and Glaser stress the importance of *trauma-informed care coordination* that is "a client-centered, assessment-based approach to integrating health care (physical and mental) and psychosocial support as well as implementing a comprehensive care plan that addresses a client's needs, strengths, and goals" (p. 237).

The Counselor's Task With Clients

As Van Der Wende's personal account illustrates, tasks that help to stabilize clients, assist them in returning to normalcy, and build their resilience are of paramount importance. After clients have detailed the event and their reaction to it, you can provide psychoeducation to normalize their reaction to an abnormal event. You might outline the typical course of reaction and recovery with the caveat that every individual reacts and recovers differently. A major task of counseling is to assist clients in examining how they have reacted to crises in the past and in exploring ways to best recover from the trauma. Assessment involves an examination of significant past crises as well as clients' cognitive, emotional, and behavioral reactions to these events. One outgrowth of assessment should be the development of an action plan for recovering from the current (or past) crisis and responding effectively to future crises. Both mental and in vivo rehearsal can go a long way toward preparing individuals for implementation of their action plan. It is also essential to identify clients' strengths, which can be leveraged to help them not only recover from the initial trauma but also aid in their long-term recovery. In the For Clients section that follows, we explain how people generally react and respond to crisis and adversity.

Notes

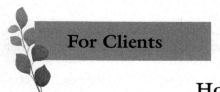

For Clients

How People React to a Disaster

We all react when faced with a crisis—a car accident, a death in the family, a divorce or separation, a report that your personal identity has been stolen, or the blow of getting fired from a job. Individuals seem to have their own ways of reacting and responding, and no two people react in the same way. In the same situation, one person might feel overwhelmed and at a loss for how to respond while the next person remains calm and collected and responds in an objective and effective manner and recovers quickly from the shock of the event. Why is it that two people can react to the same set of circumstances so differently? Many factors go into that process. We focus on helping you examine how you react in a crisis and what you can do to improve your ability to respond calmly and to recover as quickly as possible.

Take a few minutes to think about a crisis to which you were exposed and how you reacted. Then read the following description of factors that tend to influence an individual's response to a disaster. This may give you insights into why we all react so differently. These concepts are adapted from *Becoming a Helper* (Corey & Corey, 2021) and *Take Control of Life's Crises Today! A Practical Guide* (Haynes, 2014).

- Human-caused events generally elicit a stronger emotional response than a natural disaster such as a hurricane. You may feel helpless and angry at the circumstances of a hurricane, but a mass shooting may lead to feelings of anger, hopelessness, a desire to assign blame, and a need for answers as well as for justice and revenge.
- An unexpected event brings about the most emotional and mental disruption.
- In general, the closer you are to the event, the stronger the reaction.
- Events that involve injury and death have a greater impact than ones that do not.
- Your current life situation and personal level of stress can affect how well you respond in a crisis. The greater the level of distress in your life, the less effective you will be in handling a current crisis.
- The more accurately you are able to identify what is occurring during a crisis, the more likely it is that you can respond effectively. However, humans have a tendency to "normalize" situations, even if that involves distorting reality and believing nothing bad is happening despite evidence to the contrary (e.g., witnessing a robbery). Our minds try to tell us that everything is OK. We do this for self-preservation.
- The first reaction to a crisis situation may be a sense of disbelief and a feeling of disorientation. The sooner you can overcome those reactions and attempt to objectively assess the circumstances, the more quickly and effectively you can respond.
- The bottom line is that crisis situations such as natural and human-caused disasters often result in cognitive disruption and impairment, which can cause you to become immobilized and "frozen." It is as though an earthquake has occurred in your brain, and it can take considerable time to get things back in place and functioning properly.
- The better you are prepared cognitively, emotionally, and behaviorally for a disaster, the more likely it is that you will respond effectively. Learning from previous situations and practicing for future disasters is key to your success.
- The stress reaction, or fight-or-flight reaction, is a common element in a crisis. Typically, individuals experience an increase in the flow of epinephrine resulting in increases in heart rate, blood pressure, breathing, and muscle tension, all of which prepare the body for responding to threats. The downside of the fight-or-flight response is that it may impair your ability to objectively and rationally resolve the situation (Wagner & Ivey, 2018).
- Genetic makeup very likely plays a role in your response to crisis. For example, serotonin, a chemical that occurs in the synapse between nerve cells in the brain, helps regulate mood and sleep patterns. Individuals with the gene for the long-form serotonin transporter between nerve cells may be able to remain calm and to objectively assess a crisis situation, whereas those with the gene for the short-

form serotonin transporter react more impulsively (Touchette, 2003). Although you cannot do anything to change your genetic makeup, it can be useful to be aware of possible genetic factors that affect your reaction and response.

- The neurochemistry of the individual stress response involves neurotransmitters, hormones, and cortical areas of the brain (James & Gilliland, 2017). Continual exposure to stressful situations—such as the work of first responders or military personnel in a war zone—can cause permanent changes in the brain and may play a role in the development of PTSD.
- Physical symptoms and ailments are not uncommon for an individual who has experienced a stressful crisis and may intensify as additional crises are experienced over time.
- Time distortion also can occur. An event that lasted a minute can feel like an hour to a participant in the situation. Events often feel as though they are happening in slow motion, and you may feel as though you are removed from the event, as if watching from outside.
- You can expect to react to a crisis situation cognitively, emotionally, and behaviorally and that you will recover with time. These are normal reactions to abnormal events.
- The best predictor of future behavior is past behavior. Successfully managing a crisis situation makes it more likely that you will be successful in future situations. The same is generally the case for those who handle the situation poorly. However, new skills can be taught and learned, and that should be your overriding goal in counseling.

Key Thought

If you have experienced some sort of a disaster, your response is a normal reaction to an abnormal event. Most people experiencing what you have would have a reaction as well.

Workbook Material for the Client

The following questions and exercises are designed to help you examine the topic of reacting to crisis situations in your life. There are no right or wrong answers. This is an opportunity for you to spend some time thinking about how well you react to adverse events in your own life. Some questions and exercises may be easy for you, and others may require more time and thought on your part. We hope you will take plenty of time to consider each topic or question that your counselor has asked you to complete. The value in the activities and questions comes from your careful consideration about your position on the topic. The goal is for you to learn as much as you can outside the counseling setting. If you are better prepared to explore these issues, your session time will be more productive. We suggest that you keep a journal as you contemplate making changes in your life with regard to dealing with crises. Purchase a notebook or journal or record your responses to selected questions and activities on your computer. Remember to print your responses and bring them with you to your next counseling session.

Exercises and Activities

1. Consider how you might handle this situation. You are driving along a city street and a pedestrian suddenly darts out in front of your car. It takes you a fraction of a second to realize what is happening and then slam on the brakes to avoid the pedestrian who did not see your car coming when he entered the crosswalk. As your car comes to a halt, you feel a slight bump as you seem to tap the pedestrian. At the same time, you hear the screech of brakes as the driver behind you was not paying attention and slams into the rear of your car. You get out of your car and see that the pedestrian appears more shocked than injured, but then you also see that your car is seriously damaged in the rear.

   a. What are you feelings about the situation? Anger toward the person who slammed into you? Shock or a state of disbelief? Defensive about the situation and feeling upset that the pedestrian wasn't more careful? Feeling guilty or concerned about the well-being of the pedestrian? What do you think your most prominent emotion would be?

   _____

   _____

b. What do you believe your initial reaction would be? What action would you take in this situation? How would you decide on that course of action?

_____

_____

c. Have you faced a similar situation in the past? Describe what happened. How well do you think you handled it? If you could do it over again, would you handle the situation differently? If so, in what ways?

_____

_____

d. What do you need to learn to be better prepared to handle such situations in the future?

_____

_____

2. Describe a crisis situation in your life that you think you reacted to *effectively*.
   a. What was the event that triggered the crisis?

_____

_____

b. How did you react? What were your initial thoughts and feelings? How did you act or behave?

_____

_____

c. How did you first learn or become aware of the situation? How long did it take until you were able to respond to the situation?

_____

_____

d. What did you like about the way you reacted? What enabled you to draw upon your internal and external resources to react the way you did?

_____

_____

3. Describe a crisis situation in your life in which you feel your reaction and response was *unacceptable*, then answer the following questions.
   a. What was the crisis situation? How did you react?

_____

_____

b. What were the thoughts running through your mind during the crisis?

_____

_____

c. What do you wish you had done differently in the way you reacted?

_____

_____

d. How would you like to be able to react in future crisis situations?

_____

_____

e. What will it take for you to be able to react that way?

_____

_____

f. What is it that might get in your way of being able to react that way?

_____

_____

4. Select a recent crisis or trauma you experienced. Gather colored pencils, pens, chalk, or watercolors and draw or paint a picture of what that experience looked and felt like to you. As an alternative, you could create a picture of what you look and feel like as a result of that trauma. This activity is *not* a test of your artistic ability. The goal is to use nonverbal means to help process your trauma. Your picture might include objects, people, places, and so on, or it might include a more abstract image using colors and shapes and designs to depict what you are trying to represent. You might turn on some relaxing music in the background as you draw or paint your picture. Upon finishing your artwork, describe what this creative experience was like for you. We encourage you to bring the drawing or painting to your next counseling session to discuss with your counselor.

_____

_____

5. When you were growing up, think about how your family generally reacted to a crisis.
   a. Were they calm? Were they upset or overwhelmed? Were they in denial? Were they slow or quick in reacting?

   _____

   _____

   b. Who in your family handled crises most effectively? Least effectively?

   _____

   _____

   c. Which family member(s) had the greatest influence on you in terms of modeling how to handle crises?

   _____

   _____

6. Who in your present-day immediate family is the role model in reacting to crisis? How does that person handle crisis?

   _____

   _____

7. In your mind's eye, think about characters in movies or TV shows who handle crises well. In other words, which characters could be your positive role models? What is it that enables them to react so effectively to stressful situations?

   _____

   _____

8. One characteristic of effective leaders is their ability to respond well in times of crisis. Identify leaders that you look up to who handle crises effectively. They might be leaders you personally know, or they might be nationally recognized leaders in politics, education, sports, or other career fields. Describe what makes them such great leaders and, in particular, what you admire in how they approach crisis situations.

   _____

   _____

9. In thinking about a particular crisis that you experienced, reflect on whether you have any "unfinished business" to work through that weighs heavily on you. Did you say or do anything during the crisis that you regret? Did others say or do anything during the crisis that you find difficult to let go of and forgive? Forgiveness of ourselves and of others can go a long way in helping us heal and can bring us great relief.

a. Who, if anyone, do you need or want to forgive in order to move on with your life? This could be yourself or someone else.

_____

_____

b. Describe why it is important for you to forgive yourself or the other person? How do you hope your life will be enhanced by taking this step?

_____

_____

c. What, if anything, makes it challenging for you to forgive yourself or the other person?

_____

_____

d. If a miracle happened or you magically were able to offer forgiveness, how do you imagine it would feel? How would your life be different?

_____

_____

e. How motivated are you at this time to offer forgiveness?

Scale: 1   2   3   4   5   6   7   8   9   10
      Not in a   *Ready and*
      million years!   *extremely motivated*

Explain your response.

_____

10. Write a letter of forgiveness to yourself or the other person for how you or they mishandled the crisis. The goal of this exercise is *not* for you to write a letter that you will actually send. (You may or may not ultimately decide to do so, but this exercise is designed to let you express your thoughts and feelings on paper unfiltered. If you feel ready to send a letter in the future, you may want to revise it after stepping back and gaining perspective.) Bring the letter to counseling and process your reaction to doing this exercise with your counselor.

_____

_____

11. What skills or practical knowledge do you need to learn to improve your response to specific crises you may encounter in the future?

_____

_____

12. People's personalities and temperaments can play a role in the manner in which they respond to difficult situations, including crises. For instance, some individuals may not be rattled by stressors easily whereas others are quickly triggered by stress. How would you describe your personality and temperament? How have they affected the way you react during crisis situations?

_____

_____

13. The stress reaction (fight-or-flight reaction) is a common element in a crisis. When you are in distressing situations, are you more inclined to fight or escape? How does this help or hurt you?

_____

_____

14. Tragedies such as mass shootings and acts of violence have become all too common in society.
    a. What is your reaction when you hear of a mass shooting or tragedy?

    _____

    _____

    b. Do you fear that kind of tragedy could happen to you or to someone you care about?

    _____

    _____

    c. If you have children, how concerned are you for their safety in school or in public areas such as concerts?

    _____

    _____

    d. What do you do to manage these concerns?

    _____

    _____

15. How could you best react in a shooting incident?

    _____

    _____

    a. What do you anticipate you would do and think?

    _____

    _____

    For tips on how to respond in such crises, visit the website of the U.S. Department of Homeland Security and review their booklet "Active Shooter: How to Respond" (https://www.dhs.gov/xlibrary/assets/active_shooter_booklet.pdf).

Chapter 9

Trauma Recovery
and Posttraumatic Growth

The greatest glory in living lies not in never falling,
but in rising every time we fall.

—Nelson Mandela

• • •

For Counselors

With time and support, most individuals recover from traumatic events. The recovery process is as individualized as people's reaction to the crisis. Some people bounce back quickly, and others require considerably more time to recover. In this chapter, we focus on the trauma recovery process, and Mark Stebnicki, a military and trauma counseling expert, describes an innovative approach for working with victims of trauma.

People who experience a disaster may develop any number of symptoms and disorders, including PTSD, depression, generalized anxiety, simmering anger, sleep disturbances, and physical or somatic symptoms such as headaches, digestive problems, or dizziness. Individuals who have experienced a disaster will have an emotional reaction to it, but they should expect to recover in time. It is helpful to remind clients that they are experiencing a normal reaction to an abnormal event. Encourage clients to give themselves permission to take time and to accept help in their recovery. Those who have experienced a highly traumatizing event may need an extended period to recover, may need assistance in that recovery process, and may continue to be affected by the event in some form for years. Remind clients that positive changes may occur even though they experienced a negative event. There are countless stories of individuals who experienced severe trauma and used their adversity as the impetus for growth. Some of these individuals are contributing to their communities and to the world in ways they never had imagined: Oprah Winfrey, Jaycee Duggar, Elizabeth Smart,

Chesley (Sully) Sullenberger, war veterans, domestic violence victims, and many more. Above all, resilience, support, and healthy self-care are essential in the recovery process.

An important part of the recovery process involves clients being able to do something constructive with their pain. They may choose to donate to a cause, join a support or community group, sign a petition, write a letter to state representatives, organize events, or become social activists. These activities reinforce the message that they are not powerless, and others benefit from their help and giving back. For example, fire crews set up a fund for the parents whose child was seriously injured. Some individuals changed their educational and career path and channeled their passion or grief into helping others who experience a similar crisis and recovery process. The activities of the students attending Marjory Stoneman Douglas High School in Parkland, Florida, are a prime example of this call to action. Following the highly publicized 2018 school shooting that resulted in the deaths of 17 students and staff members and injured many others, the student survivors organized marches, met with legislators, challenged politicians who accepted monetary contributions from the National Rifle Association, and participated in televised town halls and interviews. Social activism became an outlet for their pain and outrage. Becoming a change agent is one way to regain a feeling of empowerment that promotes healing.

Assessing Clients' Needs During Recovery

The key to assessing the recovery of clients is to be watchful for emotional, cognitive, or behavioral changes that indicate progress. Clients who seem stuck for a lengthy period may be good candidates for more specialized treatment and should be given a referral. Clients who experience serious medical issues must be referred for medical care.

PTSD—a trauma- and stress-related disorder following direct or indirect exposure to a terrifying event—has gained increased attention in recent decades, in part due to the prolonged wars in Iraq and Afghanistan. PTSD is a serious disorder that tragically leads some trauma victims to end their pain by committing suicide. The *DSM-5* (American Psychiatric Association, 2013) states that PTSD may occur following exposure to death, threatened death, actual or serious injury, or actual or threatened sexual violence. Individuals reexperience the traumatic event through memories, nightmares, and flashbacks, and clients may suffer from anxiety, panic attacks, emotional numbness, depression, anger, or rage. Symptoms typically begin to occur within 3 months after exposure to the trauma, with distress and impairment lasting more than 1 month. Treatment may include medication, cognitive therapy, eye movement desensitization and reprocessing, and other supportive therapies.

The exercises and activities in this chapter are designed to assist clients in thinking about their trauma experiences so they can (a) make meaning of their suffering and trauma and (b) learn how to better prepare for encountering future crises. Just as emergency preparedness training occurs in communities, clients can practice and prepare for future crises. People can use everyday stressors and small crises to practice and fine-tune their skills in responding quickly and effectively.

The following piece by Mark A. Stebnicki describes a solution-focused approach developed to assist clients who have experienced trauma. This approach offers many exercises, activities, and questions for clients to help them explore their reaction to and recovery from traumatic situations. Feel free to adapt the reflective questions Stebnicki suggests as well as the exercises in the For Clients section for use in session or as therapeutic homework for your clients.

A Personal Growth Program to Heal Trauma (PGP-HT)

Mark A. Stebnicki

The personal growth program to heal trauma (PGP-HT) is a dynamic, interactive, and solution-focused approach for exploring posttraumatic growth and resiliency. This approach, described fully in Stebnicki (2017), provides an opportunity for early identification, assessment, and interventions that deal with a full range of issues affecting the mind, body, and spirit of trauma survivors. The PGP-HT approach is based on my own personal growth experiences and clinical experiences in rehabilitation and mental health counseling. This approach is particularly focused on treating those who have had exposure to extraordinarily stressful and traumatic life events. Also integrated in PGP-HT are 30 years of teaching and research experiences that I would describe as holistic in nature. The theories, models, and approaches of PGP-HT were drawn from a range of humanistic, cognitive behavioral, mindfulness and stress reduction, and culturally indigenous healing methods. The PGP-HT model is also influenced by stages of change theory. Prochaska and DiClemente (1982), Prochaska, DiClemente, and Norcross (1992), as well as their colleagues developed the foundational research in this area, explaining how individuals progress through five stages of change when transforming their pattern of simple and complex behaviors: precontemplation, contemplation, preparation, action, and maintenance. The PGP-HT model offers a unique way to assess, predict, and monitor activities that relate to clients' self-care, which will assist them in moving beyond being a trauma victim and becoming a trauma survivor.

People exposed to extraordinarily stressful and traumatic experiences require the highest level of attention, compassion, and empathy by skilled and competent mental health professionals who can act as a conduit for facilitating healing resources. Trauma survivors may also benefit from nontraditional interventions. Attuned mental health professionals have the knowledge and skills to work competently with trauma survivors, some of whom may be culturally different. Some individuals may choose a nontraditional healing path as opposed to therapy in clinical settings, such as biofeedback, animal-assisted therapy, expressive arts, acupuncture, prayer, or religious rituals. Reaching out for help and cocreating a plan with other trusted and natural supports is where the healing journey begins.

PGP-HT invites clients to change something in their life (e.g., their way of thinking, feeling, perceiving others, relationships, job settings/work environment, or mental, physical, or spiritual health). This is similar to the therapeutic stages of change individuals go through as they transition to optimal levels of wellness. PGP-HT also encourages clients to chart their experiences using techniques of expressive writing, such as a journal. Clients can benefit from recording and processing their feelings, thoughts, and experiences in this way.

Phases of PGP-HT

Phase 1: Showing Up

In this phase of PGP-HT, establishing rapport is of paramount importance. The goal is to develop a working alliance but to recognize that some survivors may not be ready for structured clinical interventions. For some survivors of trauma, several weeks and months may pass before they have any intensive interactions with mental health professionals or other culturally relevant support systems. Motivation to change the way you feel, think, and act posttrauma takes time to process, and it is quite natural for trauma survivors to isolate themselves from family, friends, and coworkers and to detach socially and emotionally. Indeed, it is important to understand the concept of *readiness* as a precursor before trauma survivors are ready to *show up*.

The discovery of client readiness is ongoing. It may change from day to day. Prior to any interventions, skilled and competent mental health professionals evaluate the degree of stress, posttraumatic stress, depression, anxiety, substance use, mood and emotional regulation, coping skills, and any level of suicide ideation. Monitoring any medical, physical, or chronic health conditions is also critical, and referrals need to be made to the appropriate health care providers. It is also critical to consider the impact your client has had with exposure to pretrauma critical events (e.g., ongoing sexual, verbal, physical abuse; exposure to violence in the neighborhood; chronic health conditions). For many clients, showing up is a challenging step. The primary emphasis in this phase of PGP-HT is for clients to be physically, mentally, cognitively, and spiritually present in the here and now. Invite your clients to be open, honest, and flexible and begin to conceptualize how they might deal more effectively or creatively with some specific issues related to their traumatic experiences.

Professional helpers can begin the PGP-HT process by asking clients to pay attention and be mindful of the things they want to change (e.g., thoughts, feelings, cognitions, relationships, and physical and mental health). Invite clients to find a quiet place in their home, outdoor environment, or go on a retreat to explore the following questions:

- What do I currently feel emotionally, physically, spiritually, educationally, academically, professionally, and in my relationships with others?
- In what areas of my life do I want to grow? What do I want to transform?
- What can I do to change or grow in specific life areas?
- What are some things I need from myself or others to achieve my goals?
- How will I know when I've arrived and have met what I set out to accomplish?

In this first phase, clients may want to be open to the idea that they can choose a more conscious and intentional way to live by being mindful in the moment. In this phase of contemplation, the professional helper should invite clients to write things down to help them express and remember what they choose to change.

Solution-Focused Questions

Highly skilled professionals know the importance of implementing the right strategies to facilitate client change. Professional helpers listen to their client's story and assess the client's motivation for change before they facilitate specific counseling theories and techniques. For many clients in therapy, learning coping skills and techniques alone will not sustain their motivation and ability to heal. Thus it is essential to have a direction that will lead to successful coping or problem-solving strategies. The following solution-focused questions are offered as a way for professional helpers to facilitate deeper creative thought with trauma survivors and to assist them in a clearer understanding of what they would like to change.

- What is it that I would like to change?
- Given my present situation, what changes make sense?
- If I made these changes, what would I be doing differently right now?
- What would these changes look like?
- What particular behaviors, thoughts, and emotions would I experience that would be healthier and reflect mental, physical, and spiritual wellness?
- What would I be doing differently that I am not doing currently?
- What resources have I thought about that would help support my goals/vision?
- If I no longer had these issues, what would others notice that was different about me?

Phase 2: Paying Attention

Paying attention, or being mindful, is more than a cognitive level of awareness and understanding. This second phase of PGP-HT requires a shift in clients' level of consciousness, becoming aware of how they regulate their mood and affect. Paying attention to deeper levels of consciousness through activities such as meditation, focusing, quieting the mind, or expressive arts will help clients cultivate a felt-sense of meaning and purpose in their life. Paying attention also has the potential to open the door to deeper states of consciousness. Inviting clients to access their intuitive sense and creativity will assist in contemplating how to transform trauma survival with a different meaning.

The primary emphasis in this phase of the PGP-HT approach is for clients to communicate a plan of action to self and others. To begin this process, it is helpful for clients to engage in expressive writing, perhaps keeping a daily journal. The journal entries may be a combination of words, symbols, sentences, drawings, sketches, or other forms of expression. Having clients document their thoughts, feelings, emotions, cognitions, and experiences will allow them to analyze some of their problem issues. After clients have written down any thoughts, emotions, or experiences, you can assist them in the interpretation, translation, and analysis with the intention of finding new meaning in their healing journey.

Paying attention is at the heart of integrating spiritual approaches in counseling practice. Spirituality is different from religiosity; one does not have to be a religious person to benefit from quieting the mind, body, and spirit. If clients engage in a program of wellness, personal growth, or spiritual or religious ritual, they are already paying attention. To nurture ones' mind, body, and spirit requires individuals to pay attention to deeper levels of consciousness. Professional helpers who have been trained in mindfulness, stress reduction, or breathing meditation can assist clients in paying attention, particularly, to identify unused opportunities and resources.

Clients have many opportunities to engage therapeutically outside of the 50-minute therapy session. Some seek mentors, spiritual guides, older family members, or peer support groups to discuss and share their trauma experiences. Professional helpers understand the various learning styles and coping experiences of their clients. You might encourage some clients to pose a question in their journal to process at a later time. Other clients may verbally state or journal about a plan of self-care with specific measurable goals supporting their healing journey into posttraumatic growth. It is clients who decide how to disclose their vision, goals, and plans for change. As the therapist, you can act in the roles of teacher, consultant, or facilitator. Clients who communicate their self-care plan take responsibility by consciously paying attention to thoughts, feelings, and behaviors that increase optimal adjustment as a posttrauma survivor.

Questions That Cultivate a Deeper Meaning and Purpose

Healing trauma requires much more than reading a self-help book or attending a counseling session. Some of the most prolific spiritual leaders of our time strongly believe that transformation of the mind, body, and spirit happens when we create a place in our consciousness that takes us to a much deeper level. Access to the human spirit happens from a meditative or nonordinary state of consciousness rather than during an ordinary or everyday state of consciousness.

The following existential and spiritual questions may be helpful to your clients as they begin cultivating a program of self-care. Some of these questions have been developed through personal interviews (see Elliott, 1996) from some of the world's greatest spiritual healers (i.e., Mother Teresa, Norman Vincent Peale, Dalai Lama, Ram Das, and Rabbi Zalman Schachter-Shalomi). Clients who listen and pay attention to their inner voice experiences may bring a higher level of wisdom and insight to their journey toward posttraumatic growth, resiliency, and healing trauma.

Ask clients the following questions, using the deeper reaches of all five senses:

- On what main beliefs, truths, or values do I base my life?
- Do I believe in a divine source of power, Great Spirit, or Supreme Being who has ultimate compassion for my life and its purpose? How do I experience this spirit entity?
- How would I characterize or describe the ultimate purpose of my life?
- What is the highest ideal that a person can reach in life?
- How have I achieved or attained a goal that I really desired? What was the process I went through to achieve this goal for myself?
- What has been or what is the greatest obstacle to obtaining what I want in my life?
- Do I see myself achieving ultimate happiness or harmony in life? If not, what are some things that may be an obstacle for me?
- What is the meaning or purpose of my life at this moment?
- If I could change anything about my life, what would I want to change?
- What advice has a family member, close friend, mentor, consultant, or spiritual leader given me in regard to my particular life issues? Has any of this been valid?
- If I could meet anyone throughout history, whom would I want to meet? What would I want to know or ask this person?
- What was the most significant thing or event (positive or negative) that ever happened in my life? How did this affect me, and what lessons did it teach me?
- Some people believe that certain things interfere with reaching personal growth. What things have I noticed in my life that have hindered my abilities to achieve?
- If I only had a few days left on earth before I passed on to some other dimension, what advice would I have for my friends, family, children, or others?
- If I only had a few days left on earth before I passed on to some other dimension, what would I want others to know or say about me when I'm gone?

Some of these deeper questions require thoughts, feelings, cognitions, insights, and reflections that may challenge clients. There are no right or wrong responses to these questions. Despite the uncertainty that exists as we contemplate the nature of these questions, it is critical that trauma survivors find meaning in their trauma experiences by probing the deeper reaches of mind, body, and spirit. This may require a weekend meditation retreat or finding a natural environment in which to write in a journal. A journey of inner healing requires that we come out of the darkness and into the light to face the fear of changing something in our life.

Phase 3: Being Open to Outcomes

In this final phase of the PGP-HT program, review any action plans or goals you and your clients have developed. This may take the form of journal entries, expressive writings, or any significant themes or meanings they have acquired during therapy. You may also want to review any progress or process notes you have written after sessions. The challenge for both clients and counselor is to search beyond the literal meaning of what has transpired during therapeutic engagements. Both clients and the counselor may look for daily or weekly progress, creative ideas that have resulted in slight and significant changes, successes, unused opportunities discovered, and coping skills and resiliency traits that have been developed. Explore clients' progress, challenges, and any obstacles clients may have encountered throughout their work. Challenge clients with things they can and cannot control.

Overall, in this final phase, it is essential to address (a) things clients perceive that have trapped them, (b) how they become stuck and unstuck, and (c) how they learned to let go—not forgetting the trauma experience but moving forward through the trauma. PGP-HT is an intentional way of guiding clients into an open and honest assessment of posttraumatic growth and resiliency. Continued exploration and maintenance of how clients can let go and grasp the things in life that nurture and support their mind, body, and spirit moving forward is at the heart of this final phase.

Assessing Outcomes in Personal Growth

PGP-HT does not endorse any one particular measure to define success. There are many tools for assessing personal growth and evidence-based practices. These take the form of structured assessments, the presence of the increase/decrease in clinical characteristics and mental health symptoms, as well as many functional assessment measures. Competent and ethical professional helpers select appropriate tools based on what they are measuring (e.g., improvement in mood and affect, relief from PTSD symptoms, completion of a smoking cessation or weight loss program, reading a self-help book, or attending a substance use support group). For many professionals and clients alike, natural support systems are valuable in measuring what others see as success with concern for overall wellness (i.e., spouse, partner, or family members).

Making the necessary changes in ones' life takes weeks and months to achieve. Many mental health researchers and clinicians emphasize that individual change and personal growth do not occur spontaneously. There are an enormous number of trauma survivor testimonials in books, articles, and online posts/blogs that communicate significant life changes and transformative experiences in mental, physical, and spiritual well-being. Typically, individuals communicate what has been successful for self and others around them. Qualitative studies in peer-reviewed journals also report and highlight details about therapeutic interventions that have made significant and profound transformative changes in a client's life. In the outcome phase of PGP-HT, professional helpers must decide what variables to measure based on a combination of professional discipline, training, client self-report, communication with family members, and other ways that may define client success.

Conclusion

The personal growth program to heal trauma approach provides an opportunity for early identification, assessment, and recommended strategies that deal with a range of issues affecting the mind, body, and spirit of trauma survivors. PGP-HT is adaptive, flexible, and organized, and it offers guidelines to professional helpers who choose to adopt a somewhat structured approach for cultivating resiliency and healing trauma. For further detailed information regarding PGP-HT, see Stebnicki (2017, pp. 313–337).

• • •

What We Have Learned About Helping Clients Therapeutically

Our firsthand experiences in working with trauma survivors have been rewarding, and progress from the initial trauma and shock of the event through recovery can be quite dramatic. Counselors must be prepared for any kind of reaction—from quiet denial to explosive anger. We must be prepared first to listen and not give advice about what clients should do. During the initial stage of recovery, clients need to tell their story, including their perceptions and initial thoughts about the event. We have seen counselors try to direct the process and give advice about what clients need to do, but this approach has not been successful. We cannot emphasize enough how important it is for clients to tell their story about the event or situation. As the recovery process proceeds, clients can be assisted with education about what to expect throughout recovery and suggestions for what they can do to expedite the process. Our goal is to help clients safely return to their daily routine and to reacquire a sense of order and stability in their life.

Some clients may be so traumatized and shaken to their core that they question their own values, beliefs, purpose, and the meaning of life. These clients may well need to be referred for more specialized trauma-informed treatment.

The Counselor's Task With Clients

A strong support system of family, friends, faith-based groups, and community is extremely helpful for most clients in their recovery from trauma. One major task for counselors is to help clients identify people in their life who can function in this supportive capacity. Some clients may need to be reminded to make use of their support network. To promote growth and resilience, the counselor can build on clients' inherent strengths and teach them new skills to assist them in developing greater confidence in their ability to handle future crises. (For more on cultivating resilience, refer to Chapter 2.) Practicing effective self-care is a major component of recovering from a crisis. Encouraging clients to eat well, get a good night's sleep, exercise, participate in relaxation and mindfulness activities, and simply participate in activities they enjoy goes a long way toward ensuring a successful recovery process. Working with clients recovering from a crisis can take a toll on the counselor, and it is imperative that counselors engage in self-care. (This topic is covered extensively in Chapter 14.)

Notes

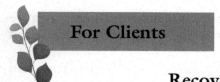

For Clients

Recovering From a Disaster or Trauma

Recovery from a disaster is an individualized process much like one's reaction to a crisis. Some people bounce back quickly, and others require considerably more time to recover. Those traumatized by a disaster may develop depression, generalized anxiety, simmering anger, and sleep disturbances as well as physical symptoms and disorders such as headaches, digestive problems, or dizziness. Some people may develop PTSD.

When stress exceeds your ability to cope with it, it is natural that symptoms may emerge. If you experience a disaster or trauma, you should expect to have an emotional reaction, and you should expect to recover in time. What you are experiencing is a normal reaction to an abnormal event. Anyone experiencing what you have would have a reaction as well. Give yourself permission to take the time and to seek the support you need. If you have experienced a highly traumatizing event, you may need an extended period to recover, and you may need assistance in that recovery process. Reaching out for support when you need it is one important way of taking care of yourself. Although it may not seem possible, you may experience a positive change in your life even though you have been through a negative event. Above all, resilience, support, and healthy self-care are essential in the recovery process.

Key Steps in Recovering From a Crisis Event

To help yourself recover from a crisis in a timely and effective manner, consider taking some of the following steps.

1. Examine the crisis and your reaction to it. What was involved, and how did you react, respond, and recover? Were you able to recover in a timely manner given the severity of the event? Do you believe you are a resilient person who is able to bounce back in a reasonable amount of time?
2. Identify and accept the feelings you are experiencing about the event. Being able to assess your true feelings about the event will help you recover more quickly.
3. Talk about your feelings regarding the event. One of the best ways to recover from a crisis is to talk with supportive individuals about the event and your reactions, your thoughts, and your feelings about it. Suppressing your feelings will only prolong your recovery.
4. Examine your self-talk about the crisis and your response to it. What you tell yourself about the situation can have a major impact on how you feel, respond, and recover. Be kind to yourself in your self-talk, and try not to berate yourself for what you did or did not do in the situation. Watch out for those "shoulds" and "oughts" that can make you feel worse.
5. Get back to your daily routine as quickly as possible with regard to work, school, eating, sleeping, exercise, and the like.
6. Practice healthy self-care. One of the best means of recovering from a crisis is to give yourself permission and time to do things you enjoy, but possibly have not been doing often enough, and to eat well, get adequate rest and exercise, and do those things that are good for your body and the soul.

The New Stress of Climate Change

Scientists agree that our climate is changing and that it is beginning to have a major impact on us (Rice, 2017). We look around us and see more severe hurricanes, prolonged droughts and wildfires, record high temperatures, melting ice caps, and rising sea levels. The seas are rising as greenhouse gases from burning fossil fuels cause glaciers and ice sheets to melt, and 311,000 coastal homes are at risk of flooding in the next 30 years (Rice, 2018). Whitmore-Williams et al. (2017) state that climate change is and will continue to be an additional source of significant stress in our everyday lives, adding to the other stresses we encounter daily. That can lead to anxiety, worry, depression, and health impacts as the world warms and sea levels rise. In addition to taking actions to counter the effects of climate change, individuals must prepare themselves for adversity, develop resilience and optimism, and work with their community, family, and social support systems.

Develop a family emergency response and communication plan in preparation for a disaster. Your plan should include what to take, where to go, and who to contact in case of an emergency such as a wildfire, hurricane, earthquake, flood, or other disaster, whether human-caused or natural. All members of your family should be aware of the plan and the emergency meeting locations. Without a plan, people often grab meaningless articles such as pots and pans, a football, or a scarf just to have something to take. Be prepared with a *go-bag* that contains key items in case you must leave immediately, a list of items to gather if you have just a few minutes, and another list of items to gather if you have an hour or two to evacuate. Place key documents such as insurance policies, estate papers, financial statements, and so forth on a flash drive in your go-bag. We encourage you to visit the Department of Homeland Security website (www.ready.gov/plan) for more information regarding developing an emergency response plan.

Workbook Material for Clients

The following questions and exercises are designed to help you examine the topic of recovering from crisis situations in your life. There are no right or wrong answers. This is an opportunity for you to spend some time thinking about how well you bounce back from adverse events in your own life. Some of the questions and exercises may be easy for you, and others may require more time and thought on your part. We hope you will take plenty of time to consider each topic or question that your counselor has asked you to complete. The value of the activities and questions comes from your careful consideration about your position on the topic. The goal is for you to learn as much as you can outside the counseling setting. If you are better prepared to explore these issues, your session time will be more productive. We suggest that you keep a journal as you contemplate how you can improve your approach to recovering from crises. Purchase a notebook or journal or record your responses to selected questions and activities on your computer. Remember to print your responses and bring them with you to your next counseling session.

Exercises and Activities

1. Think about the crisis situation you are most concerned about. What was the situation? Who was involved? How did you react?

   _____

   _____

2. Fear, shock, disbelief, guilt, confusion, sadness, panic, anger, and frustration are common emotional reactions in response to a crisis.
   a. Did you initially experience any of these emotions during or immediately after the crisis? If so, which ones were most prominent?

   _____

   _____

   b. As you recover from the crisis, have these emotions diminished in strength?

   _____

   _____

   c. Have any become more intense? Have any new emotions surfaced?

   _____

   _____

3. How are you feeling now about the event? How is the recovery process going for you? How has the past crisis changed your life situation today?

   _____

   _____

4. As you reflect on your recovery, consider whether there is anything you would like to do or approach differently.
   a. How satisfied are you with your recovery?

   _____

   _____

   b. What aspects of it are within your control, and what aspects are beyond your control to change?

   _____

   _____

5. We silently talk to ourselves about almost everything we do. That *self-talk* (internal dialogue) can influence how we react emotionally and how we respond in a crisis.
   a. What is your self-talk about the incident or crisis, your initial response, and your ongoing recovery?

   _____

   _____

   b. Is your self-talk working for you or against your recovery?

   _____

   _____

   c. If it is not working for you, what would you like to do to change that?

   _____

   _____

   d. How could your self-talk be more positive and constructive?

   _____

   _____

6. Keep a log of your self-talk for one week. At the end of the week, describe some of the key patterns you can identify.
   a. Are you a catastrophizer or a problem solver?

   _____

   _____

   b. A perfectionist or a realist?

   _____

   _____

   c. Are you kind to yourself, or are you judgmental and critical of yourself?

   _____

   _____

7. Reflect on your self-talk patterns and learn to replace negative self-statements (e.g., "I will never succeed!") with more constructive and positive self-statements (e.g., "With effort and preparation, I can succeed!"). Now it is time to get some practice. Apply your newfound self-talk and thinking patterns in everyday life situations. The more you practice in lower stakes situations, the more automatic this new approach is likely to be when the stakes are higher in consequential situations. Describe how you are doing in modifying your self-talk for everyday situations.

_____

_____

8. Is something preventing you from getting back to your daily routine? What will it take to get things back to normal for you?

_____

_____

9. Those practicing *narrative therapy* suggest that we live our lives by the stories we tell about ourselves and that others tell about us. According to this approach, "reality" is shaped by these stories because they construct and constitute what we think, feel, and do. As you recover from your traumatic experience, reflect on the problem-saturated story you often tell yourself about the crisis event and about how you and others handled it. Write it down with as much specificity as possible. Then rewrite or revise your story in a more empowering way. By viewing your story through a different lens, you may discover alternative meanings for events. (For example, instead of replaying the narrative in your mind that your family deserted you because they were ashamed of you, you might reauthor your story and replace that narrative with a more constructive one—that your family distanced themselves from you because they were absorbed in their own pain and that, even without their support, you handled the crisis well.)

_____

_____

10. Taking good care of yourself by practicing healthy self-care is one of the best ways to help yourself recover from a crisis. Most of us know what we need to do in these areas but resist doing it.
    a. How well do you take care of yourself in terms of diet, exercise, sleep/rest, and relaxation?

_____

_____

    b. In what areas could you improve?

_____

_____

    c. In what areas are you most motivated to make changes at this time?

_____

_____

11. How much of a crisis is climate change for you personally? For your family and people you care about? For the future?

_____

_____

12. What fears or concerns related to climate change do you have about living conditions for the future? List strategies you can use to manage your fears or reduce your anxiety.

_____

_____

13. Some consider climate change to be the defining issue of our time. It is expected to have dire consequences, especially if left unaddressed. What role can you play in the plan to mitigate climate change? What are some concrete actions you can take?

   _____

   _____

14. Describe the contents of a go-bag that you can assemble in case of an emergency. Write a list of items to gather if you have just a few minutes and another list of items to gather if you have an hour or two to evacuate. Where would you keep this go-bag? After writing these lists, reflect on how it was to do this exercise.

   _____

   _____

15. This chapter emphasizes the importance of developing an action plan and then practicing it so you can activate it in the event of a disaster. Reflect on your experience of doing this. How was it to practice your emergency action plan? Does any part of your plan need to be modified to improve it?

   _____

   _____

16. What are some ways you could become involved in social activism as a route to healing? Which nonprofit organizations address issues or causes that are important to you? List them below.

   _____

   _____

17. If becoming more active in social issues interests you, reflect on the skills, qualities, and strengths you have that may help you in this role.

   _____

   _____

18. What do you anticipate would be most challenging for you if you become involved in social activism? How could you address these challenges?

   _____

   _____

Chapter 10

Coping With Chronic Illness and Health Issues

To live is to suffer, to survive is to find some meaning in the suffering.
—Friedrich Nietzsche
...

For Counselors

I will never forget the stories one of my (Michelle's) dear friends told me as she was battling Stage 3 breast cancer a few years ago. In addition to the physical toll cancer and multiple rounds of chemotherapy took on her body and soul, she experienced complications after undergoing a surgical procedure. Medications to manage symptoms led to other unfortunate side effects, and she became severely depressed. She felt that her life had spiraled out of control! This truly was an ordeal for my friend, her family, and for others who care about her. On a positive note, she survived this traumatic experience and has experienced posttraumatic growth. She has found meaning through her suffering and has supported others facing health crises.

One story that stands out for me was her negative experience with a counselor during that time. My friend, who had not previously sought counseling services, wanted professional support to help her cope with her cancer crisis. She said that the counselor probed intrusively into her past childhood trauma and seemed to steer sessions in that direction. Eventually, my friend called her counselor out on this and told her that she wanted to address her depression related to cancer, not her childhood experiences. She stopped attending counseling sessions soon after because the counselor persisted in broaching the topic of her past when she needed to process what was happening in the present. As a helping professional, this is a prime example of the importance of meeting clients where they are—not where you think they should be.

Illnesses, diseases, and chronic medical conditions are a significant source of stress for people and their loved ones. Chronic illnesses are conditions lasting a year or more that require continuous medical treatment or limit daily living activities (National Center for Chronic Disease Prevention and Health Promotion, 2019a). In the United States, 6 in 10 adults have a chronic illness and 4 in 10 have two or more chronic illnesses (National Center for Chronic Disease Prevention and Health Promotion, 2019b), which might include cancer, heart disease, diabetes, stroke, lung disease, Alzheimer's disease, and kidney disease, just to name a few. Add to these illnesses, opioid use and abuse, which has been increasing dramatically in the United States. In fact, 1 in 5 Americans suffers from chronic pain, and many rely on pain medications, including opiates, for relief as they desperately search for safer and more effective treatments (Carr, 2019). In all, illnesses result in $3.3 trillion in annual health care costs. The key lifestyle risk factors for chronic disease are tobacco and alcohol use, obesity, poor nutrition, and lack of exercise.

When clients receive a diagnosis of a major illness or condition, they are challenged to respond to that crisis much like they would to any crisis or disaster. Having learned about the condition—signs, symptoms, causes, and treatments—clients also must cope with their emotional response and how this situation affects them and their family and friends. Responses to chronic illness and other serious medical issues may include shock, disbelief, anger, frustration, sadness, and depression. In addition, preexisting mental health conditions may be exacerbated. By the time an individual suffering the psychological fallout from a medical condition seeks counseling, the medical situation may have worsened and the emotional and psychological toll that has been accumulating may be affecting family, work, school, and the client's general outlook on life.

Anger and depression are common emotions among those who receive a serious medical diagnosis. Clients often direct their anger at themselves, the medical profession, the treatments, the exorbitant cost, the causes, the insurance company, and their seeming "bad luck." As people deal with a serious illness or chronic condition, depression may develop. Clients should expect to be concerned and feel sad or down due to the circumstances, but if these feelings persist for an extended period, it may become clinical depression. Symptoms of depression include feeling sad, down, empty, hopeless, helpless, and fatigued, and the person may have trouble concentrating or sleeping. A depressed person may also experience headaches, digestive issues, thoughts of suicide, or a preoccupation with death (NIMH, 2018b).

We must also acknowledge the extreme stress that family members experience who serve as caregivers for individuals with a chronic or debilitating medical condition. They are likely to feel a range of emotions about their loved one's poor health and their role as caregiver, and they may also need support and respite.

I (Bob) have dealt with the crisis of being diagnosed with cancer. That event caused me to examine not just my feelings about cancer but also my feelings about life, death, family, courage, rational decision-making, and the priorities in my life. This disaster seemed to turn my life upside down. Priorities I thought were important were discarded when the chips were down. Along with surgery, which remedied the situation, many new avenues opened in my life as I reassessed my values, my goals, my connections, and my time.

Personally experiencing a serious illness or caring for a person who is going through such an ordeal can be traumatic. To make matters even more difficult, many people lack the necessary funds for medical treatment and have difficulty gaining access to adequate health care coverage. Far too many families have amassed major debt, and some have claimed bankruptcy due to high medical bills. As Carr (2019) notes, "For many chronic pain sufferers, it can be challenging to find long-term care that is also covered by insurance" (p. 27).

Another barrier to receiving proper treatment is that many physicians dismiss pain symptoms based on the person's gender and race (Dusenbery, 2019). Ninety-one percent of U.S. women with chronic pain believe "the healthcare system discriminates against female patients" (p. 33). Dusenbery also recognizes the role of racial bias in influencing how physicians assess and treat pain. Some physicians, for instance, falsely believe that people of color are more inclined to abuse prescription painkillers. Doctors all too often underestimate the pain level of minority patients. These systemic inequities only exacerbate matters for people of color who are trying to navigate the health care system and find relief from pain.

What We Have Learned About Helping Clients Therapeutically

Clients with serious medical conditions exhibit a range of reactions, emotions, and outlooks for their future. As counselors, we hope clients will see us as part of their support team of helpers. In addition to the client, who is an integral member of the team, the counselor or social worker, medical staff, family members, the client's partner and children, and others may be involved. Creative approaches to providing support and assistance are sometimes needed, and at times help from various "team" members may be needed. It is crucial to remember, though, that any efforts to provide support must be approved by the client along with consultation with medical professionals. Clients burdened with serious medical issues often feel they have been robbed of control in many ways; it is imperative that clients have agency and control over as much as possible in their treatment and their life.

Kellie Nicole Kirksey, a certified rehabilitation counselor and holistic psychotherapist at the Cleveland Clinic Center for Integrative and Lifestyle Medicine, shares a few creative ideas for how she incorporates out-of-session activities into her practice with pain management clients.

Holistic Healing in a Pain Management Clinic

Kellie Nicole Kirksey

I am a holistic psychotherapist at a major hospital. My work focuses on mind-body techniques for emotional healing and well-being. I work primarily with an adult population, and pain management is a large part of my practice.

I give clients several homework assignments that usually begin in session and are then extended to the home. In one activity, clients draw three large circles on a piece of paper and label them Mind, Body, and Spirit. I play some soft music or we stay in silence, and I encourage clients to use their active imagination to list activities in each category that they can practice at home for self-soothing, distress tolerance, and increasing their participation in their healing process. The list often includes meditation, walking, journaling, time with friends, dancing, and deep breathing. Clients highlight the activities they will practice during the week, exploring what feels possible for them. Clients are usually surprised by the number of activities they have listed. It illustrates that they have more inner resources than they believed they did, and it gives clients a concrete plan of their own creation to assist them in managing their discomfort. When clients generate these activities, there is more ownership and a greater sense of empowerment.

A simple out-of-session activity is the cleansing shower or healing bath. Epsom salts or their favorite essential oil can be added to the bath if not contraindicated by a physician. I ask clients to fully engage their active imagination in this process. I ask them to expand their mind and imagine they are washing away the emotional stress and physical tension and seeing it exit down the drain. Although it may seem a bit silly, I usually tell them to give themselves permission to laugh and release the tension. I tell them to talk to the stress as it leaves the tub or shower and bid it goodbye. I ask them to visualize the water loosening and softening the challenges they have been carrying. Clients usually find this soothing and will practice this ritual before bedtime.

Another simple homework exercise is for clients to move gently as they listen to music to loosen their body and mind. For clients in pain management, this can be an act of permission-giving to move the body in a gentle manner to assist in easing tightness at their own pace. Their homework is to create a home playlist that lifts their energy or relaxes them. I use a few standard songs in session: "I Haven't Got Time for the Pain," by Carly Simon, or "Shake It Off," by Taylor Swift, or "I Am Light," by India Arie. I ask clients to explore music that inspires them and to bring in the song(s) the next week. I encourage them to listen to the music and to ask their body what it needs in the moment. Does the body need to stretch, recline, or do something else? This activity assists clients in getting in touch with another modality that can shift their mood and energy level, and it provides an opportunity for healthy movement. I also encourage clients to journal about how they felt during the practice.

Giving homework can assist clients in expanding their resources. All homework must be assigned with caution and awareness of past trauma and medical issues. The goal is to increase wellness and to encourage clients to practice new behaviors and healing out of session. Discussion of their homework is also a nice way to begin the next session.

• • •

The Counselor's Task With Clients

To some degree, the counselor becomes a case manager for the client with an illness or medical condition. One key task is to learn about the nature of the illness. You will need to understand the diagnosis, course of treatment, and prognosis; the effect of the illness on the individual's life, work, family, and relationships; and the emotional and psychological toll on the client's psyche, general outlook on life, and emotional state. Be vigilant in looking for signs of anxiety, anger, and depression. The most salient task is to hear the client's story, experience, emotions, precipitating reason for coming to counseling, and goals for the counseling process. A full array of treatment approaches and strategies may be employed to match the nature of the client's situation, goals, and needs.

The Crisis of Chronic Illness and Other Health Issues

Being diagnosed with a serious medical condition or chronic illness is one of the most frightening and life-changing events you can experience. In many cases, it turns your life upside down, like having a rug pulled out from under you. A few years ago, I (Bob) was diagnosed with cancer, and that event was the catalyst for much soul-searching! Not only did I think about the impact of having cancer, but I also did some intense self-exploration about life, death, family, courage, rational decision-making, and my priorities in life.

If you are reading this section because you are in counseling to discuss or process your medical situation, you have already taken a huge first step toward managing the situation. Emotions seem more intense when you are dealing with a chronic condition or another serious illness. Shock and disbelief are common reactions when you first learn of your diagnosis, treatment options, and prognosis. Anger and frustration commonly go along with adapting to this new reality, and longer term effects may include sadness and depression as you consider what this all means for you and your family, work/career, and life plans. Dealing with the diagnosis of a serious medical condition is like learning that your house is on an eroding cliff. Try your best to focus on shoring up the house to prevent it from slipping, and do not allow yourself to become preoccupied, overwhelmed, or immobilized by the fact that the house could slip down the cliff in the end.

Chronic illness adds to the daily stressors and challenges of life and may include managing your physical situation, coping with pain and discomfort, and dealing with family members, friends, doctors, nurses, therapists, clinic and hospital staff, insurance companies, and others in the health care system. Stress may result from the added financial burden associated with medical bills, the cost of prescription drugs, and being out of work. Of course, the painful emotions that often accompany a medical diagnosis also intensify stress considerably.

In addition to counseling, here are some things you can do to help you cope with your medical situation (Madell, 2015):

- Do as much as you can to fully understand your medical situation and various treatment options. Ask questions of your doctor, research your illness, and learn as much as you can. Keeping a journal recording your course of treatment and changes to your condition can help you monitor your progress in treatment.
- Manage your treatment and your medications to help you gain a sense of control.
- Monitor your emotions, and discuss what you observe in counseling. Try out different ways of managing stress, and see what works for you and what doesn't.
- Focus on key relationships. You may have less time and energy than you are used to having, so focus on the relationships that are most meaningful to you.
- Adapt to your situation the best you can. Fighting it probably will not help. Your attitude and outlook of hope will go a long way toward helping you manage your medical situation.

My (Bob) brother Gary, who passed away in 2019, had prostate cancer and colon cancer, and chemotherapy and hormonal treatments continued over the entire 11 years of the course of these illnesses. Originally, doctors gave him a few months to a few years to live—yet he lived another 11 years. For most of those years, he had chemotherapy infusions for colon cancer every 4 weeks. In addition, he had many other related medical crises, including a broken hip and atrial fibrillation, for a total of seven surgeries. The side effects of the treatments, the pain, and the emotional toll were enormous. Not long before he died, I asked Gary how he did it, how he persevered and did not give up in the face of overwhelming odds. The story that follows tells of Gary's resilience and how hope enriches a life.

The Role of Hope in Living With Chronic Illness and Health Issues

Gary Haynes (as told to Robert Haynes)

Gary said several factors kept him going over the 11-year course of his illness. One factor was his family, especially his children and grandchildren. He wanted to be around to enjoy them and their accomplishments as long as possible. He also volunteered for years as an aide at a local hospital. In that capacity, he directed patients to relevant services, comforted patients and family members who were having a tough time, and spent time with gravely ill patients who seemed lonely and depressed. His personal experience with long-term life-threatening illness and chronic pain had given him a new appreciation for patients in the hospital and, in fact, for anyone with a serious medical condition. He liked to bring love and kindness to these patients because that is what was (and is) missing in our world. He tried to give them hope by sharing his journey and giving them a dose of joy in a sterile hospital environment that often felt impersonal and frightening.

Gary's sense of purpose and will to keep battling his illness was enhanced through his work supporting, loving, and encouraging others who were enduring similar conditions. When he felt down, lonely, and discouraged, the prospect of *hope* that he could help and support others kept him going. He occasionally stopped to honor the battle that he had taken in his fight against cancer. Near the end of his life, I asked Gary what advice he would give to anyone up against chronic pain or serious medical issues. Gary's spirit of loving support is easy to see in his response to my question, and we now pass his advice along to you.

- Give yourself time to digest all the information. When you first hear the diagnosis and treatment options, it can be overwhelming, and a thousand thoughts will be running through your mind. Take a breath, step back, and carefully consider your options.
- Don't listen to the statistics and percentages the medical professionals give you. They are averages and say nothing about your individual journey or the battles you may fight and win. I have defied all the odds and statistics, and I am still going strong.
- Try to focus on what you can do about your situation rather than on any limitations that your condition may create for you.
- Negative experiences can have positive by-products. As a result of my fight with cancer, surgeries, and chemotherapy, I have been able to offer support and encouragement to hundreds of patients in the hospital where I volunteer. This would not have occurred had I not experienced these medical issues.
- You must have hope. It may take time to build that hope for a positive outcome and a resilient outlook, but it can be done. When you give up hope, you surrender your will to live.

• • •

Workbook Material for the Client

The following questions and exercises are designed to help you examine the topic of coping with chronic illness in your life, whether it is your own health crisis or that of someone you care about. There are no right or wrong answers. This is an opportunity for you to spend time thinking about how well you are managing your own health/medical issues or coping with the serious illness of a family member or friend. Some questions and exercises may be easy for you, and others may require more time and thought on your part. We hope you will take plenty of time to consider each topic or question that your counselor has asked you to complete. The value of the activities and questions comes from your careful consideration about your position on the topic. The goal is for you to learn as much as you can about yourself outside the counseling setting. If you are better prepared to explore these issues, your session time will be more productive. We suggest that you keep a journal as you contemplate how you can reduce your stress as you navigate these difficult circumstances. Purchase a notebook or journal or record your responses to selected questions and activities on your computer. Remember to print your responses and bring them with you to your next counseling session.

Exercises and Activities

Questions for Clients With Health Issues

The following activities are designed to help you and your counselor examine your health issues and learn how they are affecting you and your significant others.

1. Are you dealing with a disease, disorder, or chronic health issue? Explain:

   _____

   _____

2. What is the severity/seriousness of your situation?
   ❏ Minor   ❏ Serious, but temporary   ❏ Long-term and serious   ❏ Life-threatening

3. To get a better picture of the occurrence of your symptoms, track them in a log book and summarize the symptoms you experience in the morning, the afternoon, and in the evening. Describe any differences in the severity or painfulness throughout the day.

   _____

   _____

4. Describe your illness over your life span, including childhood, young adulthood, middle adulthood, and late/older adulthood. Describe the symptoms that were present during each of these life stages, the treatments you received, and how well they worked for you. (If the onset of your illness was at a later stage, begin there.)

   _____

   _____

5. To what extent do your family members understand and accept your illness?

   _____

   _____

   a. Are they embarrassed by your illness? If so, how do they communicate this?

      _____

      _____

   b. Do you think your family members resent your illness?

      _____

      _____

   c. Do they try to control your decisions related to managing your illness?

      _____

      _____

   d. Describe how the following questions apply in general to your family and also to individual family members (Fennell, 2012).

      _____

      _____

6. How has your illness affected your primary relationship with your significant other/spouse in terms of communication? Mutual support? Sex and intimacy? Roles and responsibilities? Finances? (Fennell, 2012).

_____

_____

7. How has this illness affected you physically and emotionally in the short term? In the long term?

_____

_____

8. How has the illness affected your self-confidence and self-image/self-concept in the following domains of life: work or school, recreation, sex and intimacy, parenting?

_____

_____

   a. Are there other areas in which your self-confidence and self-concept have been affected by your illness or condition? Describe.

_____

_____

9. How has this affected those close to you?

_____

_____

   a. Do you feel a need to take care of those people in regard to this illness? If so, explain.

_____

_____

10. How have you been able to cope with the circumstances around your illness?

_____

_____

   a. What has been the hardest part?

_____

_____

   b. What has been the least stressful part?

_____

_____

11. What were your initial thoughts about the situation? What are you thinking now?

_____

_____

12. What emotions have you experienced as a result of this diagnosis? Check all that apply.

❑ Anger   ❑ Confusion   ❑ Rage
❑ Shock   ❑ Fear   ❑ Hopelessness
❑ Disbelief   ❑ Grief   ❑ Helplessness
❑ Sadness   ❑ Anxiety   ❑ Determination
❑ Depression   ❑ Hopefulness   ❑ Optimism

13. Which of the emotions you checked off have caused you the most difficulty? In what way?

_____

_____

14. Describe any personality changes you have experienced as a result of your illness.

_____

_____

15. Depression is common for someone dealing with chronic and other debilitating illnesses. How would you rate yourself in terms of feeling depressed at the present time?

Scale: 1   2   3   4   5   6   7   8   9   10
       Not at all   *Extremely*
       depressed   *depressed*

Explain your response.

_____

16. Have you ever had thoughts of ending your life due to feelings resulting from your medical condition? If so, describe what that was/is like for you. If you currently feel suicidal, be sure to reach out for help. Contact the National Suicide Prevention Lifeline (https://suicidepreventionlifeline.org/) or 9-1-1 in case of an emergency.

_____

_____

17. If you are at all depressed, what have you tried that has helped you with this depression? (Refer to the exercises in Chapter 4 for more on depression.)

_____

_____

18. What would you like to do more of in the future to help you cope with depression?

_____

_____

19. Do you have a plan of action for coping with this health issue? If so, describe your plan. If not, create a positive plan that replaces negative and limiting feelings and thoughts with more constructive ones.

_____

_____

20. Refer to the case example of Gary waging a decade-long battle with life-threatening cancers, and answer the following questions:
    a. What was your general reaction to the case example? Could you identify with what Gary experienced? Would you concur with his words of advice? Are there any additional words of advice that you would add to the list based on your own experiences?

    _____

    _____

    b. What is the driving force that keeps you motivated and continuing with your treatment? If you could capture it in a bottle, what would you label it?

    _____

    _____

    c. Do you have hope for the future? What instills you with hope?

_____

_____

    d. How lonely is the place where you are in terms of your health issues? What helps you cope with and counter that loneliness?

_____

_____

21. How has this illness changed your thinking about life's priorities?

_____

_____

    a. If you ordered your priorities, which ones would be at the top of your list?

_____

_____

22. Write a letter to your illness or health condition as if it was a person. Consider what you would most want to convey about how it has impacted your life. After writing the letter, reflect on the experience and be prepared to talk about it with your counselor.

_____

_____

23. How are you feeling about your future and the outcome of this health issue?

_____

_____

Questions for Caregivers

1. If you are a caregiver of a family member who has a chronic illness or serious medical condition, what do you do for self-care or respite?

_____

_____

    a. To what degree does this relieve your stress?

_____

_____

    b. How often do you engage in this activity?

_____

_____

2. As the primary caregiver, how has this role changed your life and your outlook on life? These may include both positive and negative changes. What feelings and thoughts come up for you as you think about this?

_____

_____

3. What is most challenging about being a caregiver? Are there any abilities, skills, or strengths you have developed as a result of taking on this role?

_____

_____

4. As a caregiver, you are constantly giving your time, effort, and care to another person. Who supports you?

_____

_____

   a. Are you satisfied with your support system, or do you need to develop a stronger one?

_____

_____

   b. Who would you like to add to your support system?

_____

_____

5. To what extent has being a caregiver shaped or affected your identity and self-concept?

_____

_____

   a. If your loved one is facing a terminal illness, how do you think your identity and self-concept will be affected when this person eventually dies?

_____

_____

   b. What feelings, fears, and thoughts come up for you?

_____

_____

Part IV

Emerging Crises and Intensifying Stressors

In Part IV we discuss ways of coping with modern society and the stress that it engenders. We are living in a world that has changed dramatically due to globalization and modernization. At the risk of oversimplifying matters, the social, political, and technological shifts that have occurred in recent years have given rise to disturbing phenomena that create considerable stress for people. These include tribalism, divisiveness, fake news, cyberbullying, an abundance of cybersecurity threats, and technology addictions, just to name a few. Moreover, hate crimes are increasing, and tacit, if not explicit, permission has been given to unleash ugly rhetoric and implement inhumane policies toward marginalized groups such as people of color, immigrants and refugees, and the LGBTQ+ community. An Anti-Defamation League study found that more than half of Americans reported being subjected to online harassment and hateful speech in 2018 (Guynn, 2019). Despite advocacy efforts, racism, sexism, xenophobia, homophobia, and transphobia persist, and clients may be on the receiving end of these forms of oppression and discrimination.

Our emphasis in Part IV is on clients struggling or suffering from these phenomena and on providing out-of-session activities to help them process their reactions and move forward in their lives. Each chapter includes an overview of the issues, discusses how people typically react, and provides a range of exercises and activities to use with your client either in session or out of session (or a combination of both). These activities may be used as written or modified to better fit the needs of your clients. They are designed to facilitate the therapeutic process and are not a substitute for effective counseling and psychotherapy. As in all other portions of this workbook, we urge you to use your best clinical judgment in assessing whether a given exercise is appropriate for a particular client. Additional therapeutic exercises for clients are provided in Appendix A. See Appendix B for an annotated list of useful websites and online resources.

Therapeutic homework assignments are designed to assist clients in reducing stress and strengthening their resilience in today's social context in which tribalism, divisiveness, and hostility seem to flourish. Chapter 11 focuses on the tribalism that has been exacerbated by political differences and value conflicts. Chapter 12 tackles the topic of social injustice against marginalized groups, including people of color, religious minorities, immigrants and refugees, women, and the LGBTQ+ population. These are not new phenomena and may seem out of place in a section dealing with emerging crises, but we include them here because many of these tensions have increased in recent years. Chapter 13 focuses on new stresses amplified by the uses to which social media is put today, and technological innovations continue to change our world at a rapid pace.

The Unraveling of Civil Society in America

New political and social developments are reported hourly in the fast-paced 24/7 news cycle, and it is impossible to keep up with it all and not become exhausted. Technological advances make it possible for us to know what is happening around the world in real time. Developments that occurred a week or two ago often seem like they happened an eternity ago, and we cannot help but wonder about the extent to which technology and the media (including social media) contribute to the intensity of the stress we experience daily.

Having access to this incredible technology is useful in so many ways, but it inundates us with stressful information and disturbing images at a much accelerated pace. All at once, images of a hate crime committed against one group in a particular community may compete in the news media with images of another horrific act carried out somewhere else in the United States or around the world. The Christchurch, New Zealand, mosque shootings on March 15, 2019, claimed 50 lives and injured dozens more, and this tragedy was live-streamed by the shooter on social media. People around the world were outraged and condemned this attack. Mass casualty tragedies are occurring around the world daily (Miller & McCoy, 2018). Within a span of 13 hours, two mass-casualty shootings occurred in the United States, one in El Paso, Texas, August 3, 2019, in a Walmart (leaving 22 dead and 24 injured) and another in the Oregon District of Dayton, Ohio, August 4 (leaving 10 dead and 27 injured).

It is likely that many more shocking acts will occur, leaving us all wondering if conditions in society will ever improve. Will this violence and hate ever stop? No one is immune to the toxicity of today's stressful social and political climate. Even if you are not the target of a hate crime or personally subjected to systemic oppression, it is reasonable to wonder if or when an act of violence will occur near you, whether it be in the real or the virtual world. Bullying, for example, has entered the realm of cyberspace, leaving victims feeling unsafe around the clock, even in their own homes, and vulnerable to developing symptoms of PTSD, depression, and anxiety (Bauman, 2011). Social media has become a major part of many people's lives. It has enhanced our ability to connect with people, but it has also been used as a vehicle to spread hate and to torment others.

We do not want to leave you with the impression that media and technology are responsible for all of society's woes. Without question, complex forces in society (both rational and irrational, conscious and unconscious) have created conditions that have given rise to increased divisiveness, tribalism, and a sense of moral bewilderment. But few would argue that the rapid transmission of information via electronic media, which was made possible through technological advances and is now accepted as a part of normal life, does indeed play a role in adding to our daily stress.

What price do we pay when we continuously experience information overload and become saturated with troubling images, ideas, opinions, and questionable facts? And what confusion does this "post-truth" era instill in us if we must be vigilant and question the accuracy and validity of the "facts" presented? Coming to terms with these disturbing phenomena in our personal lives is hard enough, but we must also consider what this means and how we can help the clients we serve. Counselors must become skilled in identifying clients who are affected by stressful social or political developments and help them process or unpack their reactions and cope more effectively with them. It is just as important for counselors to monitor their own countertransference triggers. Counselors must be aware of how their own worldview may distort their perception of clients who hold opposing worldviews.

Scope of the Problem

Some of the disturbing trends we are experiencing in American society today reflect changes happening throughout the world. With the rise of populism and White nationalism in liberal democracies such as the United States and the United Kingdom, many people are left wondering if democracy itself is in peril. The stress that many of us experience today in our daily lives is likely exacerbated by what we see happening on a societal and a global level.

Whether around the dinner table, in an online chatroom, or in the workplace, conversations with family members, friends, or coworkers can suddenly take a negative turn and ignite powerful emotions if certain "hot button" topics are introduced. Political polarization is by no means a new phenomenon, yet the passions many politicians arouse today extend beyond the usual divide (Eckel, 2017). In his insightful essay about identity politics, Fukuyama (2018) concludes that "identity can be used to divide, but it can also be used to unify. That, in the end, will be the remedy for the populist politics of the present" (p. 114). We urge helping professionals to remain hopeful about the future and to embrace unity, not only for the sake of our clients but for our own sake and that of our loved ones as well.

Part IV focuses on emerging issues of our time and includes exercises to guide clients in examining their thoughts, feelings, and behaviors related to these issues. Although societal and global problems are unlikely to be "fixed" in the short term, we can help clients manage their stress and develop more sustainable coping strategies in this unsettled time.

Chapter 11

Political Differences, Value Conflicts, and Tribalism

*In our finest hours, though, the soul of the country manifests itself
in an inclination to open our arms
rather than to clench our fists.*

—Jon Meacham

· · ·

For Counselors

Many authors have analyzed our political situation and the current administration in recent years. Based on book titles alone, it is easy to see just how divisive national politics has become. When we factor in the tsunami of news articles, editorials, and social media posts related to politics that flood in daily, it becomes abundantly clear that politics permeates our lives in ways that matter and that our society has become increasingly tribal and polarized.

The assumption that politics is far removed from our personal lives and experiences is patently false. Political agendas and policies have a direct impact on our basic needs. A prime example is the government shutdown in 2018-19 (35 days, the longest shutdown in U.S. history). An estimated 800,000 federal employees did not receive their paychecks, causing many of them (and their families) great financial and emotional hardship. For these individuals, politics suddenly became a very personal matter. This shutdown also affected the rest of us in direct and indirect ways. Bettelheim (2019) explained that the shutdown curtailed drug reviews and food safety inspections, froze court cases, and shelved investigations into matters such as Facebook's data security practices. It also delayed the Internal Revenue Service's preparations to process millions of tax returns and led the Environmental Protection Agency to twice delay a public hearing on a proposal to roll back a major climate rule for future power plants.

Mental health professionals are likely to encounter clients who are stressed, dismayed, and bewildered by all that is going on in society today—a society that has become increasingly fractured by divisive politics and deep value differences. In the words of one psychotherapist:

> The election and subsequent rule of Donald Trump as President of the United States is an event that has had a great and perhaps unique impact on the consciousness and psyche of a large number of people in this country. In my own clinical practice, it has generated far more anxiety and upset than any other historical event except the 9/11 destruction of the World Trade Center. . . . [Unlike the attacks of 9/11], the Trump presidency is ongoing, with hourly news reports often focusing on his every comment and action however large or small. It has an "in your face" quality that is hard to avoid, much less ignore. (Yourman, 2018, p. 766)

It is unlikely that the hyperpartisan political climate we are experiencing today will end with the next election cycle. Psychotherapists and counselors must be especially vigilant and pay attention to their own values, beliefs, and political leanings—and what their impact may have on the helping process. Intrigued by this topic, Solomonov and Barber (2018) investigated patients' perspectives on the infiltration of the political climate into the therapeutic space. In a survey of 604 self-described Democratic and Republican patients residing throughout the United States, 64% said they discuss politics with their therapists, and many of them, both Democrats and Republicans, would have liked to discuss politics even more in their sessions. In addition, "stronger patient-reported alliance levels were found for patients who (a) perceived political similarity; (b) reported *implicit* [rather than *explicit*] therapist political disclosure; and (c) found in-session political discussions helpful" (p. 779). Reflecting on clinical interventions with clients wishing to discuss politics in session, Yourman (2018) indicated that in some instances "it may be useful to disclose one's own strongly held political beliefs in the service of psychotherapeutic aims" (p. 772). He concluded, however, that he would not want to be self-disclosing with clients unless he was confident he could contain his emotions regarding political differences. In his view, trying to influence client's political views rather than client's emotional outlook would be a misuse of the process.

So what does this all mean for you? It is especially important to be aware of potential transference and countertransference issues that may surface in relation to local, regional, national, or international politics. Just as "the personal is political, so may the political be intensely personal" (Farber, 2018, p. 720). You should anticipate having conversations about political and social issues that may be a source of stress and anxiety for your clients. Have a plan in place to process your thoughts and emotions with a clinical supervisor, a trusted colleague, or your own therapist to manage countertransference reactions appropriately.

Divided We Stand

In less divisive times, the popular phrase "let's agree to disagree" may have seemed like sage advice. Perhaps it still is, but that recommendation may be especially difficult to put into practice in today's world. To agree to disagree for the sake of peace and harmony is much easier said than done.

One author noted, "I am finding more and more people who say they have fallen out with friends and family members over politics and have simply stopped trying to understand those with whom they disagree. Many have retreated to their ideological bubbles, in terms of both the media they consume and the people with whom they associate" (Allott, 2018, p. 10). In a recent conversation with a friend, I (Bob) learned about a 60-year-old man who became estranged from his entire family of origin as well as his wife due to his staunch convictions and unwavering ideological beliefs. Although he had been close to his family prior to the 2016 election, afterward he moved to a different state in a desperate effort to distance himself both geographically and emotionally from anyone who didn't hold the political values he embraced. In another case, a husband and wife decided to separate until the end of the current political term because it was just too hard to live together and disagree vehemently.

These stories are not anomalies. Right-leaning individuals express hostility toward liberals, and liberal-leaning individuals reject the ideas of today's conservatives. Many people are searching for ways to deal with political ruptures in their relationships, and Eckel (2017) claims that one reason this is "uniquely challenging is that they're basing their views on differing facts" (p. 42). In the words of clinical psychologist Ben Michaelis, "this is a choose-your-own-reality situation. I've been in practice a long time, and people have definitely disagreed about politics before. But now there is very little sense of shared reality. This is an uncertain time for everyone" (cited in Eckel, 2017, p. 42). Perhaps it will come as no surprise that a growing body of literature "indicates that the American public is affectively polarized. Partisan strength is up, feelings toward the two parties are more extreme, and partisans are more intolerant of the other side" (Luttig, 2017, p. 866).

A discussion about the rise in partisan politics and social conflict would be incomplete without acknowledging the emergence of fake news and the alternative media:

> Call it misinformation, fake news, junk news, or deliberately distributed deception, the stuff has been around since the first protohuman whispered the first malicious gossip. . . . But today's technologies, with their elaborate infrastructures for uploading, commenting, liking, and sharing, have created an almost ideal environment for manipulation and abuse—one that arguably threatens any sense of shared truth. "If everyone is entitled to their own facts," says Yochai Benkler, codirector of the Berkman Klein Center for Internet & Society at Harvard University, echoing a fear expressed by many, "you can no longer have reasoned disagreements and productive compromise." You're "left with raw power," he says, a war over who gets to decide what truth is. (Waldrop, 2017, p. 12632)

LaFrance, Raicu, and Goldman (2017) posed two fundamental questions:

Is technology hurting democracy?
And can technology help save democracy?

In response to the latter question, for all of our sakes, we certainly hope so.

What We Have Learned About Helping Others Therapeutically

A basic principle that both of us have taught our trainees and supervisees to embrace is to meet clients where they are. Perhaps you recall hearing this same advice from clinical supervisors during your graduate training. Counselors are most helpful when they are able to enter the inner lives or worlds of their clients, not the other way around! Clearly, as Yourman (2018) pointed out, if clients hold an opposing political view, your role is not to challenge them to embrace your view. That would be a misuse of the therapeutic process. It may seem unnecessary to state this fundamental ethical principle—counselors avoid imposing their values on clients—but partisan beliefs (both to the left and the right) in this era of polarized politics are deeply entrenched, and you may be tempted, even subtly, to persuade clients to adopt what you consider a healthier political mind-set. Paying close attention to countertransference triggers as well as to your clients' projections onto you is of the utmost importance.

In a compelling article about the complex dynamics of a Palestinian therapist serving a Jewish patient, Srour (2015) explains that in "a world of political conflict, mental-health professionals are often called upon to help patients from the opposite camp" (p. 407). Palestinians and Israelis have faced long-term political conflict and have had years of experience coping with tribalism and polarization. In such situations, Srour believes therapists must process their sense of threat, anger, and guilt and develop a good containment vessel during therapy. Moreover, he believes therapists must work on integrating different and denied parts of their own identity "to be able to hear other, more internal dynamics in the patient's mind, which are conveyed via the political conflict reality and transference issues" (p. 407).

In our view, the quality of the therapeutic alliance and the therapist's ability to cultivate a safe and welcoming space for clients to do their work matters most. The current political climate has reawakened old psychological wounds, has exacerbated clinical symptoms of fear, anxiety, and depression, and has reactivated feelings of victimization for some clients (Farber, 2018). We believe healing approaches can help clients' process their thoughts and emotions and make meaningful connections between their reactions to politics and their long-standing issues.

The Counselor's Task With Clients

You may wonder how to help clients avoid the trap of succumbing to tribalism and other negative forces that plague society today. Realistically, your clients must live in this world (and not in a cocoon), so it is unlikely that you can prevent them from being exposed to fake news, and it is increasingly difficult to distinguish accurate information from falsified information. One task for counselors is to encourage clients to assess how they obtain their information, the frequency with which they are consuming it, how likely it is to be real or valid, and what reasonable steps they can take to determine its validity. Help clients evaluate the impact this information is having on their stress level, mental health and well-being, and worldview. If clients report feeling burdened by the information they are consuming regardless of how they are receiving it, help them devise an effective strategy for setting boundaries.

If a client is stressed or outraged by politics but constantly watches political pundits get into heated debates with each other on cable news programs or checks her Twitter account for political tweets throughout the day, it may be beneficial for the client to limit her access to news. You might suggest that she go on a "news diet"—limiting her consumption of information that fuels her negativity and stress. Instead of accessing the news a few times every day, you might suggest that she set aside a particular time once a day to catch up on the day's events. After processing this homework in counseling, she might also recognize that digesting information in one form is more palatable than another. For instance, she might discover that constant exposure to "breaking news" on TV (with its dramatic and attention-grabbing background music) arouses her anxiety, whereas reading the news in print from a credible and reliable news source is less triggering. She might also recognize that some of the content on social media does not add much pleasure to her life and could contain fake news.

The main task for counselors is to empower clients to take charge of their life by learning to set limits on their consumption of upsetting or distressing information. Until the technology industry and social media companies do a better job of regulating the information disseminated online and address the real problem of fake news, the responsibility falls on each of us to regulate our consumption of information. We may not be able to control the amount of real or fake information that comes our way, but we can control what we do with it and encourage our clients to do the same.

Dealing With Political Differences, Value Conflicts, and Tribalism

After her older brother posted comments on Facebook minimizing the pain of survivors of gun violence, Stephanie decided to confront Keith on social media. She thought she could be more candid online than in person, and she wrote a scathing post, which offended her brother deeply. Keith felt personally attacked and thought Stephanie was overreacting. Although they had a close relationship growing up and were respectful of each other despite value differences, tensions escalated after the 2016 election. Stephanie and Keith could hardly be civil toward each other and became estranged. This is just one of many stories describing the toll the current political climate is having on family relationships. If you feel stressed about today's climate of divisiveness, hatred, and bullying, and are concerned about its impact on relationships, you are not alone!

Although there is much to disagree about in today's polarized world, few would disagree that the United States of America has become a deeply divided nation. (At least most of us can agree on that!) Whether you lean to the left or the right in your political views or regard yourself as middle of the road or as an independent, it is hard to ignore the fact that tribalism is flourishing in our society. Rather than working in a bipartisan manner, those affiliated with the major political parties (or tribes) seem to be approaching politics as a zero-sum game, in which one party's victory signifies the other party's loss. Political differences have long generated lively debate and created tension, if not outright hostility, among those who feel passionately about their beliefs, but the divisiveness and hatred we are witnessing today is more widespread and more deeply entrenched. To make matters worse, a dislike of the "other tribe" has created a context in which the phenomenon of *fake news* has gained traction and attracted a mass audience (Lazer et al., 2018). We often think about fake news in a political context, but false information is also spread about a range of topics, including vaccination scares, nutritional advice, and stock market values. Undermining the credibility of legitimate news outlets that we count on to provide accurate information is dangerous to our democracy, and sometimes false information claims lives.

The Stress of Living in Polarizing Times

If you have wondered whether the divisions in society have become wider and deeper, you are not alone. The current state of our democracy, which some argue is in peril as are other democracies around the world (e.g., Fukuyama, 2018), is a source of stress for many Americans. The recent Stress in America survey (APA, 2017b) found that "nearly six in 10 adults (59 percent) report that the current social divisiveness causes them stress" (p. 1). A majority of adults from both political parties say the future of the nation is a source of stress.

You may well be wondering, "What the heck is going on? What is driving all of this divisiveness and tribalism?" The answer to these questions is complex, in fact, far more complex than we can address in this workbook. However, some developments that have led us to our current state "relate in some way to the economic and technological shifts of globalization. But they are also rooted in a different phenomenon: the rise of identity politics" (Fukuyama, 2018, p. 91). According to Brand (2017), "The crisis in our politics is fed in no small part by a widespread crisis in identity felt by millions of people [and] brought on by social change" (p. 215). We all need to know that we have a secure place in society. When people believe that their social status and sense of belonging and identity are threatened, they may experience fear, resentment, and anger. At its extreme, troubled individuals commit hate crimes, targeting innocent people. Their actions are fueled by ugly forces such as racism, xenophobia, homophobia, religious intolerance, and other forms of bigotry and oppression. At the risk of oversimplifying a very complex matter, these perpetrators seem to believe that others (often people from marginalized groups) are to blame for their lot in life and for that of others like them. Fortunately, the vast majority of people do not act out violently.

A more common occurrence in these polarizing times is the ruptures people experience in their personal relationships over political differences. Many people regard these schisms in their relationships as a source of stress. Reports of people choosing to purge their friend groups of anyone outside their political tribe are all too common today (Allott, 2018). It may be helpful for you to reflect on the important relationships in your life and assess the extent to which politics at the local, state, national, or international level have negatively affected your interactions with or attitudes toward people you care about.

Key Thought

Abraham Lincoln once stated, "A house divided against itself, cannot stand." Thus all Americans stand to gain by healing the ruptures that have damaged us as a nation. A good place to start is with our relationships with family, friends, and coworkers.

Suggestions for Coping With Political Differences, Value Conflicts, and Tribalism

Allott (2018) claims that our political tribalism is damaging our relationships, and in his view, "the remedy is not only to engage our political opponents but to do so with humility, patience and a real desire to understand" (p. 10). Here are some of his suggestions for improving political discussions with others and increasing civility:

1. Consider spending less time on social media discussing politics. You may find it much easier to have respectful and civil conversations in person rather than through the anonymity of social media.
2. Be sure you are engaging in political discussions for the right reasons. If you are challenging a friend because you are trying to understand his or her perspective, ask fair questions and listen, and then listen some more. Also, be aware if your intention is merely to prove that your friend's viewpoint is wrong.
3. Embrace the struggle between what may initially seem to be competing truths. In referring to competing truths, Allott is not referring to "alternative facts." He suggests looking a bit deeper when assessing the merits of ideas that you may not agree with on the surface. We must remember that we are capable of holding two opposing ideas in mind at the same time.

In this era of fake news, it is also important to be vigilant about your patterns of consuming information. Analyze your consumption of news and information, and consider doing the following:

1. Do a self-inventory and assess how you are obtaining your news, the frequency with which you are consuming it, and how likely it is to be real or valid versus fabricated. Consider taking some reasonable steps to determine the validity or credibility of the news source.
2. Evaluate the impact the information or news you are consuming is having on your stress level, mental health and well-being, relationships, and worldview. If it feels burdensome or is detracting from your quality of life, consult with your therapist and devise an effective strategy for setting boundaries on it.
3. Be mindful of the biases that people commonly have. Research by Lazer and colleagues (2018) found that people favor information that confirms their preexisting attitudes and find this information to be persuasive (confirmation bias). People are also prone to accept information that pleases them (desirability bias). None of us is immune from developing these biases, so try to be honest with yourself and monitor your biases.
4. Be aware of websites that may be publishing fake news. Internet platforms are "the most important enablers and primary conduits of fake news" (Lazer et al., 2018, p. 1095). Websites that have the appearance of legitimate news organizations are inexpensive to launch, and the content on these sites is monetized through online ads and social media dissemination.

Unquestionably, the technology industry faces a Herculean task to fix this real problem of fake news. They owe it to the public (and to democracy itself!). These internet platforms operate like robber barons of times past, accepting little responsibility for what they do and monetizing your personal information to increase their profits. Today the responsibility falls on each of us to regulate how we consume information. You can set boundaries on your consumption of fake news by becoming a more informed consumer, and you can empower yourself by limiting your consumption of real news that triggers you in unhealthy ways. Your personal relationships are worth protecting from false or even malicious information. Wouldn't it be a shame to sacrifice meaningful relationships over disputes that stem from toxic social media posts and information that may not be accurate?

Workbook Material for the Client

The following questions and exercises are designed to help you examine the topic of coping with political differences and value conflicts with others. There are no right or wrong answers. This is an opportunity for you to spend time thinking about how well you cope in your own life. Some questions and exercises may be easy for you, and others may require more thought on your part. We hope you will take plenty of time to consider each topic or question that your counselor has asked you to complete. The value of the activities and questions comes from your careful consideration about your position on the topic. The goal is for you to learn as much as you can outside the counseling setting. If you are better prepared to explore these issues, your session time will be more productive. We suggest that you keep a journal as you contemplate changing the way you interact with others who hold differing political viewpoints or with whom you might have value conflicts. Purchase a notebook or journal or record your responses to selected questions and activities on your computer. Remember to print your responses and bring them with you to your next counseling session.

Exercises and Activities

1. People are experiencing varying amounts of stress, anxiety, anger, frustration, exhaustion, and more in the divisiveness and political infighting in the United States today. How would you describe your feelings and reactions to all that is going on?

   _____

   _____

2. How stressed are you over the state of divisiveness, political infighting, hatred, and tribalism (people taking sides on issues)?

   Scale: 1   2   3   4   5   6   7   8   9   10
   　　　　 Not at all　　　　　　　　　　　　　 *Extremely*
   　　　　 stressed　　　　　　　　　　　　　　 *stressed*

   Explain your response.

   _____

3. How would you have rated yourself on the same scale 1 year ago? Three years ago? Five years ago?

   Scale: 1   2   3   4   5   6   7   8   9   10
   　　　　 Not at all　　　　　　　　　　　　　 *Extremely*
   　　　　 stressed　　　　　　　　　　　　　　 *stressed*

   Explain your response.

   _____

4. To what extent do you think things will change for better or for worse as we go through future election cycles? Do you think basic values are changing in society? If so, how do you anticipate that will affect U.S. politics? Explain.

   _____

   _____

5. Have you encountered differences of opinions and values with friends that are related to politics? With family members? With your partner/spouse? With coworkers? Describe those encounters. What are your feelings and reactions as you write about them?

_____

_____

6. In attempting to resolve these differences, what has worked for you and what has not?

_____

_____

7. Have you cut off communication with some people as a result of sharp political differences or value conflicts? What was it like to take this action, and how has this affected your daily life? Do you envision this as a temporary break in communication, or are you prepared to sever ties permanently with these individuals? How do you feel about this?

_____

_____

8. Have some people cut off communication with you as a result of sharp political differences or value conflicts? How has this affected your life on a daily basis? What would you most like to say to the person(s) who cut off contact with you?

_____

_____

9. You can take action to reduce your level of stress and frustration. Which of the following actions would you like to do? Pick one and try that for a period of time.
   - ❏ Reduce your exposure to the news.
   - ❏ Reduce your exposure to social media.
   - ❏ Volunteer with people and groups that do more of what you believe in.
   - ❏ Get involved in a political campaign effort.
   - ❏ Spend time each day in meditation and mindfulness.
   - ❏ Develop a daily program of relaxation.
   - ❏ Exercise on a regular basis.
   - ❏ Try to eat a more balanced and healthy diet.
   - ❏ Other: _____

10. It is possible that you are projecting some of your feelings regarding political differences onto another person. Keep a log of your reactions to others in your daily life. Pay attention to reactions that seem especially strong. Write down your assumptions about that person. Who or what do they remind you of?

_____

_____

11. The goal of this exercise is to help you find *common ground* with others toward whom you sense division. If you harbor intense negative feelings toward someone who holds a different viewpoint, take time to reflect on this series of questions:
    a. How are the person's views different from yours? What does it tap into for you? What assumptions do you have about the person who holds the different viewpoint?

_____

_____

b. If the person was here right now and was not behaving defensively, what do you suppose that person would say to you?

_____

_____

c. What would you most want to say to that person if you knew she or he would hear you?

_____

_____

d. What bothers you most about the person or that point of view?

_____

_____

e. How do you suppose the person might perceive you as a result of holding a different view?

_____

_____

f. What is at risk if you become further polarized or divided? While maintaining your values and views, how could you move toward more unity?

_____

_____

g. On what topics or issues could you find common ground with this individual? Do you think that is even possible? If so, is this something you would want to do?

_____

_____

12. Some people who harbor strong negative feelings toward others on the basis of their membership with a particular group (based on gender, race, ethnicity, sexual orientation, religion, and so forth) are afraid underneath it all that the "other" is responsible for taking something of value from them (e.g., jobs, status).
    a. What do you think about this idea?

_____

_____

b. Have you experienced or witnessed this? If so, say more about that.

_____

_____

13. If you do harbor strong negative feelings toward others on the basis of their membership with a particular group (e.g., their gender, race, ethnicity, sexual orientation, religion, etc.), where did these views originate? How did/do your family members influence your views about people who were/are different from you?

_____

_____

14. People tend to favor information that confirms their preexisting attitudes and find this information to be persuasive (confirmation bias). People are also prone to accept information that pleases them (desirability bias). None of us is immune to these forms of bias. Reflect on how you have been influenced to accept certain information.

_____

_____

15. When you engage in conversations about social and political issues that you feel passionate about, how would you rate your level of open-mindedness and willingness to listen to others' views?

Scale: 1   2   3   4   5   6   7   8   9   10
         Extremely   *Extremely*
         low   *high*

Explain your response.

_____

16. If you become defensive when discussing "hot button" topics (e.g., current events, politics), answer the following questions:
    a. How would you rate the severity of your defensiveness? Then rate how you think others would rate your defensiveness.

Scale: 1   2   3   4   5   6   7   8   9   10
         Extremely   *Extremely*
         low   *high*

Explain your response.

_____

    b. How would you describe your internal experience of being defensive or protective of yourself? Feel free to use a metaphor if that works for you (for example, "My defenses are like a steel armor or a bullet-proof vest—nothing will penetrate them!" or "My defenses are like a light jacket that I rarely need to wear."). What does your defensive behavior or attitude do for you? Does it serve your best interests or get in your way?

_____

_____

    c. How does your defensiveness affect your relationships with others? Is this something you would like to change or improve?

_____

_____

Social Injustice
Against Marginalized Groups

Injustice anywhere is a threat to justice everywhere.
—Martin Luther King Jr.

I think the first duty of society is justice.
—Alexander Hamilton

...

For Counselors

All forms of injustice are unique and devastating in their own ways, but they share the common feature of the powerful and privileged abusing their power to exploit the vulnerable. As a counselor or helping professional, the probability is quite high that you will serve clients who have experienced at least one form of social injustice. Perhaps you or your loved ones have been on the receiving end of one or more forms of oppression as well.

The themes of power, privilege, and oppression are of paramount importance when discussing matters related to social injustice against marginalized populations (Ratts, Singh, Butler, Nassar-McMillan, & Rafferty McCullough, 2016). To have a meaningful and productive conversation about racism in the United States, for instance, we must be open to discussing White supremacy and privilege as integral topics. Anything less would be a glaring omission. Discussions about racism and other forms of systemic oppression may unleash strong emotions and raise people's defenses, so some people simply avoid having these conversations. Robin DiAngelo conducts workshops on race and broaches the topic of implicit bias with participants: "Addressing racism makes many White people feel anger, fear and guilt, which leads to denial, minimization and defensiveness, . . . even though racism touches everyone" (as cited in Dastagir, 2018, p. 3a). Some people may find these courageous conversations uncomfortable, but if progress is to be made in combating injustice and bringing about equality, these conversations are essential.

When addressing themes of social injustice, remember that both clients and counselors alike present with *multiple identities* that may interact in complex ways. Ratts (2017) summed it up like this: "All individuals present a multiplicity of intersecting identities, as well as privileged and marginalized statuses, shaped by motivating forces both internal (e.g., sense of self) and external (e.g., societal oppression) that need consideration" (p. 88). Some people are marginalized in one or two ways, such as on the basis of their racial and/or gender status, whereas others are "multiply marginalized" (p. 88), which is likely to compound their stress. For example, a young person who identifies as Latino and gay and also is an undocumented immigrant who fears deportation may feel exponentially more stress.

We must think about the impact of political actions on the lives of human beings. Patler and Laster Pirtle (2018) conducted research on the psychological well-being of immigrant youth who either applied or considered applying to the Deferred Action for Childhood Arrivals (DACA) program. The investigators "found a strong, positive, and significant effect of legal status on psychological wellbeing. Receiving DACA reduced the odds of distress, negative emotions, and worry about self-deportation by 76–87%, compared to respondents without DACA" (p. 44).

What We Have Learned About Helping Others Therapeutically

Over the decades, counselors and other helping professionals have increasingly recognized the need to advocate for client populations that have been historically oppressed and marginalized. Under the umbrella of the American Counseling Association, for instance, divisions such as the Association for Multicultural Counseling and Development, the Association for Lesbian, Gay, Bisexual, and Transgender Issues in Counseling, and Counselors for Social Justice champion the rights of clients who have not held power in society. Multicultural and Social Justice Counseling Competencies were developed and are now widely regarded as essential to effective counseling (Ratts et al., 2016). We strongly encourage you to become familiar with these competencies if you are not already and to use them to guide your practice.

Substantial progress has been made by scholars and practitioners in advancing our understanding of how to respond therapeutically to clients from marginalized groups, but this field is still evolving and there is more to learn. Ratts (2017) points out that we need to deepen our understanding of individuals who experience multiple forms of marginalization, and we need to learn how privilege and marginalization intersect in people's daily lives. For example, the experiences of a woman of color who identifies as lesbian will be different from those of a heterosexual woman of color. A White gay male working as a trader on Wall Street, who is privileged in terms of his race, gender, and socioeconomic status, may be marginalized based on his sexual orientation. However, his life experiences are most certainly going to be quite different from those of a poor Black gay man who lives in a small, conservative community. When working with clients, it is critical to help them explore how their multiple identities interact and affect their lives and presenting issues.

Learning What We Don't Know and Leaning Into Discomfort

To serve clients effectively, we must be willing to seek *specialized knowledge* when working with specific populations. To illustrate this point, let's consider the needs of refugees. Bemak and Chung (2017) have expertise in helping refugees from war-torn countries who often experience numerous traumas; many have either witnessed or been subjected to torture, incarceration, atrocities, killings, starvation and other forms of deprivation, rape, and sexual and physical assaults. "Refugees fear persecution and are forced to involuntarily flee their homes to escape intolerable conditions," and Bemak and Chung stress that "displacement and premigration trauma are critical considerations when working with refugees" (p. 299). One team of researchers found that more than 85% of the 179 Burmese refugees interviewed for their study experienced life-threatening war trauma (Cook, Shannon, Vinson, Letts, & Dwee, 2015). These traumas included having their homes and villages destroyed, being orphaned, sustaining debilitating injuries from stepping on landmines, experiencing widespread community fear, and being exposed to dead bodies. They concluded that

> [refugees] want health providers to understand the political context of their trauma, validate their experiences, and provide education about the impact of trauma on health as well as treatment options. Due to a lack of knowledge about mental health and treatment options, shame, mistrust, or cultural norms that value deference to authority, refugees may not initiate the conversation and prefer that providers inquire about these experiences. (p. 10)

Refugees and other marginalized clients may be reluctant to initiate conversations about their traumatic experiences. When helpers cultivate an emotionally safe space within the counseling relationship and convey that they are open to having these conversations, clients may self-disclose more intimately about their experiences. Day-Vines and her colleagues (2007) discuss the importance of broaching the topics of race, ethnicity, and culture during the counseling process, which helps clients examine the extent to which sociopolitical factors influence their presenting issues.

Day-Vines, Ammah, Steen, and Arnold (2018) urge counselors to get comfortable with *discomfort* and note that acknowledging cultural factors strengthens counselor credibility, deepens client disclosure, and increases client satisfaction. Counselors carry distinct power within the counselor-client dyad, and we must be mindful that "we live in a racially charged society where topics about race and representation are often considered taboo and that clients may not directly address racial, ethnic, and cultural concerns unless specifically invited to do so" (p. 97).

A couple of important caveats are necessary. First and foremost, in our efforts to provide culturally competent counseling to clients, we must avoid the trap of stereotyping them and adopting a monolithic perspective (Lee, 2019). Becoming more knowledgeable about factors that may have an impact on clients (e.g., sociopolitical and cultural considerations) is a good step, but we must not jump to the conclusion that everyone from a particular cultural group shares the same reality. Clients are individuals and have their own unique perspectives and stories to tell. One way to enhance our knowledge of diversity is to read literature that broadens our worldview and exposes us to the lived experiences of people whose backgrounds and life circumstances are vastly different from our own. An excellent book about the refugee and immigrant experience is *The Newcomers: Finding Refuge, Friendship, and Hope in America* by Helen Thorpe (2017). Second, we must be willing to consciously examine our own "cultural baggage" (Lee, 2019). If we are able to understand its origins, acknowledge it, and move beyond it, Lee believes we will be in a much better position to effectively interact with those who are different from us.

Counseling Marginalized Clients in a Changing World

Scholars devoted to social justice have developed comprehensive models of counseling to address the needs of marginalized clients in a changing world. Chung and Bemak (2012) created the multiphase model (MPM) of psychotherapy, counseling, human rights, and social justice to account for the ecological context of the modern world that affects people's everyday lives. Our world has been profoundly changed by trends such as globalization, the worldwide movement of people, and shifting demographics. A whole host of serious problems, both individual and systemic, have come along with these changes, and a multipronged approach is needed. The complex problems and challenges clients face today require multilayered interventions that target both the individual and systemic levels, and the MPM does just that. It includes five phases: (a) mental health education; (b) group, family, and individual psychotherapy; (c) cultural empowerment; (d) integration of Western and indigenous healing methodologies; and (e) social justice and human rights. You can find in-depth coverage of this comprehensive framework in *Social Justice Counseling: The Next Steps Beyond Multiculturalism* by Chung and Bemak (2012). Other leading scholars on multicultural and social justice counseling include Ratts and Pedersen (2014) and Lee (2018).

The Counselor's Task With Clients

Counselors play a vital role in combating social injustice when they serve as advocates for clients who have experienced oppression or unfairness. Aside from engaging in productive and courageous conversations about racism, xenophobia, homophobia, sexism, or other sensitive topics with those who have power to change oppressive systems, you can empower your clients with tools and strategies to ease their suffering. Fred Bemak, cofounder of the Diversity Research and Action Center at George Mason University and founder of the nonprofit organization Counselors Without Borders, stated that "advocacy and counseling are fundamentally intertwined" (as cited in Meyers, 2014, p. 35); they are two parts of a whole. Counselors who embrace a more traditional view of the helping process may need to broaden their idea about what constitutes "helping." Individual, group, and family therapy give clients the therapeutic space to process their experiences, improve their interpersonal functioning, and learn new positive coping skills, but traditional counseling services may fall short of meeting individual needs—needs we cannot afford to overlook. Counselors can help ease clients' stress by teaching them practical skills that will help them navigate the world more easily. That might entail helping them figure out the public transportation system so they can get to and from a job, helping them apply for a job, or helping clients find more affordable and safe housing. If clients' basic needs remain unmet, how can we expect them to focus on meeting higher level needs such as self-actualization?

For Clients

Social Injustice Against Marginalized Groups

In an ideal and fair society, those in positions of power would commit to distributing resources more evenly. Everyone would have equal access to safe and affordable housing; healthy food; quality education, health care, and legal representation; well-paying jobs; reliable transportation; and ample opportunity to develop their interests and talents. People would not have to work three jobs to barely make ends meet, while others, though few in number, enjoy most of society's wealth and opportunities. The gap between society's richest and poorest would be shrinking instead of getting wider and deeper. People would not be discriminated against or oppressed based on their race, ethnicity, gender, sexual orientation, age, religion, ability status, or any other dimension of their identity. Diversity would be embraced and viewed as one of society's greatest strengths—not as a weakness or as a threat to overcome.

The issues that have brought you into counseling may be exacerbated by, if not directly related to, instances of social injustice that you have directly encountered or witnessed in your own life. We all have complex *multiple identities* that are shaped by our affiliations with certain groups. Our identities may be related to race, ethnicity, nationality, religion, age, socioeconomic status/social class, political leanings, education level, gender identity, sexual orientation, and so forth. None of us is just one thing. For instance, you might be a Black, well-educated, heterosexual, Muslim male; a biracial, gender fluid, well-educated atheist; or a White, Christian, blue-collar, middle-class, conservative female; or some other assortment entirely. You may give more weight or importance to certain dimensions of yourself than to others. As you think about your own multiple identities and which aspects of your identity have more prominence in your life, we hope you will also reflect on the extent to which these identities interact with each other and how they affect your life.

Suggestions for Coping With Social Injustice

If you are the victim of human rights abuses or have been subjected to oppression or discrimination in any of its forms, keep the following guidelines in mind.

1. Know your rights. You will find a lot of credible information about your rights at the American Civil Liberties Union website (https://www.aclu.org/know-your-rights), which contains information pertaining to criminal law reform and prisoners' rights, disability rights, LGBTQ+ rights, voters' rights, and more.
2. Consult with your counselor or therapist for support and guidance. If you have been traumatized and are slow to trust, talking about your reluctance to trust may be a great place to start. Trauma-informed counseling approaches have been developed and may help you process your experiences and move forward with your life.
3. It may be important for you to work with an advocate or to seek legal guidance. Some communities have agencies or organizations to assist clients in finding the resources they need. For instance, in Baltimore, Maryland, the Intercultural Counseling Connection is a resource for refugees who have settled in the area.
4. If you have difficulty asking for support, examine the underlying belief that prevents you from reaching out and challenge that belief. Ask yourself: "Although people in my life have disappointed me, does it mean that everyone will disappoint me in the future if I ask for their assistance?" Be sure to credit yourself for taking steps to challenge beliefs that may be getting in your way.
5. Get involved in social activism. It is empowering to connect with others who share your passion for changing oppressive systems. Whether you have a lot of energy and time to devote to a cause or little to none, there are ways to become involved. It may take a village to effect change, but you can play a role and be part of those efforts.
6. Take care of yourself. Be sure to "check in" with yourself every day to ensure that your essential needs are met. Monitor your stress level, and take steps to keep your stress under control.

Workbook Material for the Client

The following questions and exercises are designed to help you examine the topic of coping with social injustice. There are no right or wrong answers. This is an opportunity for you to spend time thinking about social justice issues that affect your life and strategies for feeling more empowered. Some questions and exercises may be easy for you, and others may require more thought on your part or may evoke some emotions. We hope you will take plenty of time to consider each topic or question that your counselor has asked you to complete. The value of the activities and questions comes from your careful consideration about your position on the topic. The goal is for you to learn as much as you can outside of the counseling setting. If you are better prepared to explore these issues, your session time will be more productive. We suggest that you keep a journal as you contemplate social injustice issues. Purchase a notebook or journal or record your responses to selected questions and activities on your computer. Remember to print your responses and bring them with you to your next counseling session.

Exercises and Activities

These terms frame the discussion around rights and privileges. Consider them as you complete the exercises and activities that follow.

Cultural Empowerment: Your ability to connect with your own power to overcome cultural barriers and advocate for yourself.

Marginalization: Individuals or groups of people are afforded less importance in society and feel cast aside to the margins with no voice or power. Marginalized groups may be made to feel as if they are of little value and may be relegated to a subordinate or inferior position.

Microaggressions: Commonplace verbal, nonverbal, and environmental insults and slights that communicate disparaging, hostile, or negative messages.

Privilege: Benefiting from unearned assets, such as being White, being born into affluence, or being male or heterosexual. Privilege advantages and confers dominance and power on those who possess it, even as they deny it but remain protected by it (McIntosh, 1989).

Social Justice: All people have equal access to opportunities, wealth, and privileges within a society.

Social Injustice: Individuals are denied access and subjected to unfair practices such as ageism, racism, and sexism and are denied basic human rights.

1. We all have multiple identities that are shaped by our associations with various groups. Some aspects of your identity may have more importance to you than others. You may regard gender identity and ethnicity as playing prominent roles in your life, whereas another person may place more emphasis on racial identity and educational status.

   a. Make a list of the parts of your identity that you cherish the most, and describe why each one is so important.

   _____

   _____

   b. If you had to rank order them, which of your identities would be at the top of your list?

   _____

   _____

   c. Which would be next on your list?

   _____

   _____

d. If you prefer, represent your identities on a pie chart. Which identities would constitute the largest pieces of the pie?

_____

_____

2. If you were forced to give up an aspect of your identity, which one(s) would be the easiest to let go, and which would be the hardest to part with? Explain. How is it to even imagine giving up an aspect of your identity?

_____

_____

3. Think about your multiple identities. Are there ways in which you are *privileged* as a result of your affiliation with the dominant group (those who hold more power) in society? For instance, if you are White, male, or heterosexual in this society, you would enjoy privileges (i.e., unearned assets) that people of color, females, or individuals in the LGBTQ+ community simply don't have. What is your reaction to answering this question?

_____

_____

4. Again, think about your multiple identities. Are there ways in which you are *marginalized* due to your affiliation with one or more minority or underrepresented groups in society? For instance, if you identify as a person of color, an immigrant or refugee, or a member of the LGBTQ+ community, you may be deprived of privileges (i.e., unearned assets) that people from the dominant group (those who hold more power) are afforded simply based on their group affiliation. What is your reaction to answering this question?

_____

_____

5. How do your unique identities and experiences with being privileged or marginalized (based on these identities) affect your mental health and well-being?

_____

_____

6. If you identify as belonging to a marginalized group, what are your greatest concerns about interacting with people from the dominant culture?

_____

_____

a. What are your greatest concerns about interacting with people from other marginalized groups?

_____

_____

b. Describe the context in which these interactions are likely to happen (e.g., at work, school, home, other places).

_____

_____

7. If you are part of the dominant culture, what are your greatest concerns about interacting with people from marginalized groups? Describe the context in which these interactions are likely to happen (e.g., at work, school, home, other places).

_____

_____

8. Describe a social injustice that has been a source of stress for you.

_____

_____

   a. Has this situation affected you or those you care about (either directly or indirectly)? Explain.

_____

_____

   b. What aspects of the situation have caused you the greatest stress?

_____

_____

9. How severe is your stress related to the injustice you have described?

Scale: 1   2   3   4   5   6   7   8   9   10
        Not stressed   *Extremely stressed*

   What do you think needs to happen for your stress to become manageable?

_____

10. What strategies have you used to cope with the stress resulting from the injustice you described?

_____

_____

   a. How well have they worked for you?

_____

_____

   b. How empowering have these strategies been?

_____

_____

11. Microaggressions, which can be conscious or unconscious, come in many forms and may be directed at a person based on race, sexual orientation, or other marginalized status.
   a. What messages have you received related to your status as a minority group member that have been invalidating or offensive?

_____

_____

   b. How did/do you internalize these hurtful remarks?

_____

_____

12. Some people of color experience internalized racism, and some members of the LGBTQ+ community experience internalized homophobia or transphobia. Have you internalized any negative stereotypes about your culture (as you define it) from the dominant culture? If so, describe your experience.

    _____

    _____

13. Past and present discrimination against certain groups is the basis for distrust of the majority society. People from the dominant culture may be perceived by those who hold less power in society as potential oppressors unless proven otherwise.
    a. If you are part of the dominant culture and your trustworthiness is tested by a person from a marginalized group who feels hostility, resentment, suspicion, or apprehension, how are you likely to react?

    _____

    _____

    b. Do you tend to become defensive, or are you able to respond with empathy and compassion?

    _____

    _____

14. Fighting injustice can be demanding and stressful. It is crucial to engage in self-care to maintain your stamina.
    a. What are some ways you take care of yourself that are consistent with your culture and values?

    _____

    _____

    b. In what ways could you improve your self-care?

    _____

    _____

15. One way to empower yourself is to become active in organizations and causes that combat injustice.
    a. How do you feel about getting involved in social activism?

    _____

    _____

    b. In which issues would you be most inclined to invest your resources (e.g., time, money, energy, passion)?

    _____

    _____

    c. What tasks would you envision yourself doing as an activist?

    _____

    _____

16. Consider writing a letter or making a call to your congressperson.
    a. If you contacted a local, state, or federal elected official, what message would you most want to convey?

    _____

    _____

    b. Which social justice issues would be at the top of your list?

    _____

    _____

   c. If you had to "pick your battles," which points would you most want to emphasize?

_____

_____

17. Courage is often required to challenge oppression and stand up for what you believe in. Part of your healing process may entail such action.
   a. Do you see yourself as a courageous person? Identify times in your life when you have shown courage.

_____

_____

   b. What was that like for you?

_____

_____

   c. How did others react to your courageous actions?

_____

_____

   d. What strengths did you draw on to get through that difficult time?

_____

_____

Chapter 13

Forces of Social Media
and Technology

Technology is, of course, a double-edged sword.
Fire can cook our food but also burn us.

—Jason Silva

It has become appallingly obvious that our technology has exceeded our humanity.
—Albert Einstein

• • •

For Counselors

Technology has revolutionized the world in ways that have had both positive and negative consequences. Broadly construed, technology enables people to connect with others around the world in an instant. As a society, we increasingly rely on innovative technologies to address major global challenges and threats such as climate change. In our personal lives, advanced technologies enable us to access information expediently, no matter how obscure. Whether we need a weather forecast, driving directions to a particular destination, or the answer to a trivia question, the information is at our fingertips. Technology has transformed the pace of life, increased the information flow available to us, and changed how we receive and transmit information. How much do you rely on technology in your practice and in your personal life? Do you find yourself at a loss if you leave your smartphone behind or if the internet is down for a period of time? How do you react when the Wi-Fi connection isn't working properly?

Technology has made truly mindboggling advancements in our ability to communicate around the world, but we would be remiss if we failed to acknowledge some glaring negative consequences of living in the digital age. For example, our attention span is shorter, we are prone to distractions, and being so plugged-in to our smartphones has undermined face-to-face interactions with others (Dwyera, Kushlevb, & Dunna, 2018). When in public spaces such as the grocery store, a shopping mall, or a restaurant, I (Michelle) notice that it is now the norm for people to be looking at or talking on their phones rather than making eye contact with others. Dwyera and colleagues warn that "despite their ability to connect us to others across the globe, phones may undermine the benefits we derive from interacting with those across the table" (p. 233).

Smartphone use has become problematic and even addictive for many people, including children (Ihm, 2018). Some individuals develop *nomophobia*—the fear of being unable to access and communicate with their mobile devices (King et al., 2013). Those who exhibit nomophobic behaviors can experience a range of psychosocial, behavior, and anxiety symptoms that affect their lives when they are away from their mobile devices (Yildiz Durak, 2018). This behavior can hinder academic performance, level of motivation to learn, and relationships with family members and peers. Ihm (2018) has found that the more children become addicted to smartphones the less they engage socially with others.

Researchers at the University of Pennsylvania discovered a causal link between decreasing social media use and improvements in depression and loneliness: "It is ironic, but perhaps not surprising, that reducing social media, which promised to help us connect with others, actually helps people feel less lonely and depressed" (Hunt et al., 2018, p. 767). One possible reason for this is that many social media users compare themselves and their lives unfavorably with others they view on social media posts, which usually highlight only positive experiences and successes. "Some of the existing literature on social media suggests there's an enormous amount of social comparison that happens. When you look at other people's lives, particularly on Instagram, it's easy to conclude that everyone else's life is cooler or better than yours" (Hunt as cited in Berger, 2018). On a related note, results of a University of Pittsburgh national survey demonstrated that people who report using between 7 and 11 social media platforms have more than three times the risk of developing anxiety and depression than those who use two or fewer platforms—even after adjusting for the time spent on social media overall (James, Shensa, Barrett, Sidani, & Colditz, 2019).

Another unfortunate by-product of living in the digital age is the rise of other types of online addictions or patterns of problematic use. Many people have developed addictions to video games (Mathews, Morrell, & Molle, 2019), and others frequent online gambling and shopping websites excessively (Lee, Park, & Lee, 2016). These compulsive habits can lead to distress for the individual as well as for those who care about them. Other problematic online behaviors include cyberbullying, cyberstalking, cybercrimes, and online harassment. In today's technology-focused world, more than 80% of teens use cell phones on a regular basis, and Lancaster (2018) found that about half of these young people claim to have experienced cyberbullying. Cybervictimization has been linked to a constellation of problems, including stress, suicidal ideation, depression, anxiety, loneliness, self-esteem issues, somatic symptoms, conduct problems, and drug and alcohol use, and being a perpetrator of cyberbullying has been linked to many of the same negative outcomes (Kowalski, Giumetti, Schroeder, & Lattanner, 2014; Lancaster, 2018). Those who commit financial cybercrimes, such as identity theft, may have been victimized themselves at some point. One study showed that the victim-perpetrator overlap for financial cybercrime is considerable (Kerstens & Jansen, 2016) and may result from feelings of retaliation, low self-control, and online disinhibition.

Unfortunately, technology is being used in even more nefarious ways, with foreign governments spreading disinformation and interfering in elections, as the Russian government demonstrated in the 2016 U.S. presidential election (Mueller, 2019). Moreover, people with sinister motivations have begun to weaponize social media and technology platforms, drawing massive audiences to witness their criminal behaviors. An Australian citizen who harbored White extremist hatred live-streamed the mass murder of 50 people and the wounding of dozens more in two New Zealand mosques in March 2019. Although Facebook closed the attacker's account within an hour, the video was available long enough to be shared on Facebook, Twitter, and YouTube, and it lives on digitally today.

Technology continues to advance at an accelerated pace, and societal forces such as tribalism, hatred, and divisiveness appear to be gaining momentum. Problems related to the misuse of social media and technology will continue to rise, and we anticipate that counseling and other mental health services will be in greater demand.

What We Have Learned About Helping Others Therapeutically

Many problems likely to affect clients are emerging in this technological world. Some issues may seem more benign than others (at least on the surface); however, they should all be taken seriously. For instance, some clients may be distressed because of the low number of "Likes" they receive on their social media posts in comparison to their Facebook friends. Other clients may be distressed because of cyberstalking or be perpetrators of aggressive acts online. It is important not to minimize the severity of clients' concerns. Clients upset about their lackluster social media presence may have deeper self-esteem issues (e.g., Burrow & Rainone, 2017) or could be experiencing depression or other mental health concerns that are exacerbated by the social comparison effect, a common phenomenon among social media users.

Technological forces are pervasive in everyone's daily lives today. If you are not technologically savvy, we encourage you to learn the basics so you will be equipped to help clients with social media issues or online addictions. In addition, we need to continue to learn about these emerging issues as new research that will undoubtedly inform our practices becomes available.

Individual- and System-Level Interventions

People interact with and use technology in many ways, and no one intervention can address all the related technology and social media problems clients may present in session. Solutions to client problems should be tailored to the individual dynamics, circumstances, and culture of the client. Some programs have been developed to address specific issues, such as cyberbullying, but as yet there is no consensus on which treatment approaches work best. Lancaster (2018) notes that "despite the significant concern about cyberbullying and its potential problematic outcomes, there seems to be a glaring lack of effective evidence-based programs that have been implemented in the United States" (p. 593). She does offer the sage advice that clinicians should be sure to administer programs that target the appropriate systemic level. In schools, for example, cyberbullying interventions should not focus solely on individual-level change. Rather, they should target the school climate as a whole and focus on enacting change at the peer, teacher, parent, and school administration level. As Lancaster (2018) points out, "Change that occurs at the system level may lead to more sustainable individual-level changes" (p. 600). In addition to providing counseling services in schools, Bauman (2011) believes that acceptable use policies can be developed to reduce or prevent cyberbullying in the schools. Installing filter software on computers or using parental control tools on smartphones may also be helpful. Bauman also proposes setting up anonymous reporting systems in schools and workplaces.

The Counselor's Task With Clients

The counselor's task will be determined based on the nature of the issue that burdens your client. Some clients may benefit from exploring how their social media use affects their self-esteem, self-concept, and well-being. Based on research about social media use and depression and anxiety, it may be helpful to encourage clients to keep a log of their social media use and journal about their reactions to others' posts and the meaning they ascribe to what they read online. For instance, if a client believes a Facebook friend's image of marital bliss makes her own marriage seem worse by comparison, the counselor can use that perception as a launching point to explore the client's marital satisfaction. By maintaining a log of actual time spent on social media sites and tracking fluctuations in her mood, your client may realize that she would feel better about her life and marriage if she reduced her social media use.

Some clients may be dealing with cyberbullying, either from the perspective of victim or perpetrator. Victims may benefit from psychoeducation on cyberbullying and learning techniques they can use to protect themselves online. Counselors can also connect clients with legal resources, if necessary. Above all, counselors should commend their cyberbullied clients for having the courage to report the problem, and counselors should remind clients that they are not at fault for their victimization. Victims of cyberbullying may have underlying psychological issues, and efforts should be made to evaluate clients for preexisting or concurrent disorders. Counselors should also assist their clients in finding healthy peer relationships to reduce their sense of loneliness and alienation (Bauman, 2011; Campbell, 2007). "Group counseling may be a particularly effective milieu for cybervictims" (Bauman, 2011, p. 145).

Some cyberbullying offenses may rise to a severity that warrants prosecution, but "lesser" incidents require other remedies. Bauman (2011) cautions counselors about unintended negative outcomes that can result from using punishment, and she promotes strategies that are less likely to engender a defensive posture. A major task is to help cyberbullies develop empathy, and Bauman suggests using stories and video clips about publicized cases to aid this awareness. It is also advisable to involve others in the process, such as family members and peers, rather than working with cyberbullies in isolation. For a more detailed description of this approach, we encourage you to read Bauman's (2011) book, *Cyberbullying: What Counselors Need to Know.*

We strongly encourage you to seek further knowledge on online addictions, financial cybercrimes, and other issues. You may find this information in scholarly journals and research reports, at professional meetings, and, of course, no pun intended, online!

For Clients

Forces of Social Media and Technology

If you are a *digital native* and have grown up using information technology, advancements in the rapidly evolving technology fields may not seem extraordinary. However, if you are a *digital immigrant* (like both of us) and were not introduced to personal computers and smartphones until young adulthood or later, your reaction may be vastly different. You may struggle with how dramatically technological advances have changed the world and the ways people interact today. Surely you have noticed how common it is to see people on their phones and how infrequent it has become for people to make eye contact with each other. We certainly have! Recently, I (Michelle) was in a grocery store and was reaching for a pint of ice cream in the freezer section when another customer—looking intently at her phone—reached in and grabbed it without ever acknowledging that a person (me) was standing right there. I was invisible to her, and she was so absorbed in whatever she was looking at on her phone that she lost sight of her surroundings. How often, I wonder, does this happen? Are people so transfixed by the virtual world that they have little concern for interacting with others in the real world?

Technology: For Better or For Worse

Technology is a wonderful tool, and it has revolutionized many aspects of life, ranging from the way we communicate with others to the type of medical care we receive. Advances in technology help people live longer lives and make life convenient in ways that were never possible before. Our voice-activated devices from Apple, Amazon, or Google have become our helpmates. Technology gives us the opportunity to know what is happening around the world as it is unfolding, and it has equipped us with the tools to do many remarkable things. We can get detailed information about our DNA by simply spitting in a tube and sending it away—something we never could have imagined even a few years ago!

Despite these marvels, technology has also become a major source of stress for people. Those who are active on social media sites may look at other users' photos and postings, which often capture happy moments and successes, and compare themselves unfavorably. Researchers have found a connection between social media use and a risk for depression and anxiety through these *social comparison effects*. These platforms are meant to help us connect with others, but ironically they are leaving us with feelings of isolation, loneliness, and depression. Four out of 5 adults in the United States state that they frequently check their email, text messages, and social media connections (APA, 2017a). Those who identify themselves as "constant checkers" report a higher level of stress than those who do not constantly check. It is worth taking a look to see if dialing back your technology use helps your physical and mental health. Online platforms have also become sources of addiction or problematic use for many people. Some have developed addictions or compulsive behaviors related to online gambling, shopping, gaming, or pornography. Others have been targets or perpetrators of cybercrimes such as identity theft or *cyberbullying*. Because technological forces are so pervasive in all of our lives today, they may be a source of your stress.

Key Thought

You are inundated with technology and social media on your phones, computers, and tablets. It is important to take a step back and look at the impact that is having on your life, your relationships, and your children's lives.

Suggestions for Coping With Forces of Social Media and Technology

The use of technology and the role of social media in our lives is a relatively new field of study and investigation; however, some suggestions for better coping strategies have been identified:

- Track your time on social media.
- Think about your use of social media and what need it fulfills.
- Resist the temptation to compare yourself and your life with that of others on social media platforms.
- Develop a time limit for online use and how often you check in.
- Limit your accounts to those with whom it is essential to stay in touch.
- Assess where social media fits on your priority list in life.
- Identify areas of your life you would like to be spending more time on if you limit your time on social media.
- Drop people from your accounts who harass or bully you online.
- Place smartphones, tablets, and other electronic devices outside of your bedroom while you are sleeping so your sleep is not disrupted.
- Stop using your devices at least an hour before bedtime to reduce psychological stimulation and blue light exposure, which can disturb your sleep.

Workbook Material for the Client

The following questions and exercises are designed to help you examine the topic of coping with technology and social media in your life. There are no right or wrong answers. This is an opportunity for you to spend time thinking about how well you deal with this technology. Some questions and exercises may be easy for you, and others may require more time and thought on your part. We hope you will take plenty of time to consider each topic or question that your counselor has asked you to complete. The value of the activities and questions comes from your careful consideration about your position on the topic. The goal is for you to learn as much as you can outside the counseling setting. If you are better prepared to explore these issues, your session time will be more productive. We suggest that you keep a journal as you contemplate making changes related to your social media and technology use. Purchase a notebook or journal or record your responses to selected questions and activities on your computer. Remember to print your responses and bring them with you to your next counseling session.

Exercises and Activities

1. Track your time to determine how much time you are spending online in that activity. How many hours/minutes per day on average do you spend

    _____ on your smartphone?
    _____ using a tablet/laptop/PC?
    _____ surfing the internet?
    _____ accessing your social media accounts?
    _____ playing video or computer games?

2. Describe how your use of technology, the internet, and social media helps or hinders you in your life. Which aspects/domains of your life are most affected by this use, either positively or negatively?

    _____

    _____

3. Take a break from social media for a few hours and see how you feel. Do you feel anxious and stressed? Do you feel an uncontrollable urge to log on? If you do, you might have a social media addiction. Do you think you may have an addiction to social media?

    _____

    _____

4. If you think you use social media excessively or may even be "addicted" to it, why do you think that

_____

_____

5. When you receive a notification for something online, do you feel a need to check it immediately? How stressful is it for you if you do not check it right away?

_____

_____

6. A common experience in the use of social media is the *fear of missing out* (FOMO).
   a. To what extent do you experience FOMO?

   _____

   _____

   b. What do you think you might be missing out on?

   _____

   _____

   c. What do you fear would happen if you weren't in the know or kept in the loop?

   _____

   _____

   d. Do you always feel the need to know what's going on?

   _____

   _____

7. Describe any feelings of stress, anxiety, depression, loneliness, or anger associated with your use of social media or technology. How mild or severe are these feelings?

   Scale: 1   2   3   4   5   6   7   8   9   10
             Mild   *Severe*

   Describe your feelings:

   _____

8. What is your reaction when you read online that a friend of yours is having a "perfect life," is always happy and successful, and has a ton of friends?

   _____

   _____

9. Have you ever been harassed or bullied online?

   _____

   _____

   a. What was that like for you? How did you cope with it?

   _____

   _____

   b Was there anyone in particular who offered you support during that time?

   _____

   _____

   c. What would you have most wanted to convey to the person who perpetrated this act?

_____

_____

10. Have you ever posted defamatory comments online about a person?

_____

   a. If so, what prompted you to do this?

_____

   b. How did you feel afterward?

_____

   c. Would you have been as inclined to make the same comments if you addressed the person face to face? Explain your response.

_____

11. What impact do you hope your words and online posts will have on others?

_____

   a. What does it mean to you when others respond to your posts in the way you desire?

_____

   b. Conversely, what does it mean to you when others do not respond to your posts in the way that you had hoped, or if others do not respond at all?

_____

12. Take a pause from social media and think about what need it fills in your life. Is it something you do for fun, or do you seem to be checking and comparing yourself to what others post and say online?

_____

13. In general, how would you say the use of social media has affected your self-esteem and self-concept?

_____

14. What would your life be like without using any online technology or accounts?

_____

15. With what people, activities, or hobbies would you like to spend more time if you were to limit your time online?

_____

_____

16. Jessica Bliss (2018), a counselor in Tennessee, often recommends a 30-day blackout from technology when families come to counseling for problems with technology use and online connectivity. That means no cell phones, no computer use, and no television (for the entire family)! The only exception is for school-related or work-related issues. Bliss tells her clients that the first week will be "hell on earth," but the net result is typically restored family relationships and a realization that online is not real life.

   a. What do you think about that idea? Could you do that?

   _____

   _____

   b. Think about having your family take a technology break for a week (or a month if you think the family can manage), and describe how that is for everyone.

   _____

   _____

   c. What did you learn?

   _____

   _____

17. Where does technology fit on your list of priorities for life for you and your family? What are some things you can do to make family time and relationships more of a priority?

   _____

   _____

18. Some people were not introduced to personal computers and smartphones until young adulthood or later and are referred to as *digital immigrants*. If you consider yourself a digital immigrant, how is it to navigate a world that seems increasingly wedded to technology?

   _____

   _____

19. To what degree does your presence on social media help you to feel connected to others?

   Scale: 1   2   3   4   5   6   7   8   9   10
         Disconnected   *Connected*

   Explain:

   _____

20. To what degree does your activity on social media help you feel productive?

   Scale: 1   2   3   4   5   6   7   8   9   10
                                                 Extremely
         Nonproductive   *productive*

   Explain:

   _____

21. To what degree does your presence on social media make you feel happy?

   Scale: 1   2   3   4   5   6   7   8   9   10
          Extremely   *Extremely*
          unhappy   *happy*

   Explain:

   _____

Part V

Going Forward: Counselor Self-Care and Client Life After Counseling

In Part V we turn our attention to the mental health and well-being of counselors and to issues related to terminating with clients. Serving clients in distress for hours on end can be exhausting, especially if counselors do not have a good self-care regimen in place to combat stress and prevent burnout. Having a career in helping others does not make us immune from the pressures and stresses that affect others. Counselors may experience interpersonal conflicts with family members, friends, and colleagues, divorce and custody battles, financial troubles, physical and mental health problems, the death of family members and loved ones, discrimination and social injustices, and struggles to find a healthy work-life balance (Corey & Corey, 2016).

In some instances, we might be able to anticipate stressors (e.g., a loved one's death after a long battle with a terminal illness); at other times these stressors catch us off guard. Therapist Judy Van Der Wende described the horror and disbelief she experienced when both a mass shooting and a catastrophic wildfire devastated her community within 24 hours (see Chapter 8).

> As a therapist, you are constantly torn between taking care of yourself and being available to assist suffering clients. Every single person I spoke with at this point was going through the same panicked process.

Days later she reported,

> I heard other therapists were overwhelmed and experiencing burnout. It was unsettling to hear that therapists were struggling, even though I shared the struggle. Therapy became combined with funerals and grief counseling. The grief at times was unbearable.

After the Sandy Hook Elementary School shooting in 2012, counselor Deb Del Vecchio-Scully (2018) was shocked when she learned that the unthinkable had happened in her community:

I can vividly remember that day in my office, when one of the staff told me the news. I turned to social media to learn the details, and I was shocked by what I read . . . 12 kindergartners were among those killed . . . the death toll continued to climb to 26 and then 28, and the children killed were changed to first graders. I sat at my desk stunned and sickened. I had to see clients that afternoon; many chose to stay at home as they struggled with their own feelings of sadness. (p. 249)

We are mere mortals, and although our arsenal of coping strategies may be more robust and sophisticated than those of our clients due to our advantage of education and training in counseling or psychotherapy, most of us don't put our knowledge and skills into practice in our own lives at all times.

In these divisive and polarizing times, counselors may be more at risk of experiencing countertransference issues when clients discuss political and ethical values that are at odds with their own. Although our training stresses that we remain fair, objective, and unbiased, counselors may be inclined to take a position on some highly charged issues. Now, more than ever, we need to remain vigilant and self-aware and monitor the critical role our values and beliefs may play in counseling. As careful as we may be, sometimes we allow our biases to show.

Chapter 14 describes some of the hazards of helping, especially in increasingly stressful times. The exercises in this chapter focus on helping counselors effectively cope with their caseloads of stressed and traumatized clients. Chapter 15 provides information to assist counselors in processing their feelings about ending their relationships with clients. Then we focus on resources and exercises to help clients say goodbye to this counseling relationship and prepare for life after counseling.

Chapter 14

Compassion Fatigue, Vicarious Traumatization, and Burnout

Love yourself first, and everything else falls in line.
You really have to love yourself to get anything done in this world.

—Lucille Ball

...

This chapter focuses solely on counselors and the importance of having an established self-care regimen to guard against compassion fatigue, vicarious traumatization, and burnout. Counselors actively listen to clients' stories, and responding to these pain-filled stories may affect counselors' emotional balance over time. Self-care is an essential aspect of counselors' well-being.

For Counselors

Self-care is a collection of positive actions that foster wellness and effective coping (Corey, Muratori, Austin, & Austin, 2018). As a professional helper, you are probably well aware of the importance of self-care as the basis for caring for others. Although counseling graduate programs emphasize self-care for their trainees, many students find it challenging to put self-care into practice while juggling coursework, a practicum or internship, a demanding job and family responsibilities, and so on. We've known students who say, "When I graduate and start my career, I will have more time for self-care, but I am just too busy right now." Of course, after graduating and launching their careers, and without the reinforcement of professors and clinical supervisors reminding them of their ethical obligation to practice good self-care, counselors may find it easy to let self-care slip off their radar—especially those who are focused on mastering new and demanding roles in their personal and professional lives.

In recounting his challenging transition from being a doctoral student to working at a university counseling center, Julius A. Austin listed a series of major events that occurred in his life within a 1-year period. While finishing his dissertation, this young professional did a job search and accepted a position at a university, married his fiancée and learned that they were expecting their first child, and purchased a home. Austin noted: "Until this last year, I was not fully aware that even positive life changes are associated with some degree of stress. With all these major life changes, I did not find time for self-care, and I disregarded my mental and physical health" (Corey, Muratori, et al., 2018, p. 35).

When we overextend ourselves in our personal or professional lives, it can be challenging to put self-care into practice. We both have struggled at various points in our careers to make self-care our priority, and we can appreciate the challenges associated with making time for self-care.

Counselors in Pain: The Self-Care Paradox

Many counselors are inclined to put the needs of others ahead of their own needs, and they may struggle with making wellness a top priority. Whether you are a counselor trainee or a seasoned professional, you will pay a steep price for chronic neglect of your emotional, mental, physical, and spiritual well-being. One clinician, professor, and writer described his agonizing experience coping with a personal crisis. Moffatt (2018) courageously writes about how his failing marriage negatively influenced his professional competence, worldview, and sense of self because he sorely neglected caring for himself. Now, in a much healthier state of mind, Moffatt reflects on what he refers to as the *self-care paradox*:

> This is such a bizarre paradox. Counselors, of all people, should know better. We are trained to take care of ourselves, and we emphasize the importance of self-care to our clients. Yet my self-confidence in those days caused me to naively believe that crisis wouldn't knock on my door. I think in some ways, when counselors talk about self-care it is more of an academic conversation than a real one. It may be something like the fact that we all know we are going to die someday, but it isn't real to us until we stare it square in the face. (p. 54)

Using his own painful journey as a cautionary tale, Moffatt provides useful tips for other helpers in taking preventive measures to avoid impairment. We believe that the following points he makes have merit:

- Don't wait for crisis to strike before finding your own counselor.
- To maintain good mental health, take care of your body by exercising, eating well, and getting adequate rest.
- Boost your happiness and reduce your stress by making time to play.
- Know your limits regarding how much you can manage, and set boundaries with the work commitments you make.
- Remember that being a counselor doesn't make you immune from experiencing problems in life any more than being an oncologist makes one immune from developing cancer.
- Engage in supervision or interact with a mentor (even after you have attained your license or counseling credential) to have a second set of eyes to help evaluate your competence and ability to engage with clients, especially when you are experiencing a crisis.

Reinforcing Moffatt's advice, Stebnicki (2017) points out that supervisors can play an integral role in assisting counselor trainees in developing an ongoing practice of self-assessment and self-care that decreases the risk of burnout and impairment.

Scope of the Problem: Burnout, Counselor Impairment, Fatigue Syndromes, and Vicarious Traumatization

As a counselor trainee in graduate school, you were indoctrinated with advice about self-care and were repeatedly cautioned about the hazards of burnout, and with good reason. Neglecting self-care and failing to take steps to replenish ourselves can have a debilitating effect on us. As we saw in Moffatt's case, however, understanding concepts intellectually doesn't always directly translate to having a real grasp of their importance—until you are personally affected by them.

Burnout involves much more than experiencing fleeting feelings of being tired or fatigued. It is a chronic condition that encompasses emotional exhaustion, depersonalization, and reduced personal accomplishment (Maslach, 1993; Maslach, Jackson, & Leiter, 1996). It is difficult to pinpoint how widespread burnout is today in the mental health and counseling fields, but one research group found that between 21% and 67% of mental health workers may be experiencing high levels of burnout (Morse, Salyers, Rollins, Monroe-DeVita, & Pfahler, 2012).

In *Leaving It at the Office: A Guide to Psychotherapist Self-Care*, Norcross and VandenBos (2018) address the reasons burnout is thriving. In their view, the "grim truth about behavioral health practice is that organizations create much of the exhaustion and demoralization behind burnout" (p. 185). They note a number of factors that can contribute to this condition. In institutional settings, mental health workers may perceive a lack of control in their jobs, feel overworked and insufficiently compensated or rewarded for the work they do, and believe they are not receiving fair treatment. In addition, they may experience a breakdown in community and have to contend with conflicting values in these settings. In other words, "the prevalence of burnout is exploding because of the social environments in which people work" (p. 185).

Norcross and VandenBos (2018) have also identified a variety of prominent hazards that come with the territory of conducting psychotherapy. They recognize that *patient behaviors* such as suicidal statements and attempts, violence, hostile transference, anger directed toward the therapist, intense resistance, passive-aggression, low motivation and apathy, severe depression, and other forms of psychopathology can take their toll on us and may "color our perceptions of society and humanity" (p. 45). In addition, *psychic isolation*, which comes with the ethical responsibility of maintaining confidentiality while also controlling emotions, withholding personal information, setting aside personal concerns, and engaging in one-way intimacy, can leave us feeling lonely and separate from others. Norcross and VandenBos also point to hazards inherent in *therapeutic relationships*, including responsibility for patients, a lack of gratitude from clients, countertransference, challenges in working with disturbed individuals, and other stressors. They discuss the common hazards of *emotional depletion* that can result from experiencing boredom or monotony with patients and a lack of therapeutic success, having difficulty leaving psychodynamics at the office, identifying with patients' psychopathology, and experiencing compassion fatigue or secondary traumatization. Norcross and VandenBos also remind us that mental health practitioners are not immune from the *personal disruptions* that others in society experience in everyday living. Counselors too may face illness or disability, financial problems, the death or loss of loved ones, divorce, marriage, pregnancy, parenthood, and a multitude of other positive and negative stressors.

We are keenly aware of the toxicity of the current political climate and the resultant spike in stress and anxiety that seems inescapable in today's world. Most, if not all, of us are affected by this noxious sociopolitical climate. In fact, a major impetus for embarking on this project was our observation of the toxic conditions in society—increasing tribalism, racial animus, and intolerance of "the other." Mental health professionals are exposed to a potent dose of negativity on a continuous basis these days simply by turning on the news. A large proportion of clients (64% to be precise) want to discuss politics with their therapists, and many would have liked to discuss politics even more in their sessions (Solomonov & Barber, 2018; also see Chapter 11). Consequently, even if counselors set boundaries by limiting their own news consumption, their clients are likely to remind them of what is in the news.

One of the most nerve-wracking aspects of being a mental health clinician is the inevitability of facing ethical dilemmas and the threat of ethical violations and malpractice. As Norcross and VandenBos (2018) point out, "the threat of malpractice can paralyze us and cause us to practice too defensively" (p. 49). One group of investigators studied the relationship between practicing counselors' experiences with ethical dilemmas and their stress and burnout and discovered that those who observed higher rates of ethical dilemmas were more likely to report experiencing higher levels of stress and burnout (Mullen, Morris, & Lord, 2017). Concerned about the well-being of counselors who encounter ethical quandaries, Mullen and colleagues encourage counselors to consider the collateral costs of facing and managing ethical situations and to acknowledge the stress resulting from such experiences. They caution counselors against ignoring their own emotional response and endorse incorporating coping strategies into the resolution of ethical problems to mitigate the personal effects of stress on counselors.

While maintaining a high level of ethics and professionalism, many counselors are challenged even further by the daunting number of clients who are presenting with symptoms of trauma. Compared to past years, Foreman (2018) notes that counselors are reporting a higher proportion of their caseloads being comprised of clients who have been traumatized. It is possible that there is a higher incidence rate of traumatic experiences today, but we must not rule out the possibility that traumatized people are seeking treatment more frequently, perhaps viewing counseling as less stigmatizing than in previous times. Foreman cautions that due "to the increasing number of clients seeking counseling who have experienced trauma, counselors are at a greater risk for developing vicarious traumatization and becoming impaired" (p. 142).

When engaging in intense therapeutic work with traumatized clients, counselors may experience an internal transformation of their perceptions of themselves and question their own competence, the trustworthiness of others, and the safety of all of us in the world (Foreman, 2018). The estimated prevalence rate of *vicarious traumatization* is 45.9% among counselors (Dunkley & Whelan, 2006; Foreman, 2018). Counselors who work in the disaster mental health field are especially vulnerable to stress given the nature of their work and the conditions they encounter. These counselors are affected both personally and professionally by multisystemic disasters and are advised to acknowledge their own trauma and status as "survivors." At the massive Camp Fire that scorched a vast area of California in November 2018, counselors providing assistance to the tens of thousands of victims are at a substantial risk of developing vicarious traumatization. Many of the counselors providing services were themselves victims of the fire and lost homes, businesses, possessions, and even friends or family members in that destructive fire.

In the face of increasing numbers of large-scale disasters, "the potential for [counselors] experiencing vicarious trauma is great" (Webber & Mascari, 2018a, p. 174). Helping professionals affected by their work with victims may appear to hold rigid beliefs; become cynical, anxious, and depressed; and withdraw socially. If left unaddressed, they may head down the dangerous path toward impairment.

Helping professionals may feel *compassion fatigue* or *empathy fatigue* as a result of listening compassionately and empathically to their clients' pain-saturated stories. These counselors should monitor themselves for signs of depletion, distress, and impairment. Gentry, Webber, and Baranowsky (2018) state that compassion fatigue can develop as a function of bearing witness to trauma and suffering and that it develops in phases. Initially, in the *zealot/idealist* phase, counselors may be extremely dedicated and energetic and may even work overtime. As they transition into the *irritable* phase, they may appear distracted and distant and perhaps be critical of their colleagues despite making their own mistakes. In the third phase, *withdrawal*, these stressed counselors tend to be tired and neglectful, which may have a negative impact on their family life. If they begin to feel hopeless or enraged, to hate clients and lack patience, and to lack a capacity for fun or humor, they are likely in the *zombie* phase. In this final phase, "counselors must make a choice between emotional and physical illness or a transformation toward health and growth" (p. 84).

Mark A. Stebnicki is credited with coining the term *empathy fatigue*. Here he explains the phenomenon in depth and offers sage advice to counselors for developing a personal growth program.

Empathy Fatigue: Healing Counselor Wounds

Mark A. Stebnicki

Stories told by many indigenous peoples claim that each time the shaman heals others the shaman gives away a piece of her or his own mind, body, and spirit. The journey to become a medicine man or woman requires an understanding that the healer will become wounded and require healing at some time (Tafoya

& Kouris, 2003). Henri Nouwen (1972), a Catholic priest, professor of theology, and prolific writer on psychospirituality and theology, referred to this experience as the *wounded healer*. He describes helpers as withdrawing or stepping away from their own internal issues to create a space for those they are caring for to benefit from the healers' intense empathy and compassion. Many modern day healers, such as psychologists and counselors, also encounter a wounded healer experience after working at very intense levels of person-made and natural disasters. I refer to this phenomenon as *empathy fatigue*.

Empathy fatigue results from a state of psychological, emotional, mental, physical, spiritual, and occupational exhaustion that occurs as counselors' own wounds are continually revisited by their clients' life stories of chronic illness, disability, trauma, grief, and loss (Stebnicki, 1999, 2000, 2001, 2007, 2008, 2016). It is different from compassion fatigue, burnout, and other professional fatigue syndromes because of the existential and spiritual qualities that intensify this experience. I hypothesize that this experience may be different from other types of counselor impairment primarily because empathy fatigue

1. is viewed as a form of counselor impairment that can occur early in one's career due to an interaction of variables including, but not limited to, personality traits, general coping resources, age and developmental related factors, opportunities to build resiliency, appropriate job matches and aptitudes for certain professions, organizational and other environmental supports that may or may not exist within the work culture, and the interrelationship between the person's mind, body, and spiritual development;
2. many times goes unrecognized by the individual and the professional counseling setting or environment because of its subtle characteristics;
3. may be experienced as both an acute and cumulative type of emotional, physical, and spiritual stressor that does not follow a predictable linear path to total burnout or fatigue;
4. is a highly individualized experience for most individuals because the counselor's perception toward the client's story and life events differs depending upon the issues presented during session; and
5. is a dynamic construct where the search for personal meaning in one's chronic illness, disability, traumatic experience, pain, and suffering is an existential, moral, and spiritual pursuit.

It is of paramount importance that professional counselors, counselor educators, and clinical supervisors recognize this negative shift within the professional counselor's mind, body, and spirit that may signal an experience of empathy fatigue.

Many indigenous cultures view our spiritual capacity to serve others as a type of soul loss or soul wounding experience (Stebnicki, 2016) that may require a "soul retrieval" (Harner, 1990; Ingerman, 1991). The soul loss or wounding experience makes our chi or body energy vulnerable. There is a sense that we are giving away our capacity to heal others. Consequently, when we have no protective aura, our spiritual resource is exposed. Within the context of Western counseling and psychology, we may be experiencing transference or countertransference with our clients.

Many counselors spend a tremendous amount of time and energy acting in compassionate and empathic ways, searching for the meaning of their client's soul that has been lost to trauma, addictions, and other stressful life events. Some professionals may question whether they are preordained for the counseling profession. Due to the nature of the counseling profession, counselors may become affected by the transient physical, emotional, and psychological symptoms reported by their clients. Searching through our clients' emotional scrapbooks can entail a personal physical, mental, and spiritual cost.

Measuring Empathy Fatigue

Recognizing and identifying salient features of empathy fatigue may be enhanced by the Global Assessment of Empathy Fatigue (GAEF) rating scale, which is a theoretical measure of the holistic experience of empathy fatigue (see Stebnicki, 2016). The scale categorizes five levels of functioning: Level V (most impaired) indicates the highest level, and Level I (least impaired) indicates the lowest level of empathy fatigue. Within each of the five levels, professional helpers may experience and project this felt-sense experience in seven distinct content areas: (1) cognitively, (2) behaviorally, (3) spiritually, (4) process/counseling skills, (5) emotionally, (6) physically, and (7) occupationally. GAEF assessments score each of these areas based on observations by self and others in the professional helper's environment. Overall, it is hypothesized that each professional suffering from empathy fatigue differs in his or her frequency, intensity, level of intrusion, and avoidance, and that these factors may be both acute and cumulative in nature.

Cultivating a Personal Growth Program

Taking care of yourself begins by recognizing, identifying, preventing, and preparing your mind, body, and spirit for the counseling profession. It is foundational for maintaining competent and ethical professional practice. Corey, Muratori, et al. (2018) believe it is essential for mental health professionals to attend to their physical, psychological, intellectual, social, and spiritual needs because counseling professionals are compassionate people. They are good at attending to others' self-care, but at times they neglect to nourish their own. This type of work-related stress has a psychological, physical, and behavioral cost that may result in symptoms of depression, anxiety, and emotional exhaustion (Corey & Corey, 2021).

Cultivating personal growth in the counseling profession is a dynamic and interactive process, and I have offered multiple personal growth programs to heal trauma and cultivate self-care (see Stebnicki, 2001, 2007, 2016, 2017). Each has been developed from theories, models, and approaches that range from humanistic, cognitive behavioral, and mindfulness stress reduction to culturally indigenous healing practices. Here are four ways to cultivate the seeds of personal growth that nourish your mind, body, and spirit and enhance your work in the profession you have chosen.

1. *Challenge yourself to learn a new healing approach.* As I have learned from my Level I, II, and III Reiki Master training, as well as my beginning and intermediate level shaman training, cultivating personal growth begins by trying something new, a foundational principle of resiliency. About 75% of our communication with one another is nonverbal. Becoming attuned to metacommunication from indigenous teachings brings an additive dimension to your professional practice as a therapist. Finding a mentor that matches your personal interests and spirit-to-work opens new pathways for a personal journey, adding another dimension to your counseling practice. Some other pathways include yoga, tai chi, Qi Gong, mindfulness meditation, walking a labyrinth, drumming circle, and meditative walks in natural settings.

2. *Create a sacred space to practice your profession.* I have been mindful of creating a sacred environment that matches my mind, body, and spirit in many therapeutic environments in which I have worked. You may choose to create good Feng Shui with the appropriate amount of soft lighting, introduce aromas in your sacred space with the use of a diffuser (i.e., essential oils), project sound therapy through different digital media, provide comfortable furnishings, or incorporate works of art, photos, and other meaningful items that you can draw from for inspiration throughout your day.

3. *Cultivate social and interpersonal relationships.* Cultivating meaningful social and interpersonal relationships with coworkers, friends, mentors, supervisors, and other colleagues provides a natural support system. It is critical to cultivate positive social and interpersonal supports to enhance your socioemotional well-being. Withdrawing from typical work-related activities (e.g., going to lunch with coworkers, attending after work social functions) may be a sign of professional fatigue.

4. *Get movement into your day.* Longevity studies have found that people who live to be 100 years old or more have always participated in movement in their culture and environment. You do not have to be a member of an elite fitness club to gain range of motion, physical activity, or cardiovascular health. In most urban and rural areas, riding a bike, walking to work, or walking to the store is not possible. So it is incumbent upon you to create your own movement activities in your life, which might include outdoor activities such as gardening or walking in natural areas or a structured group activity or class of like-minded people engaged in the same movement activity.

Conclusion

Professional counselors who have client exposure to extraordinarily stressful and traumatic life events may be predisposed to an empathy fatigue reaction. This can range on a continuum from low to high fatigue. Empathy fatigue is both similar and different from other types of counselor impairment or professional fatigue syndromes. It is hypothesized that the cumulative effects of multiple client sessions throughout the week may lead to a deterioration of the counselor's resiliency or coping abilities. Developing a clearer understanding of the risk factors associated with empathy fatigue is pivotal for professional counselors when developing their self-care strategies.

• • •

Mitigating the Effects of Stress and Bolstering Resilience Through Self-Care

To succeed in meeting the demands of our professional commitments in an increasingly stressful world, "our self-care should mirror the care we provide to others" (Corey, Muratori, et al., 2018, p. 1). Just as counselors individualize treatment goals and plans to meet clients' unique needs and increase the likelihood that they will comply with services, it is essential to create a self-care plan for ourselves that is tailored to our specific needs and interests. If you invest your time and energy in creating a self-care plan, it is logical to create a plan you are inspired to put into action, not simply file away in a drawer. One salient lesson I (Michelle) learned from coauthoring *Counselor Self-Care* (see Corey, Muratori, et al., 2018) is that each of the 52 guest contributors followed their own unique self-care journey. Helpers with varied experience, backgrounds, and expertise in the helping professions all reinforced the idea that "no one person has the ideal formula for optimal self-care" (p. viii).

Stress-reducing self-care strategies might include one or a combination of the following practices: meditation, mindfulness, relaxation, tai chi, yoga, Pilates, being in touch with nature, a healthy and well-balanced diet, exercise, recreation and fun, serving others, and self-reflection (Corey, Muratori, et al., 2018). The best self-care strategies for you may not be feasible or appealing to another helper—and vice versa. Of course, the possibilities are endless. It seems safe to say that the best self-care practices are in the eye of the beholder. For instance, while some of us (e.g., Bob) enjoy camping in national parks for recreation and relaxation, others (e.g., Michelle) would much prefer to stay in a hotel—far, far away from spiders and other creepy crawlers! We both enjoy spending time in nature, but we approach it differently.

Another important pathway to taking care of yourself is participating in personal psychotherapy or counseling. Norcross and VandenBos (2018) claim that approximately three-quarters of practitioners have availed themselves of personal psychotherapy and, in many cases, have done so on several occasions. They suggest that personal treatment strengthens your personal functioning and improves your professional competence. Personal therapy can also deepen your perception of personal and interpersonal dynamics and conflicts. It can lead to clearer perceptions of client dynamics and reduce countertransference and distorted or contaminated reactions. Moreover, seeking personal therapy can lessen the impact of emotional burdens that are an inherent part of conducting counseling or psychotherapy and can reinforce the validity of psychotherapy and its transformative power. Finally, placing yourself in the role of the client may sensitize you to your clients' interpersonal reactions, needs, and struggles (Norcross & VandenBos, 2018). As consumers of personal therapy prior to and at points throughout our careers in the counseling field, both of us can attest to these benefits. In addition to helping us process our own personal issues, making ourselves vulnerable as clients has given us a more nuanced understanding of the therapeutic process, which has helped us tremendously in our professional roles.

Another critical aspect of self-care is establishing and maintaining healthy boundaries both *within* and *between* the personal and professional realms of your life. This can be a formidable challenge today as technological advances continue to blur the boundaries between work and personal time (Corey, Muratori, et al., 2018). Helping professionals are also extremely attached to our devices, and we need to remind ourselves to "unplug" sometimes. Exercise good judgment in determining the parameters related to your client "availability." Clinicians "on call" at their organizations may have a professional and ethical obligation to be available to consult with clients at all hours of the night on certain days, but those working in a private practice or at an agency may choose to limit their availability outside of sessions to emergencies only. Of course, there are many other options in between. The key is to make your policies regarding these boundaries abundantly clear so others are aware of your expectations and limits. Striving to find a balance between work and recreation, even if that balance needs to shift at times, and learning to effectively manage your personal and professional responsibilities are crucial to managing stress. For more on the topic of managing boundary issues in counseling, see Herlihy and Corey (2015).

Approaching self-care by attending to the various dimensions of your life and well-being in a holistic manner rather than focusing on a single domain (such as diet and nutrition *or* social life) may help to strengthen your resilience and prevent conditions such as compassion or empathy fatigue, burnout, or vicarious traumatization from taking hold. Foreman's (2018) pilot research study found that a counselor's overall wellness predicted lower levels of vicarious traumatization. We owe it to ourselves and to our clients to embrace a lifestyle of wellness.

Jude T. Austin II, a licensed professional counselor, assistant professor at the University of Mary Hardin-Baylor, and coauthor of *Counselor Self-Care* (Corey, Muratori, et al., 2018), describes his unique perspective on self-care. Rather than viewing self-care as tasks to be completed or actions to be taken to maintain one's sense of well-being, Austin views self-care as a relational process.

One Counselor's Relationship With Self-Care

Jude T. Austin II

I engage in self-care by first building a realistic relationship with my self-care process. In relationships with people, I find patience, unconditional positive regard, flexibility, and grace to be attractive characteristics. I try to uphold these characteristics within my relationship to self-care. Just as with other real relationships, there are times throughout the day when I feel closer to or more distant from self-care. I respect this ebb and flow. I do not fight it, because when I do, I become self-critical. Judgment seeps into this relationship when I maintain a "fail/fix" relationship with self-care. For example, if I develop a workout plan and miss a day, I feel like I let myself down and I need to "fix" this by working out the following day. Of course, something comes up the next day, and I end up missing my workout, triggering a sense of "failure."

To avoid this vicious cycle, I look for activities that offer flexibility when building my relationship with self-care. For example, I recently picked up golf as a leisure activity. I did not set up a schedule in which I must play a round of golf once a week, practice a certain amount of times per month, or hit a certain number of golf balls. Instead, I committed to making golf a part of my life for this semester. I do that by listening to an audiobook about golf and tuning in the golf channel when I am sitting at home or in my office working. I bought some plastic balls, and I practice chipping them when I want to take a break from writing or grading papers. I play a round of golf when my schedule allows—once or twice a month, 4 times a month, or once every 2 months. I try to build a relationship with golf that works for me. When I try to cram self-care strategies into my life in ways that don't fit well with my lifestyle, they seem to fade away.

• • •

The following exercises and activities are designed to help you, the helper, examine how well you are taking care of yourself. We hope it will motivate you to create a realistic self-care plan to enhance your well-being. We encourage you to take an honest inventory of the ways in which you are currently nourishing and replenishing yourself and living a satisfying life as well as the ways in which you might improve.

Exercises and Activities

Counselor Self-Care, Vicarious Traumatization, and Fatigue Syndrome

1. Think about how you felt about your work when you first entered the field (or started your professional training) and how you feel about it now. Write a letter from your past professional self (PPS) to your current professional self (CPS). Write about what your hopes were when you first became a counselor and whether your career has unfolded as planned. How does your PPS feel toward your CPS? For example, have you lived up to your initial expectations or exceeded them? Include anything in the letter your PPS would like to say to your CPS. Pay attention to feelings that come up for you as you write.

_____

_____

2. Write a letter from your CPS to your past professional self. Describe some of the greatest challenges you have faced as a counselor. If your career path took an unexpected turn at any point, describe how that was for you. What messages would you most like to convey to your PPS?

_____

_____

3. Write a letter from your CPS to your future professional self (FPS). What are you hoping your FPS will accomplish? If you currently are not satisfied in your career, how would you like your FPS to feel or behave differently than you do now? What will it require for you to achieve this?

_____

_____

4. Jude T. Austin II describes having a realistic relationship with his self-care program. Describe the relationship you currently have with self-care.

_____

_____

   a. How satisfied are you with it?

_____

_____

   b. In what ways would you like to improve or change your relationship with it?

_____

_____

   c. List three to five steps you could take to move in this direction. How likely are you to take each of these steps?

_____

_____

5. We know good self-care is a desired state, but why is it so difficult to attain?

_____

_____

a. Describe your greatest barriers to achieving your self-care goals.

_____

_____

b. If you were your own client, how would you work therapeutically to change your self-care patterns?

_____

_____

6. An important aspect of self-care is the ability to establish and maintain healthy boundaries, both within and between the personal and professional realms of your life.
   a. How would you describe your boundaries?

_____

_____

   b. Is there anything you would like to change about them?

_____

_____

   c. If so, how do you think this would improve your personal or professional life?

_____

_____

7. What role does social media and technology use play in your personal and professional life?

_____

_____

   a. In what ways does it positively and negatively affect your quality of life?

_____

_____

   b. How has it affected your relationships with others?

_____

_____

   c. How has it affected your mood and self-esteem?

_____

_____

   d. Would you like to make any changes with regard to your use of social media or other electronic technologies?

_____

_____

8. One hazard of being a counselor and seeing clients all day long is insufficient movement.
   a. How much movement or physical activity do you get each day or week?

_____

_____

   b. If you are not getting enough exercise, how motivated are you to make changes in this area?

_____

_____

   c. In what forms of activity are you most inclined or least likely to engage?

_____

_____

9. Review the phases (zealot/idealist, irritable, withdrawal, zombie) described in the chapter.
   a. Have you developed compassion fatigue from your work with trauma survivors?

   _____

   _____

   b. Which phase most closely captures where you see yourself?

   _____

   _____

   c. What could you do to relieve your symptoms of compassion fatigue and regain your energy?

   _____

   _____

10. Do particular clients trigger your countertransference (including political countertransference)?

   _____

   _____

   a. Describe how you are triggered and what comes up for you when interacting with these clients.

   _____

   _____

   b. List some strategies you could use to address your reactions.

   _____

   _____

11. Stebnicki describes empathy fatigue as an acute and cumulative type of emotional, physical, and spiritual stressor in reaction to clients' life stories of chronic illness, disability, trauma, grief, and loss.
   a. Have you experienced empathy fatigue? If so, describe what the experience was like for you.

   _____

   _____

   b. What toll has it taken on you and on your relationships?

   _____

   _____

12. Stebnicki says that "cultivating meaningful social and interpersonal relationships with coworkers, friends, mentors, supervisors, and other colleagues provides a natural support system."
   a. How would you describe your support system?

   _____

   _____

   b. Are your social and interpersonal relationships with coworkers, friends, and colleagues satisfying to you?

   _____

   _____

   c. If not, what could you do to change this?

   _____

   _____

13. Stebnicki emphasizes the importance of creating a sacred environment (or physical space) where you practice counseling that is aligned with your mind, body, and spirit.
    a. How would you describe your office? Is it inviting, or does it lack warmth and aesthetic appeal?

    _____

    _____

    b. If you are not satisfied with it, what could you do to make it a more inviting space?

    _____

    _____

14. The prevalence rate of vicarious traumatization is rather steep. This phenomenon is becoming all too common as greater demands are being placed on mental health professionals who work in highly stressful settings such as disaster zones.
    a. Have you experienced vicarious traumatization?

    _____

    _____

    b. If so, what has that been like, and how has it adversely affected you personally and professionally?

    _____

    _____

15. To improve your happiness, try maintaining a gratitude journal, and list a few things you are grateful for each day. In stressful times, that may seem like a difficult task to accomplish, but even identifying life's small pleasures (e.g., eating a delicious meal or listening to inspiring music) can make a world of difference.

    _____

    _____

Chapter 15

Preparing Clients for Life After Counseling

How lucky I am to have something that makes saying goodbye so hard.
—A. A. Milne

• • •

In this chapter, we provide exercises and activities for both counselors and clients. Although counselors and clients may share some emotions in saying goodbye, the work of counselors is quite different from the work of clients at the termination of counseling. Both counselors and clients will benefit from thoughtful explorations of this phase of the therapy relationship.

For Counselors

It seems fitting to end this workbook with a chapter devoted to the termination phase of counseling. We have provided an array of homework exercises and activities to assist clients in reaching their treatment goals. When clients have made substantive progress toward their goals, counselors know that termination is on the horizon. Whether you conduct brief therapy or longer term psychotherapy, the final stage of counseling is just as important as the other stages. Clients have invested themselves in an intense therapeutic process, and they deserve to experience a satisfying end to this process in which they can make meaning of their therapeutic journey. Norcross, Zimmerman, Greenberg, and Swift (2017) examined the core termination behaviors of experienced therapists who subscribed to a range of theoretical orientations. The following tasks were endorsed by the vast majority of practitioners:

- Discuss what went well in therapy.
- Recognize both improvements and areas of growth for clients during psychotherapy.
- Encourage clients to take responsibility for their success in therapy.

- Formulate future goals and create plans to help clients achieve them.
- Abide by the ethical guidelines.

Helping clients translate their learning into action is one of the most important functions during the final phase of counseling (Corey & Corey, 2016, 2021). If clients have met their goals, the ending phase can be viewed as a *commencement*; clients are now equipped with new tools to use and new directions to explore in dealing with problems as they arise. Providing your clients with resources that may be useful to them after counseling ends is one way to support them in continuing their growth without your direct guidance.

Saying Goodbye and Parting Ways: Ending the Therapeutic Journey

In our personal lives, each of us has our own unique way of experiencing endings, and clients and counselors also have individual perceptions about ending their relationship. People form attachments to other people, and we all are affected emotionally when faced with the task of detaching or separating from others. The specific circumstances surrounding separation or detachment will influence the way we experience the loss as well as the degree of intensity of our reaction. For instance, the magnitude of the loss related to ending a long-term relationship with a partner due to infidelity will be much greater than that of ending a relationship with a casual acquaintance or a Facebook friend over political differences. Our styles of attaching and detaching from others is quite complex and may have its origins in our early development. Pioneering attachment theorists Mary Ainsworth and John Bowlby (1965) advanced our understanding of the critical importance of our early interactions with caregivers in developing attachment behaviors or styles. Those who developed a secure attachment style as children may have an easier time managing relationships and balancing separateness with togetherness as adults. Those who developed anxious-ambivalent or anxious-avoidant attachment styles early in life may struggle to navigate close relationships in adulthood.

Some counselors may have a vulnerability to loss based on their own early life experiences and may experience anxiety and depression when their clients terminate the process (Boyer & Hoffman, 1993). Humphrey (2009) recommends that "counseling professionals explore their own loss histories to enhance their understanding of the nature and impact of loss and grief in their lives" (p. 219). Boyer and Hoffman (1993) believe the counselor's perception of the client's sensitivity to loss also plays a role in heightening the counselor's anxiety during the termination phase. In working with clients who have been traumatized or exposed to multiple losses, counselors must be vigilant about monitoring their own countertransference triggers and take steps to protect themselves from absorbing or internalizing their clients' projections. As in navigating the previous stages of the therapeutic process, you must remain alert to your own unfinished business during the ending phase as you help your clients cope with all of their feelings related to termination.

We encourage you to keep the process of termination *collaborative*. One team of scholars made the following observation:

> Although many therapists seek to build a collaborative working relationship with their clients when making treatment decisions, collaboration is also an important technique that can be used to help clients plan for a successful termination. Collaborative termination strategies can first be used in the initial session in order to address clients' termination expectations. Strategies can also be used throughout treatment to help clients focus on their treatment goals. Last, collaborative termination strategies should be used in the final session to help clients take ownership of their gains and to equalize the therapeutic relationship. (Goode, Park, Parkin, Tompkins, & Swift, 2017, p. 10)

The following exercises ask you—the counselor—to focus on your own history of loss and factors that may help or hinder you in effectively facilitating termination with your clients. Some of these exercises are geared toward examining your own attachment style and the way you cope with separation and detachment.

Exercises and Activities

1. What do you know about your own attachment patterns that may influence the way you handle termination with your clients?

   _____

   _____

   a. As a child and later as a teenager, how did you cope with endings?

   _____

   _____

   b. Have any of these patterns persisted into adulthood?

   _____

   _____

2. Do you anticipate having greater difficulty terminating counseling with particular clients? If so, explain.

   _____

   _____

   a. What is it about these clients or your relationship with them that will make the process more difficult for you?

   _____

   _____

3. Do you anticipate feeling a sense of relief when particular clients (e.g., those exhibiting difficult or dangerous behaviors) terminate counseling? Say more about this.

   _____

   _____

4. Particular clients may have a vulnerability to loss or a history of dependency on others and may struggle with termination. How will you help these clients deal with ending counseling sessions with you?

   _____

   _____

5. You have listened empathically to your clients' stories and have been invested in their therapeutic journeys. How do you suppose it will be for you to not know what happens to them in the future?

   _____

   _____

6. If you run into clients 1, 5, or even 10 years after termination, what would you most want to know about their lives and the choices they've made?

   _____

   _____

   a. As you think about this question in relation to specific clients, what feelings surface for you?

   _____

   _____

7. Are there some clients with whom you feel you did your best work?

   _____

   _____

a. How was it or how will it be to terminate with them?

_____

_____

b. What messages would you most like to convey to them about the work you did together?

_____

_____

8. Do you fear you may not have served some clients as effectively as you had hoped before they terminated? If so, describe.

_____

_____

a. What would you do differently if you could do it over again?

_____

_____

9. A symbolic gesture, such as a sports trophy or a graduation certificate, is often provided to mark the end of a successful endeavor. How would you collaborate with your client to celebrate the termination of your work together in counseling with an appropriate symbol?

_____

_____

10. Write a message to your client who is terminating counseling. Tailor it to the specific client, and send your client away with a message of hope and encouragement.

_____

_____

For Clients

As you approach the termination phase in counseling, it is important to reflect on all of the hard work you have done to progress to this point. As you consolidate what you have learned, be sure to give yourself credit for making changes that have resulted in your growth. Ending counseling is likely to stir up a range of emotions, and we encourage you to allow yourself to embrace those feelings and not avoid them. The following exercises and activities are designed to help you process your experience and to acknowledge the work you have done. In addition, some activities may assist you in examining your reactions to the end of this relationship.

Exercises and Activities

1. Counseling is a unique relationship in which your counselor gets to know you on an emotionally deep level. In preparing to end your counseling sessions, reflect on what you will miss the most about this special relationship. Put into words what this therapeutic relationship has meant to you.

   _____

   _____

2. As you approach the ending of your counseling sessions, think about what you have accomplished over the course of counseling.
   a. What has changed in your life that pleases you?

   _____

   _____

   b. What has changed that does not please you?

   _____

   _____

   c. What were your goals for counseling, and did you accomplish them?

   _____

   _____

   d. What work remains to be done?

   _____

   _____

   e. What were the major lessons you learned over the course of counseling?

   _____

   _____

3. Where do you see your life headed from here? Where do you think you will be in 1 year? In 5 years? What will it take for you to accomplish these goals?

   _____

   _____

4. Did you accomplish everything you had hoped for in counseling? How would you rate the success of your counseling experience?

Scale: 1   2   3   4   5   6   7   8   9   10
         Accomplished   *Accomplished*
           nothing   *everything*

Explain:

_____

5. What, if anything, could have made counseling more useful or productive for you?

_____

_____

6. Counseling is designed to help you get your life moving in the direction you would like to go.
   a. Do you feel that has been accomplished?

_____

_____

   b. Do you feel you can now move ahead with your life without the aid of counseling?

_____

_____

7. What are some actions you hope to be taking in your life? Your work? Your relationships? Your family? Your community? Be as specific as possible.

_____

_____

8. Do you believe counseling was effective? What did you do to improve your situation? (Be sure to give yourself credit for your growth!)

_____

_____

9. Take a few minutes to relax, close your eyes, and think about the useful ideas, lessons, and messages you have taken from counseling. What are those ideas, lessons, and messages, and how will they help you in the future?

_____

_____

10. Even though counseling is coming to an end, you can return as needed. Some people like to return every 6 or 12 months for a refresher (similar to having your car serviced to be sure everything is running efficiently).
   a. Can you see yourself returning for such a refresher? Why or why not?

_____

_____

   b. What might prevent you from doing that?

_____

_____

11. Is there anything or any topic that you would like to discuss with your counselor before you conclude counseling? Is there anything left undone?

   _____

   _____

12. Think of a symbolic gesture that celebrates the termination of your work in counseling. For instance, you could attach a slip of paper (with keywords written on it about burdens you addressed in counseling) to a balloon and send it off into the sky! Or choose a small rock that symbolizes the burdens you worked through with your counselor. You might carry it with you for a short time (e.g., in your purse or jacket) to get a sense of how it has weighed you down. When you are ready to let it go, toss it into the ocean, a lake, or a river. If you prefer, keep it as a reminder of the issues that you were successfully able to resolve in counseling (but remove it from your purse or jacket so you don't end up with a new problem—back pain!). These are just two examples; use your imagination and creativity to think of a symbolic gesture that is meaningful for you.

   _____

   _____

Recommended Resources for Clients

The following websites contain valuable information about topics covered in this workbook: mental health issues and treatment, suicide prevention, social justice, and human rights. We encourage you to continue to grow in your journey through life.

- American Civil Liberties Union (ACLU): https://www.aclu.org/
- American Counseling Association (ACA): https://www.counseling.org/
- American Psychological Association (APA): https://www.apa.org/
- Human Rights Watch: https://www.hrw.org/
- National Institute of Mental Health (NIMH): https://www.nimh.nih.gov/index.shtml
- National Suicide Prevention Hotline: https://suicidepreventionlifeline.org/
- Psychology Today: https://www.psychologytoday.com/us
- Southern Poverty Law Center (SPLC): https://www.splcenter.org/
- Substance Abuse and Mental Health Services Administration (SAMHSA): https://www.samhsa.gov/
- SuicideHotlines.com: http://www.suicidehotlines.com/

References

Abel-Khalek, A. M. (2016). Introduction to the psychology of self-esteem. In F. Holloway (Ed.), *Self-esteem: Perspectives, influences and improvement strategies.* Hauppauge, NY: Nova Science.

Ainsworth, M., & Bowlby, J. (1965). *Child care and the growth of love.* London, UK: Penguin Books.

Alfonsi, S. (2019, June 23). *Paul McCartney opens up about Abbey Road, the Beatles' breakup in wide-ranging interview* [Interview]. Retrieved from https://www.cbsnews.com/news/paul-mccartney-opens-up-about-abbey-road-the-beatles-breakup-yoko-ono-in-wide-ranging-60-minutes-interview-2019-06-23/

Allott, D. (2018). Three steps to more civil political debate. *America, 219,* 10.

Alltucker, K. (2018, December 14). *Depression, suicide rates highest in Mountain West states.* Retrieved from https://www.usatoday.com/in-depth/news/health/2018/12/06/depression-rates-rise-utah-looking-slow-increase/2213071002/

American Psychiatric Association. (2013). *Diagnostic and statistical manual of mental disorders* (5th ed.). Arlington, VA: Author.

American Psychiatric Association. (2018, May 7). *Americans say they are more anxious than a year ago: Baby boomers report greatest increase in anxiety.* Retrieved from https://www.psychiatry.org/newsroom/news-releases/americans-say-they-are-more-anxious-than-a-year-ago-baby-boomers-report-greatest-increase-in-anxiety

American Psychological Association. (2017a, February 23). *APA's survey finds constantly checking electronic devices linked to significant stress for most Americans* [Press release]. Retrieved from https://www.apa.org/news/press/releases/2017/02/checking-devices

American Psychological Association. (2017b). *Stress in America: The state of our nation.* Washington, DC: Author.

American Psychological Association. (2018, November 11) *The road to resilience.* Washington, DC: Author. Retrieved from https://www.apa.org/helpcenter/road-resilience

American Psychological Association. (2019). *Strategies for controlling your anger: Keeping anger in check.* Retrieved from https://www.apa.org/helpcenter/controlling-anger

America's loneliness epidemic. (2018, May 18). *The Week, 18,* 20.

Anxiety and Depression Association of America. (n.d.). *Facts and statistics.* Retrieved from https://adaa.org/about-adaa/press-room/facts-statistics

Arden, J. (2010). *Rewire your brain.* Hoboken, NJ: Wiley.

Bacon, J. (2018, November 30). Suicide, overdoses rise in US. *Reno Gazette Journal, 39,* p. B2.

Bauman, S. (2011). *Cyberbullying: What counselors need to know.* Alexandria, VA: American Counseling Association.

Beck, A. T., Steer, R. A., & Brown, G. K. (1996). *Manual for the Beck Depression Inventory–II.* San Antonio, TX: Psychological Corporation.

Becker-Phelps, L. (2013, May 20). Stop your anxiety now! *Psychology Today.* Retrieved from https://www.psychologytoday.com/us/blog/making-change/201305/stop-your-anxiety-now

Bemak, F., & Chung, R. C-Y. (2017). Refugee trauma: Culturally responsive counseling interventions. *Journal of Counseling & Development, 95,* 299–308. doi:10.1002/jcad.12144

Berger, M. W. (2018, November 9). *Social media use increases depression and loneliness.* Retrieved from https://penntoday.upenn.edu /news/social-media-use-increases-depression-and-loneliness

Bettelheim, A. (2019, January 25). *Recovery from shutdown will be long and difficult.* Retrieved from https://www.politico.com /story/2019/01/25/studown-recovery-long-back-pay-1117804

Bliss, J. (2018, December 31). 30-day tech blackout helps families reconnect. *Reno Gazette Journal, 39,* 3.

Bourne, E. J. (2005). *The anxiety and phobia workbook* (4th ed.). Oakland, CA: New Harbinger.

Bourne, E. J. (2015). *The anxiety and phobia workbook* (6th ed.). Oakland, CA: New Harbinger.

Boyer, S. P., & Hoffman, M. A. (1993). Counselor affective reactions to termination: Impact of counselor loss history and perceived client sensitivity to loss. *Journal of Counseling Psychology, 40,* 271–277.

Brand, J. (2017). Politics, projection, and fake news. *Group: Journal of the Eastern Group Psychotherapy Society, 41,* 213–227.

Bremner, J. D. (2006). Traumatic stress: Effects on the brain. *Dialogues in Clinical Neuroscience, 8,* 445–461.

Brownlee, C. (2019, Summer). Window of opportunity. *Hopkins Bloomberg Public Health,* 26–31.

Bruk, D. (2018, December 19). *This is the biggest regret in life most people have.* Retrieved from https://www.msn.com/en-us/lifestyle/smart-living/this-is-the-biggest-regret-in-life-most-people-have/ar-BBR7QBi?li=AAa0dzB&item=module_ad_enabled%3Afalse.3

Brymer, M., Jacobs, A., Layne, C., Pynoos, R., Ruzek, J., Steinberg, A., . . . Watson, P. (2006). *Psychological first aid: Field operations guide* (2nd ed.). Los Angeles, CA: National Child Traumatic Stress Network.

Burns, D. D. (1999). *Feeling good: The new mood therapy.* New York, NY: HarperCollins.

Burrow, A. L., & Rainone, N. (2017). How many likes did I get? Purpose moderates links between positive social media feedback and self-esteem. *Journal of Experimental Social Psychology, 69,* 232–236.

Campbell, M. A. (2007). *Cyberbullying and young people: Treatment principles not simplistic advice.* Retrieved from http://www.scientist-practitioner.com

Carr, T. (June, 2019). Real pain relief, now! *Consumer Reports, 84,* 24–32.

Centers for Disease Control and Prevention. (2017). *National vital statistics report, Nov. 27, 2017.* Washington, DC: U.S. Department of Health and Human Services.

Centers for Disease Control and Prevention. (2019). *Violence prevention: CDC-Kaiser ACE study.* Retrieved from https://www.cdc.gov/violenceprevention/childabuseandneglect/acestudy/about.html

Chatterjee, R. (2018). *Americans are a lonely lot, and young people bear the heaviest burden.* Retrieved from https://www.npr.org /sections/health-shots/2018/05/01/606588504/americans-are-a-lonely-lot-and-young-people-bear-the-heaviest-burden

Chokshi, N. (2019, April 30). Americans are among the most stressed people in the world, poll finds. *New York Times,* p. D2.

Chung, R. C.-Y., & Bemak, F. (2012). *Social justice counseling: The next steps beyond multiculturalism.* Thousand Oaks, CA: Sage.

Cigna. (2018, May 1). *New Cigna study reveals loneliness at epidemic levels in America.* Retrieved from https://www.cigna.com/newsroom/news-releases/2018/new-cigna-study-reveals-loneliness-at-epidemic-levels-in-america

Clark, D. A., & Beck, A. T. (2012). *The anxiety and worry workbook: The cognitive-behavioral solution.* New York, NY: Guilford Press.

Collier, L. (2016). *Growth after trauma.* Retrieved from https://www.apa.org/monitor/2016/11/growth-trauma

Cook, T. L., Shannon, P. J., Vinson, G. A., Letts, J. P., & Dwee, E. (2015). War trauma and torture experiences reported during public health screening of newly resettled Karen refugees: A qualitative study. *BMC International Health and Human Rights, 15,* 1–13. doi:10.1186/s12914-015-0046-y

Corey, G., Corey, M. S., & Corey, C. (2019). *Issues and ethics in the helping professions* (10th ed.). Boston, MA: Cengage.

Corey, G., Corey, M. S., & Muratori, M. (2018). *I never knew I had a choice: Explorations in personal growth* (11th ed.). Boston, MA: Cengage.

Corey, G., Muratori, M., Austin, J. T., & Austin, J. A. (2018). *Counselor self-care*. Alexandria, VA: American Counseling Association.

Corey, M. S., & Corey, G. (2016). *Becoming a helper* (7th ed.). Boston, MA: Cengage.

Corey, M. S., & Corey, G. (2021). *Becoming a helper* (8th ed.). Boston, MA: Cengage.

Cormier, S. (2018). *Sweet sorrow: Finding enduring wholeness after loss and grief*. Lanham, MD: Rowman & Littlefield.

Dastagir, A. E. (2018, May 29). Author says bias is inevitable, but it can be faced, uprooted. *USA Today*, p. A3.

Day-Vines, N. L., Ammah, B. B., Steen, S., & Arnold, K. M. (2018). Getting comfortable with discomfort: Preparing counselor trainees to broach racial, ethnic, and cultural factors with clients during counseling. *International Journal for the Advancement of Counselling, 40*, 89–104. doi:10.1007/s10447-017-9308-9

Day-Vines, N. L., Wood, S. M., Grothaus, T., Craigen, L., Holman, A., Dotson-Blake, K., & Douglass, M. J. (2007). Broaching the subjects of race, ethnicity, and culture during the counseling process. *Journal of Counseling & Development, 85*, 401–409.

Del Vecchio-Scully, D. (2018). In our own words: Reflecting on the Sandy Hook School shooting. In J. M. Webber & J. B. Mascari (Eds.), *Disaster mental health counseling: A guide to preparing and responding* (4th ed., pp. 249–250). Alexandria, VA: American Counseling Association Foundation.

Del Vecchio-Scully, D., & Glaser, M. (2018). Disaster recovery in Newtown: The intermediate phase. In J. M. Webber & J. B. Mascari (Eds.), *Disaster mental health counseling: A guide to preparing and responding* (4th ed., pp. 233–248). Alexandria, VA: American Counseling Association Foundation.

Dobson, D., & Dobson, K. S. (2017). *Evidence-based practice of cognitive-behavioral therapy* (2nd ed.). New York, NY: Guilford Press.

Donovan, N. J., Wu, Q., Rentz, D. M., Sperling, R. A., Marshall, G. A., & Glymour, M. M. (2017). Loneliness, depression and cognitive function in older U.S. adults. *International Journal of Geriatric Psychiatry, 32*, 564–573.

Dunkley, J., & Whelan, T. A. (2006). Vicarious traumatisation: Current status and future directions. *British Journal of Guidance and Counselling, 34*, 107–116. doi:10.1080/03069880500483166

Dusenbery, M. (2019, June). It's all in your head. *Consumer Reports, 84*, 32–33.

Dwyera, R. J., Kushlevb, K., & Dunna, E. W. (2018). Smartphone use undermines enjoyment of face-to-face social interactions. *Journal of Experimental Social Psychology, 78*, 233–239. doi:10.1016/j.jesp.2017.10.007

Eckel, S. (2017, May/June). Divider-in-chief. *Psychology Today, 50*, 41–43.

Elliott, W. (1996). *Tying rocks to clouds: Meetings and conversations with wise and spiritual people*. New York, NY: Image Books/Double Day.

Farber, B. (2018). Clowns to the left of me, jokers to the right: Politics and psychotherapy. *Journal of Clinical Psychology, 74*, 714–721. doi:10.1002/jclp.22600

Fennell, P. A. (2012). *The chronic illness workbook: Strategies and solutions for taking back your life*. Latham, NY: Albany Health Management.

Foreman, T. (2018). Wellness, exposure to trauma, and vicarious traumatization: A pilot study. *Journal of Mental Health Counseling, 40*, 142–155. doi: 10.17744/mehc.40.2.04

Frances, A. (2017, October 17). *Duke psychiatrist: America is having a nervous breakdown* [Interview]. Retrieved from https://www.madinamerica.com/2017/10/america-nervous-breakdown/

Fukuyama, F. (2018, September/October). Against identity politics: The new tribalism and the crisis of democracy. *Foreign Affairs*, 90–114.

Gentry, J. E., Webber, J. M., & Baranowsky, A. B. (2018). Compassion fatigue: Our Achilles' heel. In J. M. Webber & J. B. Mascari (Eds.), *Disaster mental health counseling: A guide to preparing and responding* (4th ed., pp. 79–92). Alexandria, VA: American Counseling Association Foundation.

Goode, J., Park, J., Parkin, S., Tompkins, K. A., & Swift, J. K. (2017). A collaborative approach to psychotherapy termination. *Psychotherapy, 54*, 10–14. doi:10.1037/pst0000085

Goewey, D. J. (2017, December 7). *85 percent of what we worry about never happens.* Retrieved from https://www.huffpost.com/entry/85-of-what-we-worry-about_b_8028368

Guynn, J. (2019, February 13). Half of Americans harassed online. *USA Today,* p. A2.

Hara, K. M., Aviram, A., Constantino, M. J., Westra, H. A., & Antony, M. M. (2017). Therapist empathy, homework compliance, and outcome in cognitive behavioral therapy for generalized anxiety disorder: Partitioning within- and between-therapist effects. *Cognitive Behavior Therapy, 46,* 375–390. doi: 10.1080/16506073.2016.1253605

Harner, M. (1990). *The way of the shaman* (3rd ed.). New York, NY: Harper & Row.

Hayes, S. C. (2018, July/August). From loss to love. *Psychology Today, 51,* pp. 73–79, 90.

Haynes, R. (2014). *Take control of life's crises today! A practical guide.* Chula Vista, CA: Aventine Press.

Haynes, R., Corey, G., & Moulton, P. (2003). *Clinical supervision in the helping professions: A practical guide.* Pacific Grove, CA: Thomson-Brooks/Cole.

Herlihy, B., & Corey, G. (2015). *Boundary issues in counseling: Multiple roles and responsibilities.* Alexandria, VA: American Counseling Association.

Hobfol, S. E., Watson, P., Bell, C. C., Brymer, M. J., Friedman, M. J., & Ursano, R. J. (2007). Five essential elements of immediate and mid-term mass trauma intervention: Empirical evidence. *Psychiatry, 70,* 283–315. doi:10.1521/psyc.2007.70.4.283

Howes, R. (2008, April 16). Fundamentals of therapy #1: Who goes? *Psychology Today.* Retrieved from https://www.psychologytoday.com/us/blog/in-therapy/200804/ fundamentals-therapy-1-who-goes

Humphrey, K. M. (2009). *Counseling strategies for loss and grief.* Alexandria, VA: American Counseling Association.

Hunt, D., Robertson, D., & Pow, A. (2018). The counselor's role in the age of social media and fake news. *Journal of Creativity in Mental Health, 13,* 405–417. doi:10.1080/15401383.2018.1462748

Hunt, M. G., Marx, R., Lipson, C., & Young, J. (2018). No more FOMO: Limiting social media decreases loneliness and depression. *Journal of Social and Clinical Psychology, 37,* 751–768.

Hwang, P. O. (2000). *Other-esteem: Meaningful life in a multicultural society.* Philadelphia, PA: Accelerated Development/Taylor & Francis.

Ihm, J. (2018). Social implications of children's smartphone addiction: The role of support networks and social engagement. *Journal of Behavioral Addictions, 7,* 473–481. doi:10.1556/2006.7.2018.48

Ingerman, S. (1991). *Soul retrieval: Mending the fragmented self.* New York, NY: Harper.

Jagtiani, A., Khurana, H., & Malhotra, N. (2019). Comparison of efficacy of ketamine versus thiopentone-assisted modified electroconvulsive therapy in major depression. *Indian Journal of Psychiatry, 61,* 258–264. doi:10.4103/psychiatry.IndianJPsychiatry_386_18

James, A. E., Shensa, A., Barrett, E., Sidani, J. E., & Colditz, J. (2019, September 10). *Using lots of social media sites raises depression risk.* Retrieved from http://www.braininstitute.pitt.edu/using-lots-social-media-sites-raises-depression-risk

James, R. K., & Gilliland, B. E. (2017). *Crisis intervention strategies* (8th ed.). Boston, MA: Cengage.

Jose, S. (2016). *Progressing through grief: Guided exercises to understand your emotions and recover from loss.* San Antonio, TX: Althea Press.

Kang, Y. (2019). The relationship between contingent self-esteem and trait self-esteem. *Social Behavior and Personality: An International Journal, 47,* e7575.

Kazantzis, N., Whittington, C., & Dattilio, F. (2010). Meta-analysis of homework effects in cognitive and behavioral therapy: A replication and extension. *Clinical Psychology: Science and Practice, 17,* 144–156.

Kennard, J. (2008, February 12). *Freud 101: Psychoanalysis.* Retrieved from https://www.healthcentral.com/article/freud-101-psychoanalysis

Kerr, B. (2019, May 25). Amanda Eller, hiker lost in Hawaii forest, is found alive after 17 days. *New York Times.* Retrieved from https://www.nytimes.com /2019/05/25/us/hawaii-hiker.html

Kerstens, J., & Jansen, J. (2016). The victim–perpetrator overlap in financial cybercrime: Evidence and reflection on the overlap of youth's on-line victimization and perpetration. *Deviant Behavior, 37,* 585–600. doi:10.1080/01639625.2015.1060796

King, A. L. S., Valença, A. M., Silva, A. C. O., Baczynski, T., Carvalho, M. R., & Nardi, A. E. (2013). Nomophobia: Dependency on virtual environments or social phobia? *Computers in Human Behavior, 29,* 140–144.

Kong, J., Fang, J., Park, J., Li, S., & Rong, P. (2018). Treating depression with transcutaneous auricular vagus nerve stimulation: State of the art and future perspectives. *Frontiers in Psychiatry, 9.* Retrieved from https://www.ncbi.nlm.nih.gov/pmc/articles/PMC5807379/

Konow, D. (2018, October 30). Michael Phelps speaks out about battling depression, anxiety. *The Counseling Insider* [Interview]. Retrieved from https://www.thefix.com/michael-phelps-speaks-out-about-battling-depression-anxiety

Kowalski, R. M., Giumetti, G. W., Schroeder, A. N., & Lattanner, M. R. (2014). Bullying in the digital age: A critical review and meta-analysis of cyberbullying research among youth. *Psychological Bulletin, 140,* 1073–1137. doi:10.1037/a0035618

Kübler-Ross, E. (1969). *On death and dying.* New York, NY: Macmillan.

Kuin, N., Masthoff, E., Kramer, M., & Scherder, E. (2015). The role of risky decision-making in aggression: A systematic review. *Aggression and Violent Behavior, 25,* 159–172.

LaFrance, A., Raicu, I., & Goldman, E. (2017, May). The next great experiment. *The Atlantic.* Retrieved from https://www.theatlantic.com/technology/archive/2017/05/the-next-great-experiment/523890/

Lancaster, M. (2018). A systematic research synthesis on cyberbullying interventions in the United States. *Cyberpsychology, Behavior, and Social Networking, 21,* 593–602. doi:10.1089/cyber.2018.0307

Lazer, D. M. J., Baum, M. A., Benkler, Y., Berinsky, A. J., Greenhill, K. M., Menczer, F., . . . Zittrain, J. L. (2018, March 9). The science of fake news: Addressing fake news requires a multidisciplinary effort. *Science, 359,* 1094–1096.

Lee, C. C. (2018). *Counseling for social justice* (3rd ed.). Alexandria, VA: American Counseling Association Foundation.

Lee, C. C. (Ed.). (2019). *Multicultural issues in counseling: New approaches to diversity* (5th ed.). Alexandria, VA: American Counseling Association.

Lee, J., Blackmon, B. J., Lee, J. Y., Cochran, D. M., & Rehner, T. A. (2019). An exploration of post-traumatic growth, loneliness, depression, resilience, and social capital among survivors of Hurricane Katrina and the Deepwater Horizon oil spill. *Journal of Community Psychology, 47,* 356–370. doi:10.1002/jcop.22125

Lee, S., Park, J., & Lee, S. B. (2016). The interplay of internet addiction and compulsive shopping behaviors. *Social Behavior & Personality, 44,* 1901–1912.

Lenehan, P., Deane, F. P., Wolstencroft, K., & Kelly, P. J. (2019). Coherence between goals and therapeutic homework of clients engaging in recovery-oriented support. *Psychiatric Rehabilitation Journal, 42,* 201–205.

Lennon, J. (2017). *Reality leaves a lot to the imagination.* Retrieved from https://www.goalcast.com/2017/07/18/john-lennon-quotes-live-love/

Leutenberg, E. R. A., & Liptak, J. J. (2014). *Coping with everyday stressors workbook.* Duluth, MN: Whole Person Associates.

Linehan, M. M. (2015). *DBT skills training: Handouts and worksheets* (2nd ed.). New York, NY: Guilford Press.

Luttig, M. D. (2017). Authoritarianism and affective polarization: A new view on the origins of partisan extremism. *Public Opinion Quarterly, 81,* 866–895. doi:10.1093/poq/nfx023

Lyumbomirsky, S. (2007). *The how of happiness.* New York, NY: Penguin Books.

Ma, X., Yue, Z. Q., Gong, Z. Q., Zhang, H., Duan, N. Y., Shi, Y. T., . . . Li, Y. F. (2017). The effect of diaphragmatic breathing on attention, negative affect and stress in healthy adults. *Frontiers in Psychology, 8,* 874. doi:10.3389/fpsyg.2017.00874

Madell, R. (2015). *Battling the stress of living with chronic illness.* Retrieved from https://www.healthline.com/health/depression/chronic-illness#1

Mancini, A. (2016a). Rethinking trauma: The trouble with post-traumatic growth. *Psychology Today.* Retrieved from https://www.psychologytoday.com/us/blog/rethinking-trauma/201606/the-trouble-post-traumatic-growth

Mancini, A. (2016b). Rethinking trauma: Can trauma improve our psychological health? *Psychology Today.* Retrieved from https://www.psychologytoday.com/us/blog/rethinking-trauma/201607/can-trauma-improve-our-psychological-health

March, E., & McBean, T. (2018). New evidence shows self-esteem moderates the relationship between narcissism and selfies. *Personality and Individual Differences, 130,* 107–111. doi:10.1016/j.paid.2018.03.053

Markman, A. (2018, May 22). Narcissism is not just high self-esteem. *Psychology Today.* Retrieved from https://www.psychologytoday.com/us/blog/ulterior-motives/201805/narcissism-is-not-just-high-self-esteem

Mascari, J. B., & Webber, J. M. (2018). Disaster mental health and trauma counseling: The next decade. In J. M. Webber & J. B. Mascari (Eds.), *Disaster mental health counseling: A guide to preparing and responding* (4th ed., pp. 287–294). Alexandria, VA: American Counseling Association Foundation.

Maslach, C. (1993). Burnout: A multidimensional perspective. In W. B. Schaufeli, C. Maslach, & T. Marek (Eds.), *Professional burnout: Recent developments in theory and research* (pp. 19–32). Washington, DC: Taylor & Francis.

Maslach, C., Jackson, S. E., & Leiter, M. P. (1996). *Maslach burnout inventory manual, 3.* Palo Alto, CA: Consulting Psychologists Press.

Mather, K. (2013, May 7). Jaycee Dugard speaks of hope in wake of Cleveland kidnapping case. *LA Times.* Retrieved from https://www.latimes.com/local/lanow/la-xpm-2013-may-07-la-me-ln-jaycee-dugard-speaks-of-hope-in-wake-of-cleveland-kidnapping-20130507-story.html

Mathew, S. J., Wilkinson, S. T., Altinay, M., Asghar-Ali, A., & Anand, A. (2019, February). Electroconvulsive therapy (ECT) vs. ketamine in patients with treatment-resistant depression: The ELEKT-D study protocol. *Contemporary Clinical Trials, 77,* 19–26.

Mathews, C. L., Morrell, H. E. R., & Molle, J. E. (2019). Video game addiction, ADHD symptomatology, and video game reinforcement. *American Journal of Drug and Alcohol Abuse, 45,* 67–76. doi: 10.1080/00952990.2018.1472269

Matu, S. A. (2018). Cognitive therapy. In A. Vernon & K. A. Doyle (Eds.), *Cognitive behavior therapies: A guidebook for practitioners* (p. 77). Alexandria, VA: American Counseling Association.

Mayo Clinic. (2017, July 12). *Self-esteem check: Too low or just right?* Retrieved from https://www.mayoclinic.org/healthy-lifestyle/adult-health/in-depth/self-esteem/art-20047976

McHugh, B. C., Wisniewski, P., Rosson, M. B., & Carroll, J. M. (2018) When social media traumatizes teens: The roles of online risk exposure, coping, and post-traumatic stress. *Internet Research, 28,* 1169–1188. doi:10.1108/IntR-02-2017-0077

McIntosh, P. (1989, July/August). White privilege: Unpacking the invisible knapsack. *Peace and Freedom,* 8–10.

McRae, M. (2018, February 8). *Scientists have discovered how traumatic experiences actually rewire the brain.* Retrieved from https://www.sciencealert.com/hippocampus-inhibition-pathways-prefrontal-cortex-post-traumatic-stress-disorder-relapses

Meichenbaum, D. (2012). *Roadmap to resilience: A guide for military, trauma victims and their families.* Cary, NC: Institute Press.

Mental Health America. (2019). *Mental health in America-adult data ranking 2019.* Retrieved from https://www.mhanational.org/issues/mental-health-america-adult-data#two

Meyer, D. S., & Tarrow, S. (Ed.). (2018). Introduction. In *The resistance: The dawn of the anti-Trump opposition movement.* Cambridge, UK: Oxford University Press.

Meyers, L. (2014, May). Advocacy in action. *Counseling Today, 56,* 32–41.

Meyers, L. (2017, September) High anxiety. *Counseling Today, 60,* 39.

Meyers, L. (2018, October). Infusing hope amid despair. *Counseling Today, 61,* 18–25.

Meyers, L. (2019, January). Building client and counselor resilience. *Counseling Today, 67,* 22–27.

Miller, J. (2010). Current views on the therapeutic value of homework in counselling and psychotherapy. *Counselling Psychology Quarterly, 23,* 235–238.

Miller, S., & McCoy, K. (2018, November 8). Thousand Oaks makes 307 mass shootings in 311 days. *USA Today* [Online]. Retrieved from https://www.usatoday.com/story/news/nation/2018/11/08/thousand-oaks-california-bar-shooting-307th-mass-shooting/1928574002/

Moffatt, G. K. (2018, August). The hurting counselor. *Counseling Today, 61,* 52–56.

Molina, B. (2018, May 14). Health insurer: More Americans depressed. *Reno Gazette Journal,* p. B1.

Montero, D., & Tchekmedyian, A. (2017, October 2). More than 50 dead and 400 injured in shooting on Las Vegas strip; police say lone suspect is dead. *Los Angeles Times.* Retrieved from https://www.latimes.com/nation/la-na-las-vegas-mandalay-bay-20171001-story.html

Morse, G., Salyers, M. P., Rollins, A. L., Monroe-DeVita, M., & Pfahler, C. (2012). Burnout in mental health services: A review of the problem and its remediation. *Administration and Policy in Mental Health and Mental Health Services Research, 39,* 341–352. doi:10.1007/s10488-011-0352-1. Retrieved from https://www.ncbi.nlm.nih.gov/pmc/articles/PMC3156844/

Mueller, R. S., III. (2019). *Report on the investigation into Russian interference in the 2016 presidential election.* Washington, DC: U.S. Department of Justice.

Mullen, P. R., Morris, C., & Lord, M. (2017). The experience of ethical dilemmas, burnout, and stress among practicing counselors. *Counseling and Values, 62,* 37–56. doi: 10.1002/cvj.12048

National Aeronautics and Space Administration. (2019, September 10). *Scientific consensus: Earth's climate is warming.* Retrieved from https://climate.nasa.gov/scientific-consensus/

National Center for Chronic Disease Prevention and Health Promotion. (2019a, July 30). *About chronic diseases.* Retrieved from https://www.cdc.gov/chronicdisease/about/index.htm

National Center for Chronic Disease Prevention and Health Promotion. (2019b, April 15). *Chronic diseases in America.* Retrieved from https://www.cdc.gov/chronicdisease/resources/infographic/chronic-diseases.htm

National Center for Health Statistics. (2017). *Health, United States, 2016: With chartbook on long-term trends in health.* Washington, DC: U.S. Government Printing Office.

National Institute of Mental Health. (2018a, July). *Anxiety disorders.* Bethesda, MD: Author. Retrieved from https://www.nimh.nih.gov/health/topics/anxiety-disorders/index.shtml

National Institute of Mental Health. (2018b). *Chronic illness and mental health.* Bethesda, MD: Author.

National Institute of Mental Health. (2018c, February). *Depression.* Bethesda, MD: Author. Retrieved from https://www.nimh.nih.gov/health/topics/depression/index.shtml

Neff, K., & Germer, C. (2018). *The mindful self-compassion workbook.* New York, NY: Guilford Press.

Norcross, J. C., & VandenBos, G. R. (2018). *Leaving it at the office: A guide to psychotherapist self-care.* New York, NY: Guilford Press.

Norcross, J. C., Zimmerman, B. E., Greenberg, R. P., & Swift, J. K. (2017). Do all therapists do that when saying goodbye? A study of commonalities in termination behaviors. *Psychotherapy, 54,* 66–75.

Norwegian Nobel Committee. (2014). *The Nobel Peace Prize 2014* [Press release]. Retrieved from https://www.nobelprize.org/prizes/peace/2014/press-release/

Nouwen, H. J. M. (1972). *The wounded healer.* New York, NY: An Image Book/ Doubleday.

Novaco, R. (2003). *Novaco Anger and Provocation Inventory (NAS-PI).* Torrance, CA: Western Psychological Services.

Oxenden, M., & Zhang, C. (2019, October 9). Carjackings spike continues in Baltimore, with incidents up 30% from this time last year. *Baltimore Sun.* Retrieved from http://www.baltimoresun.com/news/crime/bs-md-ci-cr-carjackings-rise-in-baltimore-20191009-tfj4xqx4sjhuhikxxxqp5re6im-story.html

Patler, C., & Laster Pirtle, W. (2018, February). From undocumented to lawfully present: Do changes to legal status impact psychological wellbeing among Latino immigrant young adults? *Social Science & Medicine, 199,* 39–48.

Perryman, K., Blisard, P., & Moss, R. (2019, January). Using creative arts in trauma therapy: The neuroscience of healing. *Journal of Mental Health Counseling, 4,* 80–94.

Preidt, R. (2019, March 5). U.S. deaths from suicide, substance abuse reach record high. *US News & World Report.* Retrieved from https://www.usnews.com/news/health-news/articles/2019-03-05/us-deaths-from-suicide-substance-abuse-reach-record-high

Prochaska, J. O., & DiClemente, C. C. (1982). Transtheoretical therapy: Toward a more integrative model of change. *Psychotherapy: Theory, Research and Practice, 19,* 276–288.

Prochaska J. O., DiClemente C. C., & Norcross J. C. (1992). In search of how people change. *American Psychologist, 47,* 1102–1104.

Raheem, M. A., & Hart, K. A. (2019, March). Counseling individuals of African descent. *Counseling Today, 61,* 43.

Ratts, M. J. (2017). Charting the center and the margins: Addressing identity, marginalization, and privilege in counseling. *Journal of Mental Health Counseling, 39*, 87–103. doi:10.17744lmehc.39.2.01

Ratts, M. J., & Pedersen, P. B. (2014). *Counseling for multiculturalism and social justice: Integration, theory, and application* (4th ed.). Alexandria, VA: American Counseling Association.

Ratts, M. J., Singh, A. A., Butler, K., Nassar-McMillan, S., & Rafferty McCullough, J. (2016, February). Multicultural and social justice counseling competencies: Practical applications in counseling. *Counseling Today*, 40–45.

Ray, J. (2019, April 25). Americans' stress, worry and anger intensified in 2018. *Gallup 2019 Global Emotions Report*. Retrieved from https://news.gallup.com/poll/249098/americans-stress-worry-anger-intensified-2018.aspx

Reilly, P. M., & Shopshire, M. S. (2002) *Anger management for substance abuse and mental health clients: A cognitive behavioral therapy manual.* Rockville, MD: Center for Substance Abuse Treatment, Substance Abuse and Mental Health Services Administration.

Rice, D. (2017, May 27). Climate change is causing a nightmare—lost sleep. *Reno Gazette Journal*, p. B1.

Rice, D. (2018, June 19). Rising seas threaten 311K coastal homes. *Reno Gazette Journal*, p. B1.

Richardson, R., Richards, D. A., & Barkham, M. (2010). Self-help books for people with depression: The role of the therapeutic relationship. *Behavior and Cognitive Psychotherapy, 38*, 67–81. doi:10.1017/S1352465809990452

Rogers, C. R. (1951). *Client-centered therapy: Its current practice, implications, and theory.* Boston, MA: Houghton Mifflin.

Rolston, A., & Lloyd-Richardson, E. (2019). *What is emotion regulation and how do we do it?* Retrieved from http://selfinjury.bctr.cornell.edu/perch/resources/what-is-emotion-regulationsinfo-brief.pdf

Rosenblatt, K. (2018, November 11). *Nurses fleeing fast-moving Camp Fire scramble to save patients—and themselves.* Retrieved from https://www.nbcnews.com/news/us-news/nurses-fleeing-fast-moving-camp-fire-scramble-save-themselves-n934961

Schaefer, L. M., Howell, K. H., Schwartz, L. E., Bottomley, J. S., & Crossnine, C. B. (2018). A concurrent examination of protective factors associated with resilience and posttraumatic growth following childhood victimization. *Child Abuse & Neglect, 85*, 17–27. doi:10.1016/j.chiabu.2018.08.019

Scheel, M. J., Hanson, W. E., & Razzhavaikina, T. I. (2004). The process of recommending homework in psychotherapy: A review of therapist delivery methods, client acceptability, and factors that affect compliance. *Psychotherapy, 41*, 38–55.

Sedikides, C., & Gress, A. P. (2003). Portraits of the self. In M. A. Hogg & J Cooper (Eds.), *Sage handbook of social psychology* (pp. 110–138). London, UK: Sage.

Seligman, M. (2002). *Authentic happiness.* New York, NY: Atria/Simon & Shuster.

Shapiro, E. (2019, May 24). *"I took back my freedom": Jayme Closs' powerful statement read as her kidnapper gets life in prison without parole.* Retrieved from https://abcnews.go.com/US/man-abducted-13-year-jayme-closs-sentenced/story?id=63213591

Shrestha, A., Cornum, R., Vie, L. L., Scheier, L. M., Lester, P. B., & Seligman, M. E. P. (2018). Protective effects of psychological strengths against psychiatric disorders among soldiers. *Military Medicine, 183*, 386–395.

Solomonov, N., & Barber, J. P. (2018). Patients' perspectives on political self-disclosure, the therapeutic alliance, and the infiltration of politics into the therapy room in the Trump era. *Journal of Clinical Psychology, 74*, 779–787. doi:10.1002/jclp.22609

Srour, R. (2015). Transference and countertransference issues during times of violent political conflict: The Arab therapist–Jewish patient dyad. *Clinical Social Work Journal, 43*, 407–418. doi:10.1007/s10615-015-0525-6

Stebnicki, M. A. (April, 1999). *Grief reactions among rehabilitation professionals: Dealing effectively with empathy fatigue.* Presentation made at the NRCA/ ARCA Alliance Annual Training Conference, Dallas, Texas.

Stebnicki, M. A. (2000). Stress and grief reactions among rehabilitation professionals: Dealing effectively with empathy fatigue. *Journal of Rehabilitation, 6*, 23–29.

Stebnicki, M. A. (2001). Psychosocial response to extraordinary stressful and traumatic life events: Principles and practices for rehabilitation counselors. *New Directions in Rehabilitation, 12,* 57–71.

Stebnicki, M. A. (2007). Empathy fatigue: Healing the mind, body, and spirit of professional counselors. *Journal of Psychiatric Rehabilitation, 10,* 317–338.

Stebnicki, M. A. (2008). *Empathy fatigue: Healing the mind, body, and spirit of professional counselors.* New York, NY: Springer.

Stebnicki, M. A. (2016). From empathy fatigue to empathy resiliency. In I. Marini & M. A. Stebnicki (Eds.), *The professional counselor's desk reference* (2nd ed., pp. 533–545). New York, NY: Springer.

Stebnicki, M. A. (2017). *Disaster mental health counseling: Responding to trauma in a multicultural context.* New York, NY: Springer.

Steer, R. A., Rissmiller, D. J., & Beck, A. T. (2000). Use of the Beck Depression Inventory with depressed geriatric patients. *Behaviour Research and Therapy, 38,* 311–318.

Sturm, D. C., & Echterling, L. G. (2017, May). Preparing for the mental health impact of climate change. *Counseling Today, 59,* 60–63.

Suhartono, M., & Paddock, R. C. (2018, July 3). "Eat, eat, eat": Found after 10 days in Thai cave. *New York Times,* p. 1.

Tafoya, T., & Kouris, N. (2003). Dancing the circle: Native American concepts of healing. In S. G. Mijares (Ed.), *Modern psychology and ancient wisdom: Psychological healing practices from the world's religious traditions* (pp. 125–146). New York, NY: Haworth Integrative Healing Press.

Tedeschi, R. G., & Calhoun, L. G. (1995). *Trauma and transformation: Growing in the aftermath of suffering.* Thousand Oaks, CA: Sage.

Thorpe, H. (2017). *The newcomers: Finding refuge, friendship, and hope in America.* New York, NY: Scribner.

Touchette, N. (2003, July 25). *Gene variant protects against depression.* Retrieved from http://www.genomenewsnetwork.org/articles/07_03/depression.shtml

Transcript: Greta Thunberg's speech at the U.N. Climate Action Summit. (2019, September 23). Retrieved from https://www.npr.org/2019/09/23/763452863/transcript-greta-thunbergs-speech-at-the-u-n-climate-action-summit

Trask, E. V., Barounis, K., Carlisle, B. L., Garland, A. F., & Aarons, G. A. (2018). Factors associated with assignment of therapeutic homework in a large public children's mental health system. *Administration and Policy in Mental Health, 45,* 821–830. doi:10.1007/s10488-018-0867-9

Turk Nolty, A. A., Rensberger, J. K., Bosch, D. S., Hennig, N., & Buckwalter, J. G. (2018). Spirituality: A facet of residence. *Fuller Magazine, 12,* 54–57.

Twenge, J. M., Cooper, A. B., Joiner, T. E., Duffy, M. E., & Binau, S. E. (2019). Age, period, and cohort trends in mood disorder indicators and suicide-related outcomes in a nationally representative dataset, 2005–2017. *Journal of Abnormal Psychology, 128,* 185–199. http://dx.doi.org/10.1037/abn0000410

University of Pennsylvania. (2019). *Resilience training for the Army.* Retrieved from https://ppc.sas.upenn.edu/services/resilience-training-army

von Glischinski, M., von Brachel, R., & Hirschfeld, G. (2019). How depressed is "depressed"? A systematic review and diagnostic meta-analysis of optimal cut points for the Beck Depression Inventory revised (BDI-II). *Quality of Life Research, 28,* 1111–1118.

Wagner, D., & Ivey, A. (2018). Riding the wave: Helping clients live in sustainable nervous system functioning. *Counseling Today, 60* (12), 16–19.

Waldrop, M. M. (2017). The genuine problem of fake news: Intentionally deceptive news has co-opted social media to go viral and influence millions. Science and technology can suggest why and how. But can they offer solutions? *Proceedings of the National Academy of Sciences of the United States of America, 114,* 12631–12634. doi:10.1073/pnas.1719005114

Walsh, R. (2011). Lifestyle and mental health. *American Psychologist, 66,* 579–592.

Wang, J., Mann, F., Lloyd-Evans, B., Ma, R., & Johnson, S. (2018). Associations between loneliness and perceived social support and outcomes of mental health problems: A systematic review. *BMC Psychiatry, 18,* 1–16. doi:10.1186/s12888-018-1736-5

Webber, J. M., & Mascari, J. B. (Eds.). (2018a). *Disaster mental health counseling: A guide to preparing and responding* (4th ed.). Alexandria, VA: American Counseling Association Foundation.

Webber, J. M., & Mascari, J. B. (2018b). Understanding disaster mental health. In J. M. Webber & J. B. Mascari (Eds.), *Disaster mental health counseling: A guide to preparing and responding* (4th ed., pp. 3–16). Alexandria, VA: American Counseling Association Foundation.

Weck, F., Richtberg, S., Esch, S., Höfling, V., & Stangier, U. (2013). The relationship between therapist competence and homework compliance in maintenance cognitive therapy for recurrent depression: Secondary analysis of a randomized trial. *Behavior Therapy, 44*, 162–172.

Wheeler, A. M., & Bertram, B. (2019). *The counselor and the law: A guide to legal and ethical practice* (8th ed.). Alexandria, VA: American Counseling Association.

Whitehead, S. (2019, February 19). The gifts of volunteering as a disaster mental health counselor. *Counseling Today.* Retrieved from https://ct.counseling.org/2019/02/the-gifts-of-volunteering-as-a-disaster-mental-health-counselor/

Whitmore-Williams, S. C., Manning, C., Krygsman, K., & Speiser, M. (2017). *Mental health and our changing climate: Impacts, implications, and guidance.* Washington, DC: American Psychological Association and ecoAmerica.

Wubbolding, R. (2017). *Reality therapy and self-evaluation: The key to client change.* Alexandria, VA: American Counseling Association.

Yildiz Durak, H. (2018). What would you do without your smartphone? Adolescents' social media usage, locus of control, and loneliness as a predictor of nomophobia. *Addicta: The Turkish Journal on Addictions, 5*, 543–557. doi:10.15805/addicta.2018.5.3.0025

Yourman, D. B. (2018). A Marxist therapist treats a Trump-supporting client: A tale of politics and psychotherapy. *Journal of Clinical Psychology, 74*, 766–773.

Additional Exercises for Common Mental Health Issues

The following out-of-session activities and exercises can be tailored to the needs of clients experiencing a wide range of mental health issues and other stressors, including those featured in Part II of this workbook. They reflect a variety of theoretical perspectives.

1. **Self-Care.** Practice good self-care by eating right, exercising, getting adequate sleep, and relaxing so you will have the physical and mental energy and stamina to deal with crisis situations. Avoid using alcohol, drugs, food, and smoking as stress reducers. Those harmful coping mechanisms may provide short-term relief but result in your body being less able to cope physically with the stress of the crisis. Some people find that they trigger or intensify feelings of guilt and low self-esteem. Check the response that most closely describes your self-care habits regarding the following topics.

    a. How would you describe your eating habits generally?

    ❑ Unhealthy ❑ Often Unhealthy ❑ Sometimes Healthy ❑ Mostly Healthy ❑ Healthy

    b. How many times per week do you exercise?

    ❑ Never ❑ 1–2 ❑ 3–4 ❑ 5+

    c. How many hours of sleep do you get a night on average?

    ❑ 1–3 ❑ 4–6 ❑ 7–8 ❑ 9+

    d. How often do you find time to relax?

    ❑ Never ❑ Rarely ❑ Sometimes ❑ Often ❑ Frequently

    e. How often do you enjoy your hobbies?

    ❑ Never ❑ Annually ❑ Monthly ❑ Weekly ❑ Daily

Overall, how would you describe your self-care habits?

_____

_____

2. **Wellness and Self-Care.** Striving for wellness is a life-long journey. Your ability to prepare for and handle crisis situations you may encounter is greatly enhanced when you are in the best physical and mental condition possible. Some people may say that self-love and self-care are signs of selfishness; however, we must remember that it is not a matter of self-care *versus* caring for others. It surely is possible to be invested in both. In fact, your capacity to care for others will be diminished if you don't first take care of your own needs. For self-care to become a priority, it has to become a lifestyle that you practice daily rather than something you hope you will get to, but probably won't. You need to make a commitment, outline a schedule to practice it, and convince yourself that self-care is high on your priority list. Here are a few ideas to get you started on your path to improved self-care.

   a. What one thing are you willing to commit to *today* for better self-care? It does not have to be a major commitment, but taking even one step forward often serves as a motivator for you to continue in a positive direction.

   _____

   _____

   b. Walsh (2011) outlines a comprehensive review of therapeutic lifestyle changes (TLCs) that promote wellness: exercise, nutrition and diet, time in nature, relationships, recreation, relaxation, stress management, religious or spiritual involvement, and service to others. Ample research and clinical evidence supports these therapeutic lifestyle changes. Create a chart like Chart A.1 to assess where you are now and where you would like to be in terms of incorporating these TLCs into your life. For each TLC, rate yourself, and then create a plan to describe how you will achieve your goal in each domain.

Scale: 1   2   3   4   5   6   7   8   9   10
        Not achieved   *Completely*
           at all   *achieved*

Chart A.1 Therapeutic Lifestyle Changes

Therapeutic Lifestyle Changes (TLCs)	How well do you currently take care of yourself in this domain?	Rate where you would like to be in this domain.	Your plan for achieving TLCs. Be specific and include measureable actions.
Exercise			
Nutrition and diet			
Time in nature			
Relationships			
Recreation			
Relaxation			
Stress management			
Religious/spiritual involvement			
Service to others			

3. **Snapshots of Your Life.** Pictures (and images) speak a thousand words. Using your smartphone or camera, take photos of things you care about, and write about the meaning of the images and the feelings they evoke. In your journal, describe how these feelings and thoughts evoked by the images relate to your concerns. Bring your thoughts and reactions to this exercise to counseling to process with your therapist.

_____

_____

4. **A Dose of Laughter.** Make time to see the humor in stressful circumstances. We are not suggesting that you minimize the seriousness of the situation, but we all need to "come up for air" from time to time. Humor has therapeutic value as long as you are not using it to express masked hostility. Humor, when used appropriately, can help you reframe events and gain a fresh perspective and help you refuel. Whether you are into late night comedy shows on TV, enjoy live stand-up comedy acts, or burst into laughter over funny YouTube videos, seek out some laughter. It is good medicine! What makes you laugh?

_____

_____

5. **Bridging the Grand Canyon.** Do you feel immobilized and unable to take action toward a goal you want to achieve? Take a moment to imagine the spectacular Grand Canyon in Arizona. (We are using a metaphor, so why not choose an image that is breathtaking, right?) Does it feel like there is a Grand Canyon between where you stand and a particular goal you want to achieve? You may feel frozen with anxiety over pursuing a relationship (or even ending a toxic one). You may be plagued with fear about pursuing an advanced degree because you couldn't bear to be rejected by admissions, so you sabotage your chances by not applying to programs. Whatever that elusive goal is for you, the energy it takes to wrestle with your fear and anxiety is palpable. So here is an opportunity to explore what keeps you from working toward your goal and bridging that chasm.

a. What is your goal? Be specific.

_____

_____

b. What are the *realistic* constraints that prevent you from reaching or attaining your goal? Differentiate between *perceived* constraints and *actual* constraints, and ask yourself, "How can I be sure that a perceived constraint is an actual constraint? What is the evidence of that?"

_____

_____

c. Describe your feelings and emotions about achieving versus not achieving your goal. How would your quality of life be affected either way? Is it worth it to you to achieve your goal? What are you willing to risk to achieve your goal: slight discomfort, moderate discomfort, or extreme discomfort?

_____

_____

d. What are some challenges you might expect to encounter in working toward your goal? What could you do if you encountered these challenges? Whose support could you seek if you ran into these difficulties?

_____

_____

e. If your stated goal proves to be unrealistic or unachievable (like getting to the other side of the Grand Canyon), how could you modify it so it is within the realm of possibility?

_____

_____

By answering these questions, you have taken the major first step in building the infrastructure you need (a bridge that is sturdy and safe) to cross the canyon to achieve your goal. Be sure to give yourself credit for any progress you make toward attaining your goal. Even steps in the right direction should be acknowledged and celebrated!

6. **Using Expressive Arts.** You do not need to be a talented artist to complete this exercise. The only requirement is that you are willing to exercise your creativity. Think about the core issue you are struggling with, and name it. It might be depression, anger, grief, or anxiety, for example. Then describe this problem or burdensome issue by creating a collage about it; drawing a picture or creating a painting about it; choreographing a dance about it; writing a story, a poem, or cartoon about it; composing a song about it; or identifying someone else's creative product that captures your issue or your feelings about it. What did you learn about yourself and your struggle through this exercise?

_____

_____

7. **Identity Issues.** Sometimes our symptoms and mental health issues can become entangled with our identities. How has _____ become a part of your identity? What would it be like to lose this part of your identity? Are there certain aspects of it that you would miss? Explain.

_____

_____

8. **Dominant Issue.** If _____ were not such a dominant part of your life, what would replace it? How do you suppose your life would be different?

_____

_____

9. **Control of Your Recovery.** Which aspects of your recovery from _____ do you have the most control over?

_____

_____

a. How satisfied are you with how you are managing these aspects of your recovery?

_____

_____

b. Is there anything you would want to change about how you are approaching these parts of your recovery? If so, explain.

_____

_____

10. **Reconciling Different Parts of Yourself.** If you had the opportunity to talk to the part of you that thwarts your progress in recovering from_____, what would you most want to say? What would this part want to say back to you in response? Carry on a dialogue between these two parts (the part that wants to move forward in your recovery and the part that seems to get in your way and impede progress). After doing this exercise, write in your journal about the experience and any insights you gained about yourself.

_____

_____

11. **Compromising with Yourself.** If you could work out a compromise between polar opposite parts of yourself (e.g., the part that wants to take the risk to go on a date, pursue a new career path, or move to a new place, and the part of you that's afraid), what would that compromise look like?

_____

_____

12. **Bibliotherapy.** If you are an avid reader, search the internet for books that address an issue with which you are struggling. You may choose to read nonfiction, biographies, autobiographies, fiction, short stories, or collections of poetry. If you prefer books on tape, that may be a productive way to spend your time driving to and from work. Use your journal to record your reactions to these books.

_____

_____

13. **Your Crisis as a Movie or Play.** If the crisis or problem you experienced was a movie or play and you were the director, which aspects of the story line would you want to highlight? Which genre would capture your perspective best? Would it be presented as a comedy, a drama, or a horror film?

_____

_____

14. **The Story of Your Life.** If your life were a movie, a television series, or a book, what would the title be? What would the scenes, episodes, or chapters be? How is it to think about your life in this manner?

_____

_____

15. **Is Change Worth It?** If you choose *not* to change with regard to an issue that is bothering you, would that be OK?

_____

_____

a. Describe how you think your life would be if you chose not to change anything.

_____

_____

b. Is it worth it to change? Reflect on this in your journal.

_____

_____

16. **Managing Your Emotions.** Managing or regulating emotions can be difficult at times. A number of factors may contribute to this: You may lack the skills to regulate your emotions; your emotional outbursts (or your inability to reveal emotions) may be reinforced by others; you may succumb to myths about showing emotions and believe they are signs of weakness; or you may be biologically predisposed to struggle with regulating emotions. What do you think makes it difficult for you to manage your emotions?

_____

_____

17. **Worst Case Scenario.** Sometimes it helps to think of the worst case scenario and develop a plan to address a stressful situation should it occur (even if it seems unlikely). If you can address the fear directly, it may lose some of its power over you. Describe the worst case scenario for a problem or issue you are facing. Pay attention to your feelings and thoughts as you consider this, and write about them in your journal. Then develop a plan for navigating or resolving this problem/issue. After completing your plan, reflect on how you feel about it. Do you feel a bit more liberated and empowered to tackle this problem or issue if it occurs?

_____

_____

18. **Medication Fears.** If a part of your treatment plan is to take medication to manage symptoms (e.g., anti-anxiety or antidepressant medicines), but you remain hesitant about taking them, write the pros and cons in your journal.
    a. If your helping professionals believe you would benefit greatly by taking medication, what is their argument?

    _____

    _____

    b. Identify your greatest concerns about taking medication, and explore things you could do to address the "cons" on your list? For instance, if you are concerned about weight gain, perhaps you could devise an exercise or weight management program.

    _____

    _____

19. **Gender Role Analysis.** How have gender role expectations affected your well-being and self-concept? In what ways did your family of origin shape your views on gender roles? Which family members were most influential in this regard? Were there others outside of your family who influenced your views on gender? If so, describe.
    a. Have your gender role expectations changed over time? If so, how have they changed?

    _____

    _____

    b. Are there any changes you would like to make in terms of your gender role identity?

    _____

    _____

    c. What would be the consequences of making these changes?

    _____

    _____

    d. What kind of support or lack of support would you expect if you went against your socialization?

    _____

    _____

20. **Conduct a Power Analysis.** What messages did you internalize at a young age about power dynamics?

_____

_____

   a. How was power distributed in your family of origin?

_____

_____

   b. Did certain members hold more power than others, or was it about equal?

_____

_____

   c. How did family members express or use their power?

_____

_____

   d. In your view, was power used in a healthy or unhealthy way?

_____

_____

   e. Was power used to control others?

_____

_____

   f. How do you use power in your relationships today?

_____

_____

21. **Impact of Gender and Power Dynamics.** To what extent do gender and power dynamics compound any problems that are a source of stress for you today?

_____

_____

Appendix B

Internet Resources
for Counselors

American Civil Liberties Union

www.aclu.org/

Over the past century, the ACLU has been committed to defending and preserving the individual rights and liberties guaranteed by the U.S. Constitution and federal laws. This website provides invaluable information on issues ranging from immigrants' rights to racial justice to LGBTQ+ rights.

American Counseling Association

www.counseling.org/

ACA is the world's largest association representing professional counselors in various practice settings. This website has an extensive list of mental health resources, information about counselor competencies, clearinghouses for interventions, activities, and syllabi, and more.

American Psychological Association

www.apa.org/

With more than 118,000 members and 54 divisions, the APA is the nation's leading professional and scientific organization representing psychology. The APA website contains a wealth of information about a wide range of topics that are covered in this workbook.

American Red Cross Training Services: Disaster Training

www.redcross.org/take-a-class/disaster-training

The American Red Cross provides disaster training for all volunteers at no charge. Visit this site to learn about their online and in-person trainings.

Anxiety and Depression Association of America

https://adaa.org/

Since 1979, the ADAA, an international nonprofit organization, has been committed to the prevention, treatment, and cure of anxiety, depression, PTSD, OCD, and co-occurring disorders through practice, research, and education.

Bloomberg American Health Initiative

https://americanhealth.jhu.edu/

With a $300 million gift, the largest ever made to the Johns Hopkins Bloomberg School of Public Health, this initiative tackles critical, 21st-century challenges to public health in the United States, including addiction and overdose, environmental challenges, obesity and the food system, risks to adolescence health, and violence. Visit this site for resources and for American Health Podcast.

Bureau of Consumer Protection

www.ftc.gov/about-ftc/bureaus-offices/bureau-consumer-protection

Under the umbrella of the Federal Trade Commission, the BCP provides information to educate consumers about their rights and responsibilities. This site contains tips and advice for consumers about online security, identity theft, scams, and much more.

Centers for Disease Control and Prevention

www.cdc.gov/

Visit the CDC's website for information related to an expansive list of topics including diseases and health conditions, healthy living, emergency preparedness, and more.

Earth Institute, Columbia University

www.earth.columbia.edu/

The institute comprises more than two dozen research centers and hundreds of people who collaborate across numerous disciplines at Columbia University and is devoted to helping guide the world onto a path toward sustainability. Visit this website to read about exciting initiatives and research on climate, water, energy, global health, and more.

Findlegalhelp.org

www.americanbar.org/groups/legal_services/flh-home/

This website is a public service of the American Bar Association's Legal Services Division. It offers information about free legal assistance for low-income individuals as well as a directory of legal assistance resources for veterans and active-duty service members.

Global Health NOW

www.globalhealthnow.org/

This online resource, launched in 2014 as a free weekday e-newsletter by the Johns Hopkins Bloomberg School of Public Health, is a superb forum for news and information for the global health community.

Human Rights Campaign

www.hrc.org/

The HRC is the nation's largest civil rights organization working to achieve equality for the lesbian, gay, bisexual, transgender, and queer community.

Human Rights Center: UC Berkeley School of Law
https://humanrights.berkeley.edu/
Established in 1994, the center has conducted major human rights investigations in more than a dozen countries, including in the United States. A 2015 recipient of the MacArthur Award for Creative and Effective Institutions, the HRC has launched programs and projects related to sexual violence, human trafficking, and more.

Human Rights Resilience Project
www.hrresilience.org/
This site brings together research, resources, and tools to improve resilience and promote well-being within the human rights community.

Human Rights Watch
www.hrw.org/
This organization investigates and reports on human rights abuses occurring throughout the world. HRW works with organizations across the globe to protect beleaguered activists and to help hold abusers to account and bring justice to victims.

Melissa Institute for Violence Prevention and Treatment
https://melissainstitute.org/
Located on the University of Miami campus, the institute facilitates seminars and conferences and provides consultation focusing on violence prevention and related topics.

National Hospice and Palliative Care Organization
www.nhpco.org/
Representing integrated, person-centered health care, this organization provides practical guidance, legislative representation, and inspiration to palliative care and hospice providers so they can enhance experiences for patients and reduce caregiving responsibilities and emotional stress for families.

National Institute of Mental Health
www.nimh.nih.gov/index.shtml
NIMH, one of the many institutes that comprise the National Institutes of Health, offers expert-reviewed information, fact sheets, and statistics on mental disorders and related topics. Visit their website to learn more about NIMH research and science news related to mental health and illness.

National Institutes of Health
www.nih.gov/
Under the umbrella of the U.S. Department of Health and Human Services, the NIH is the nation's medical research agency, and the website provides access to extensive information and research about a multitude of health conditions. The site also provides links to NIH's 27 impressive institutes and centers, some which may be relevant to the needs of your clients.

National Palliative Care Research Center
www.npcrc.org/
The primary mission of this center is to develop and fund research aimed at improving care for seriously ill patients and their families, but the website also has many useful links to resources and organizations related to palliative care.

National Suicide Prevention Lifeline
https://suicidepreventionlifeline.org/
This invaluable resource, a national network of local crisis centers, provides free and confidential support for people in distress every day around the clock. In addition, the Lifeline offers prevention and crisis resources and best practices for professionals (call 1-800-273-8255; for those hard of hearing, call 1-800-799-4889).

Positive Psychology Center
https://ppc.sas.upenn.edu/services/penn-resilience-training
Housed at the University of Pennsylvania, this center has earned a reputation as a leading organization for evidence-based, state-of-the-art resilience and positive psychology programs.

SocialWorkersToolBox.com
www.socialworkerstoolbox.com/
Download free clinical resources for direct service with adults and children. The site includes materials related to mental health issues such as self-esteem, depression, and anger, as well as bullying, sexual abuse, and domestic abuse.

Substance Abuse and Mental Health Services Administration
www.samhsa.gov/
SAMHSA's goal is to improve the quality and delivery of behavioral health services across the United States. This site includes information about practitioner training and programs, links to grants and data, and treatment locators.

Substance Abuse and Mental Health Services Administration (SAMHSA) Disaster Distress Helpline
www.samhsa.gov/find-help/disaster-distress-helpline
Crisis counseling and support are available 24/7, 365 days a year to people experiencing emotional distress related to natural or human-caused disasters (call 1-800-985-5990).

Substance Abuse and Mental Health Services Administration (SAMHSA) National Helpline:
www.samhsa.gov/find-help/national-helpline
This confidential and free helpline is accessible 24/7, 365 days a year to individuals and families facing mental health and substance use disorders. This treatment referral and information service is available in English and Spanish (call 1-800-662-HELP [4357]).

Southern Poverty Law Center
www.splcenter.org/
The SPLC is the leading nonprofit organization monitoring the activities of domestic hate groups and other extremists in the United States. The website provides information about hate and extremism, marginalized individuals' rights, justice, and teaching tolerance.

Therapist Aid
www.therapistaid.com/
This website was created to offer mental health professionals free evidence-based therapy and education tools to improve their craft. Visit this site for worksheets, interactive tools, guides, videos, and more.

United States Environmental Protection Agency
www.epa.gov/
The mission of the EPA is to protect the environment and human health. The EPA archive contains links to environmental topics of historical interest.

United States National Suicide and Crisis Hotlines
http://suicidehotlines.com/national.html
This website offers links to and phone numbers for a range of crisis hotlines throughout the United States.